Making Isaiah Plain

An Old Testament Study Guide for the Book of Isaiah

Randal S. Chase

Making Isaiah Plain:
An Old Testament Study Guide for the Book of Isaiah
© 2010, 2011 Randal S. Chase

Send inquiries to:
Plain and Precious Publishing
3378 E. Sweetwater Springs Drive
Washington, UT 84780

Send e-mail: info@makingpreciousthingsplain.com

For more copies visit www.makingpreciousthingsplain.com

For a listing of all Plain and Precious Publishing products,
visit www.makingpreciousthingsplain.com
or call 435–251–8520.

Printed in the United States of America

ISBN: 978–1–937901–14–1

Cover: *The Prophet Isaiah*, by Gustave Doré, 1865

Making Isaiah Plain

An Old Testament Study Guide for the Book of Isaiah

Table of Contents

Acknowledgments

This book is dedicated to Church members everywhere who hunger and thirst for an understanding of the scriptures. It has been my privilege to teach literally thousands of such souls in gospel classes, as well as in CES Institute and Adult Education classes, over the years. They have all inspired me with their dedication to reading, pondering, and feasting upon the word of God. I have learned much from them in the process.

I acknowledge the help and encouragement of my sweet wife Deborah, who has assisted me in all of my endeavors to teach and to write concerning the gospel of Jesus Christ. I acknowledge the encouragement of many friends and students to write these study guides, the patient and meticulous assistance of my editor and son, Michael Chase, who has assisted in this work, and other Church scholars who have provided solid counsel about its form and substance, and who have offered invaluable insights on many topics.

I acknowledge other knowledgeable gospel scholars and teachers who have written similar study guides in the past, which I have quoted time and time again in this volume.

Many of the helps and suggestions found herein have been adapted from those provided by other Isaiah scholars. If you desire further help, you may profit from obtaining these works and reading them in their entirety.

"Understanding Isaiah" and "The World of Isaiah," in *Old Testament Student Manual, 1 Kings–Malachi*, Religion 302 (Salt Lake City: The Church of Jesus Christ of Latter-day Saints, 2003), 131–37, 171–78.

"Hebrew Literary Styles," in *Old Testament Student Manual, Genesis–2 Samuel*, Religion 301 (Salt Lake City: The Church of Jesus Christ of Latter- day Saints, 2003), 303–8.

"Nephi's Keys to Understanding Isaiah," by Donald W. Parry, in *Isaiah in the Book of Mormon* (Provo, UT: FARMS, 1998), 47–65.

Bruce R. McConkie, "Ten Keys to Understanding Isaiah," *Ensign*, Oct. 1973, 78–83.

Daniel H. Ludlow, *A Companion to Your Study of the Book of Mormon* (Salt Lake City: Deseret Book, 1976), 134–45.

Joseph Fielding McConkie and Robert L. Millet, *Doctrinal Commentary on the Book of Mormon*, 4 vols. (Salt Lake City: Deseret Book, 1987–92), 1:151–67, 232–82.

"Nephi and Isaiah," by Kent P. Jackson, in *Studies in Scripture, Vol. 7: 1 Nephi to Alma 29* (Salt Lake City: Deseret Book, 1987), 131–45.

Foreword

Both Nephi and the Savior emphasized the importance of Isaiah's writings. Nephi said, "I … write more of the words of Isaiah, for my soul delighteth in his words. For I will liken his words unto my people, and I will send them forth unto all my children, for he verily saw my Redeemer, even as I have seen him" (2 Ne. 11:2). And the Savior said, "I say unto you, that ye ought to search these things. Yea, a commandment I give unto you that ye search these things diligently; for great are the words of Isaiah" (3 Ne. 23:1). We are therefore commanded to give diligent effort to reading and understanding Isaiah, as have prophets throughout the scriptures.

The Isaiah Barrier

Elder Bruce R. McConkie said: "If, as many suppose, Isaiah ranks with the most difficult of the prophets to understand, his words are also among the most important for us to know and ponder. … It just may be that my salvation (and yours also!) does in fact depend upon our ability to understand the writings of Isaiah as fully and truly as Nephi [did]."[1]

This could be discouraging news to Old Testament and Book of Mormon readers, since everyone who has ever begun reading these books knows that the Isaiah chapters can be much more difficult to interpret than what precedes and follows them. But it is well worth the effort to try to understand them because of the rich understanding they provide and the beauty of their language.

Elder Boyd K. Packer said:

"Those who never move beyond the Isaiah chapters [in the Book of Mormon] miss the personal treasures to be gathered along the way. They miss the knowledge of:

- The purpose of mortal life and death,
- The certainty of life after death,
- What happens when the spirit leaves the body,
- The description of the Resurrection,
- How to receive and retain a remission of your sins,
- What hold justice or mercy may have on you,
- What to pray for,
- Covenants and ordinances,
- And many other jewels that make up the gospel of Jesus Christ."[2]

The author's sincere desire is to make Isaiah plain as a powerful witness of the Messiahship of Jesus Christ.

How to Use This Book

To facilitate learning, students and teachers may use this study guide in a variety of ways. I have suggested two below, in no particular order of preference. Choose the method that works best for you, but whatever method you choose, complete the assigned scripture reading for each week's lesson *before* you go to class.

Option 1. Prayerfully read the scriptures associated with the current lesson *first*, and then read the chapter in this book that corresponds to those scriptures.

Option 2. Carefully and prayerfully read the scriptures associated with the current lesson, using this study guide as a reference to help you understand the context and consequences of the scriptures *while you are reading them*. To do this, you would keep this book open and use it as a guide and commentary alongside your scriptures.

This study guide comments on many, but not all, of the scriptures in Isaiah. Rather than a verse-by-verse analysis, I have provided a summary restatement of events, divided into scripture blocks with attached explanations and quotes. An example of how these scripture blocks and comments are organized is shown below:

● **Isaiah 11:6–9** (2 Nephi 21:6–9): **Great peace will exist during the Millennium.** This is the classic description of the Millennium that all Bible readers are familiar with: "The wolf also shall dwell with the lamb, and the leopard shall lie down with the kid, and the calf and the young lion and fatling together; and a little child shall lead them" (v. 6).

The synonymous parallels and metaphors in these verses are stunningly vivid, concluding with the great promise that "they shall not hurt nor destroy in all my holy mountain, for the earth shall be full of the knowledge of the Lord, as the waters cover the sea" (v. 9). It is in verses such as these that we are most aware of Isaiah's poetic gift, which gives rise to descriptions that are so beautiful we cannot imagine them being said in any other way.

Elder Orson Pratt said:

> The knowledge of God will then cover the earth as the waters cover the mighty deep. There will be no place of ignorance, no place of darkness, no place for those that will not serve God. Why? Because Jesus, the Great Creator, and also the Great Redeemer, will be Himself on the earth, and His holy angels will be on the earth, and all the resurrected Saints that have died in former dispensations will all come forth, and they will be on the earth. What a happy earth this creation will be, when this purifying process shall come, and the earth be filled with the knowledge of God as the waters cover the great deep! What a change! Travel, then, from one end of the earth to another, you can find no wicked man, no drunken man, no man to blaspheme the name of the Great Creator, no one to lay hold on his neighbor's goods, and steal them, no one to commit whoredoms—for all who commit whoredoms will be thrust down to hell, saith the Lord God Almighty, and all persons who commit sin will be speedily visited by the judgments of the Almighty![3]

In every chapter, I have provided a historical setting for the scriptures discussed. I have also freely included other scriptural references that provide additional light on the topic. In the end, understanding the doctrine is more important than the history, though I believe it is possible to understand both, and it is better if we do.

Note to Teachers

For the convenience of readers, the chapters in this study guide are organized around the lesson topics for Isaiah that are found in the Church's Gospel Doctrine manual. However, teachers should remember that this study guide is not intended to become a substitute for the official lesson manuals of the Church. Your lessons should follow precisely the organization found in your lesson manual, and should be centered on the assigned scriptures for each lesson. Teachers should read their lesson manuals first and take note of the main doctrinal points that are listed there. After doing this, teachers may use this book as a way of enhancing their own personal understanding of the events and scriptures covered in a particular lesson, just as any other gospel scholar might do. But you should never use this book as a guide to teaching your lessons.

Notes:

1. "Ten Keys to Understanding Isaiah," *Ensign*, Oct. 1973, 80, 78.

2. In Conference Report, Apr. 1986, 77; or *Ensign*, May 1986, 61.

3. In *Journal of Discourses*, 21:325.

CHAPTER 1

An Introduction to the Prophets

THE PROPHETS

Our Savior was once asked by an insincere lawyer, "Master, which is the great commandment in the law?" And He answered by saying, "Thou shalt love the Lord thy God with all thy heart, and with all thy soul, and with all thy mind. This is the first and great commandment. And the second is like unto it, Thou shalt love thy neighbour as thyself. On these two commandments hang all the law and the prophets" (Matt. 22:36–40).

When Jesus and others referred to "the law," they were referring to the law of Moses, as given and explained in Leviticus, Numbers, and Deuteronomy. These were imbedded within a category we call today "the history" of Israel from Genesis to Nehemiah. There were also "the writings," special historical narratives about particular heroes like Esther and Job, plus the poetry of David and the wisdom literature of Solomon (see chart on the following page). These books and writings provided instruction and examples, but they did not carry the same weight as the law and the prophets in guiding Israelite religion and life.

"The prophets" were the writings of the prophets from Isaiah to Malachi. Among these there were four "major" prophets and twelve "minor" prophets (referred to as minor—meaning "small"), signifying the quantity rather than the quality of these books. Their messages are as vital as those of the major books. These minor prophets in order of their appearance in the Bible are: Hosea, Joel, Amos, Obadiah, Jonah, Micah, Nahum, Habakkuk, Zephaniah, Haggai, Zechariah, and Malachi.

John Singer Sargent painted this mural of the prophets in the Boston Public Library in 1895

Old Testament Books by Type

THE PROLOGUE	HISTORICAL CORE	THE WRITINGS	THE PROPHETS
Genesis	Exodus	Esther	*Major Prophets*
	Leviticus	Job	Isaiah
	Numbers	Psalms	Jeremiah
	Deuteronomy	Proverbs	Ezekiel
	Joshua	Ecclesiastes	Daniel
	Judges	Song of Solomon	*Minor Prophets*
	Ruth	Lamentations	Hosea
	1–2 Samuel		Joel
	1–2 Kings		Amos
	1–2 Chronicles		Obadiah
	Ezra		Jonah
	Nehemiah		Micah
			Nahum
			Habakkuk
			Zephaniah
			Haggai
			Zechariah
			Malachi

THE PROLOGUE	HISTORICAL CORE	THE WRITINGS	THE PROPHETS
Given to Moses by revelation. It reveals the source (creation), lineage (patriarchs), and destiny of Israel. It does this for both ancient and modern Israel. It was important enough to latter-day Israel that a corrected version (Book of Moses) was one of the first things, after the Book of Mormon, given to the Prophet Joseph Smith for the Restored Church.	The first four books listed here (Exodus, Leviticus, Numbers, and Deuteronomy), combined with Genesis, are referred to as the Pentateuch—the five books given to us by Moses. These historical books cover the period from the calling of Moses (1250 BC) to the last record of the doings of Nehemiah (432 BC), near the end of the Old Testament.	These books are literary works, written at the same time as the historical books but in a narrative (story-telling) form. The point is to show how the righteous can keep the commandments in all kinds of circumstances. Proverbs and Ecclesiastes are classified as "wisdom literature," providing wisdom on how to live life happily and successfully. But in all of them, wisdom is conveyed through various literary styles.	Major prophets are called major because of the length of their books, not because of their greater importance. They were written at the same time as the historical books, but with a prophetic perspective. Minor prophets wrote shorter books, some at the same time as the major prophets and others in their own time. While the other books of the Old Testament have anonymous authors, all of the books of the prophets are identified by the name of the author (except Jonah).

The Bible contains these books in roughly the order shown above, thus organizing them not in chronological order but by type. Thus, the writings concerning one of the earliest prophets, Jonah, do not appear first. As a minor prophet, his book is found in the collection of minor prophets at the end of the Bible. And even these are not in chronological order. The histories appear roughly in the middle of the Bible, ending with Nehemiah (arguably the final book of the Bible chronologically).

This organizational pattern in the Bible can be confusing to a casual reader of the Bible. Chronologically, the books appear to be scrambled. From the following chart, we can see in particular how scrambled the writings of the prophets are in our Bible.

Order in the Bible:	Chronological:		GD Lesson Order
Elijah	Psalms		28. Elijah
Elisha	Job		29. Elisha
Ezra	Proverbs		30. Solomon Temple
Nehemiah	Ecclesiastes		31. Proverbs & Eccl.
Esther	Song of Solomon		
Job	Elijah	914 BC	32. Job
Psalms	Elisha	897 BC	
Proverbs			
Ecclesiastes	*The Prophets*		
Song of Solomon	Jonah	826 BC	33. Jonah & Micah
	Amos	811 BC	34. Hosea
The Prophets	Hosea	790 BC	35. Amos & Joel
Isaiah	Isaiah	740 BC	36. Isaiah, Pt. 1
Jeremiah	Micah	722 BC	37. Isaiah, Pt. 2
Lamentations	Nahum	642 BC	38. Isaiah, Pt. 3
Ezekiel	Zephaniah	640 BC	39. Isaiah, Pt. 4
Daniel	Jeremiah	626 BC	40. Isaiah, Pt. 5
Hosea	Obadiah	609 BC	41. Jeremiah, Pt. 1
Joel	Habakkuk	609 BC	42. Jeremiah, Pt. 2
Amos	Daniel	606 BC	
Obadiah	Ezekiel	592 BC	43. Ezekiel, Pt. 1
Jonah	Lament.	587 BC	44. Ezekiel, Pt. 2
Micha	Joel	540 BC	
Nahum	Haggai	520 BC	
Habakkuk	Zechariah	520 BC	
Zephaniah	Esther	486 BC	45. Esther & Daniel
Haggai	Ezra	458 BC	46. Daniel
Zechariah	Nehemiah	444 BC	47. Ezra & Nehemiah
Malachi	Malachi	430 BC	48. Zechariah & Malachi

The Kings and Prophets of Judah and Israel

Information concerning key historical figures in the Bible appears in multiple books throughout the Bible. For example, the kings of Judah and Israel appear in the historical books as well as in the prophets—both major and minor. We have to read both the history and the prophets to get the full story. And even among these books, there are duplications. The Chronicles cover the same period of time (and more) as the books of 1 and 2 Kings, just as the large and small plates of Nephi did in Book of Mormon history. And some prophets served and wrote at the same time, though their books are found in separate places within the Bible. The chart on the following page shows the prophets after the time of Solomon and the kings to whom they ministered in both Judah and Israel. In this book, we will discuss events from the perspective of these prophets, in roughly chronological order.

The Role of Ancient Prophets

- **Matthew 16:4 The Lord referred to Jonah as a "prophet."** A "prophet" in Old Testament times had the spirit and gift of prophecy and was called by God to go forth as a spokesman for Him.

- **Revelation 19:10 John, on the Isle of Patmos, defined the spirit of prophecy as "the testimony of Jesus."** All prophets are called to bear witness of the Savior—to bring faithful believers unto Christ in all ages of the world. A prophet who does not testify of Christ is a false prophet.

- **Joseph Smith—History 1:35 Certain prophets were also "seers."** The Prophet Joseph Smith explained that the Urim and Thummim consisted of "two stones in silver bows ... fastened to a breastplate," and that "the possession and use of these stones were what constituted 'seers' in ancient or former times." These were used to learn the mind and will of God and to inquire into events past, present, and future. Jaredite prophets possessed them. Abraham

KINGDOM OF JUDAH	PROPHETS	KINGDOM OF ISRAEL	
King (* righteous) Reign from Year	Prophet (Year[s] Ministry)	Year began Reign	King
Rehoboam...... 22 yrs...... 975	**Ahijah** (975)	975...... 22 yrs..... **Jeroboam**	
Abijam.......... 3 yrs...... 957			
* **Asa** .... 41 yrs.. 955	**Obed** (954)	954...... 2 yrs. .... **Nadab**	
	Jehu (953)	953...... 24 yrs..... **Baasha**	
		930...... 2 yrs. .... **Elah**	
		929...... 7 days.... **Zimri**	
		929...... 12 yrs..... **Omri**	
		918...... 22 yrs..... **Ahab**	
* **Jehoshaphat**. ... 25 yrs...... 914	**Elijah** (914–897)		
		898...... 2 yrs. .... **Ahaziah**	
	Elisha (897–832)	897...... 12 yrs..... **Jehoram (Joram)**	
Jehoram. .... 8 yrs...... 893			
Ahaziah......... 1 yr....... 885			
Athaliah......... 7 yrs...... 884	**Jonah** (880–maybe 826)[1]	884...... 28 yrs..... **Jehu**	
* **Joash** (Jehoash).. 40 yrs...... 878	**Joel** (878–maybe 540)[2]		
		856...... 17 yrs..... **Jehoahaz**	
* **Amaziah**. .... 29 yrs...... 841		842...... 16 yrs..... **Joash (Jehoash)**	
	Jonah (826–750)[1]	826...... 41 yrs..... **Jeroboam II**	
* **Uzziah (Azariah)**52 yrs...... 811	**Amos** (811–750)		
	Hosea (790–721)		
		773...... 6 mos.... **Zachariah**	
		772...... 1 mo..... **Shallum**	
		772...... 10 yrs..... **Menahem**	
* **Jotham**.......... 16 yrs...... 758		761...... 2 yrs. .... **Pekahiah**	
		759...... 20 yrs..... **Pekah**	
Ahaz. .... 16 yrs...... 742	**Isaiah** (740–701)		
		730...... 9 yrs. .... **Hoshea**	
* **Hezekiah**........ 29 yrs...... 726	**Micah** (722)	721...... Israel taken captive by Assyria.	
Manasseh....... 55 yrs...... 697			

NOTES:

Amon. .... 2 yrs...... 642	**Nahum** (642–606)	[1] The date of Jonah's ministry is in dispute. Some place it as early as 880 BC, some as late as 826 BC, at the same time as Hosea. Either way, he was one of the earliest of prophets after Elijah and Elisha.
* **Josiah**........... 31 yrs...... 640	**Zephaniah** (640–608)	
	Jeremiah (626–586)	
Jehoahaz........ 3 mos. 609	**Obadiah** (609–586)	
Jehoiakim....... 11 yrs...... 608	**Habakkuk** (609–598)	
First Judean captivity occurs. . 605	**Daniel** (606–530, in captivity)	
Jehoiachin. ...... 3 mos..... 598	Lehi (600–598)	[2] The date of Joel's ministry is also in dispute. Some place it as early as 878 BC, some as late as 540 BC. This author believes that the later date is more likely, given the nature of the content, which is more like that of Zechariah.
Zedekiah........ 11 yrs...... 598		
	Ezekiel (592–570, in captivity)	
Judah captive by Babylon. 587		
	Joel (540–maybe as early as 878)[2]	
Cyrus decrees return of Jews. . 537		
* **Zerubbabel**................. 537		
Temple rebuilding begins	**Haggai** (520)	* Indicates a king who was right- eous during some or all of his reign.
	Zechariah (520–518)	
Ezra commission to return. ... 458	**Ezra** (458–not a prophet)	
* **Nehemiah** made governor... 444	**Nehemiah** (444–not a prophet)	
Nehemiah's 2nd visit......... 432		
	Malachi (430)	

(Adapted from standard dates in LDS Bible Dictionary, "Chronology," 637–40, and from entries for prophets in it. Note that revised dates in the chronology would change this chart, but not the sequence. All dates are approximate.)

used them. Moses gave Aaron a set to keep in the pouch behind his breastplate, and High Priests in Israel used them even when no "prophet" was available to tell them the will of God. Joseph Smith used them specifically to translate the Book of Mormon, but also for the purpose of obtaining answers from God.

● Amos 3:6–7 Amos gives important information about the call and role of a prophet of God.

> … Shall a trumpet be blown in the city, and the people not be afraid? shall there be evil in a city, and the Lord hath not done it?

> … Surely the Lord God will do nothing, but he revealeth his secret unto his servants the prophets.

The Lord is not inclined to surprise us. With every blessing or curse comes a foretelling that allows us to exercise our agency and make a choice. He calls certain individuals to be His mouthpieces on earth—to both teach and testify concerning Him and to provide guidance to all those who will hearken unto them.

The Prophet Joseph Smith said: "According to the testimony of the scriptures in all ages of the world, whenever God was about to bring a judgment upon the world or accomplish any great work, the first thing He did was to raise up a prophet, and reveal unto him the secret, and send him to warn the people, so that they may be left without excuse … Prophets … warned the people [even when] they gave no heed [and] rejected their testimony; [then] the judgments came upon the people."[1]

President Ezra Taft Benson said: "As [a] prophet reveals the truth, [he] divides the people. The honest in heart heed his words, but the unrighteous either ignore the prophet or fight him. When the prophet points out the sins of the world, the worldly either want to close the mouth of the prophet, or else act as if the prophet didn't exist, rather than repent of their sins. Popularity is never a test of truth. Many a prophet has been killed or cast out. As we come closer to the Lord's Second Coming, you can expect that as the people of the world become more wicked, the prophet will be less popular with them."[2]

The Writings of the Prophets in the Bible

The writings of the prophets in the Bible are a small portion of the total. Like the books of Mosiah, Alma, and Helaman in the Book of Mormon, they are a detailed account of a relatively short period of time.

— In the new LDS edition of the Bible, there are 1,184 pages in the Old Testament and 860 of these precede the writings of the prophets. This leaves only 324 pages from Isaiah to Malachi.

— There are more pages in the New Testament (404) than in the Old Testament prophets (324).

— The time covered by the writings of the prophets is quite short. Alltogether they cover only two major time periods of just 50 years each, except for the last three prophets in our present-day Bible.

Nevertheless, the writings of the prophets are extremely valuable. They were valuable to the people of the Old Testament who looked to these prophets for counsel. They were valuable as predictors of the great world events to come—the scattering of Israel, the birth of the Savior, His ministry, and the great latter-day work of gathering Israel once again. And they are valuable to us today as evidence of the hand of God in the affairs of men. We have already seen the fulfillment of many of their teachings and prophecies. And we can rely on them for guidance both now and in the future, right up to and including the millennial reign of the Messiah.

Notes:

1. *History of the Church*, 6:23.

2. "Fourteen Fundamentals in Following the Prophet," in *1980 Devotional Speeches of the Year* [1981], 29.

CHAPTER 2.

Understanding Isaiah

INTRODUCTION

The Book of Isaiah

The book of Isaiah covers the entire plan of salvation, from premortal councils where Lucifer's selfish pretensions were rejected, to his own day of gross wickedness in Israel, to the birth and mission of the Savior, to the great age of apostasy, to the latter-day restoration and gathering, to the Second Coming of our Lord and His glorious millennial reign. Along the way, he prophesies of the Nephites, the lost tribes of Israel, the return of Judah to the land of Canaan, and the ultimate destinies of the Old and New Jerusalems. He was, truly, a prophet for and to all dispensations.

The prophet Isaiah

Isaiah, son of Amoz, was born in the first half of the eighth century BC. He was called to be a prophet in about 740 BC, and his ministry extended for approximately 40 years, mostly in and around Jerusalem, where he counseled with the kings and people of Judah—most notably King Hezekiah of Judah.

Isaiah had great literary talents. Almost all of Isaiah's prophecies were written in fine Hebrew poetry. His prophecies focus on the house of Israel—its past, present, and future. A major theme was the Messiah—His birth and mission as the Savior who would suffer for all, and as the Great King at the last day. Isaiah's ministry was not restricted to his own time but was intended for all generations.

Isaiah is one of the "major" prophets of the Old Testament, along with Jeremiah, Ezekiel, and Daniel, so designated because of the greater length of these books.

Isaiah is the most frequently quoted Old Testament prophet in all other scriptures. And those other scriptures, both ancient and modern, shed great light on the words and prophecies of Isaiah. We find commentary by prophets and the Savior in the Book of Mormon, and several helpful commentaries by the Prophet Joseph Smith and the Lord in the Doctrine and Covenants.

● Isaiah in the Bible:

— Isaiah is quoted more often than any other prophet.

— The King James Version has 66 chapters of Isaiah, containing 1,292 verses.

— The size of his book makes him the first "major prophet" in the Old Testament.

— New Testament writers had great respect for Isaiah, quoting him 57 times.

● Isaiah in the Book of Mormon:

— Isaiah is quoted by Nephi, Jacob, Abinadi, Moroni, and the Savior.

— In all, they quote 22 chapters of Isaiah, more than any other prophet is quoted.

— Nephi alone quotes 16 chapters of Isaiah, and the Savior quotes 2 chapters.

— They quote 414 Isaiah verses (32% of Isaiah).

— They paraphrase another 34 verses (3% of Isaiah).

— In all, they put 35% of the book of Isaiah on their small, very valuable plates.

Elder Bruce R. McConkie said, "The Book of Mormon is the world's greatest commentary on the book of Isaiah."[1] We are very fortunate to have detailed interpretations of Isaiah in the Book of Mormon as an aid to understanding. But in addition, there are many helps in the Doctrine and Covenants.

● Isaiah in the Doctrine and Covenants:

— Quotes, interprets, and paraphrases Isaiah 100 times.

— D&C 101 contains keys to understanding Isaiah 65.

— D&C 113 interprets Isaiah chapters 11 and 52.

— D&C 133 elaborates on Isaiah chapters 35, 51, 63–64.

— Numerous uses of Isaiah's phraseology can also be found. For example, compare D&C 133:3, 15, 27, 40–53, 67–70 to Isaiah 52:10, 12; 51:10; 64:1–4; 63:1–9; 50:2–3, 11.

● Isaiah's continued importance in the latter days:

— Isaiah prophesied of the Apostasy and Restoration.

— He saw the scattering and gathering of Israel.

— He prophesied of the latter-day state of Israel.

— He prophesied of the Second Coming and the Millennium.

— He saw the fall of the great and abominable church.

The Major Themes of Isaiah

Isaiah was not merely a prophet unto the Israelites. He was and is a prophet unto the Nephites and unto us in our own time. The scope of his visions and prophecies reach back into premortal life and forward to the glorious Millennium of our Lord. The themes include:

— Local or historical events of Isaiah's day (15 chapters).

— Gospel restoration in the latter days through Joseph Smith.

— Israel's latter-day gathering and her final triumph and glory.

— Book of Mormon coming forth as a new witness for Christ.

— Apostate conditions of the nations in the latter days.

— Zion to be redeemed.

— Messianic prophecies (see Isa. 7:14; 9:6–7; 2 Ne. 17:14; 19:6–7), including:

- Christ's birth and mortal ministry
- Christ's visit to the spirits in prison
- The Crucifixion and Atonement
- The Second Coming of the Millennial Christ

Elder Russell M. Nelson wrote: "One scholar of Isaiah documents that no [fewer] than 391 of the verses [of Isaiah quoted in the Book of Mormon] refer to the attributes, appearance, majesty, and mission of Jesus Christ."[2]

THE LIFE AND MINISTRY OF ISAIAH

Isaiah's times were troubled times for the Israelites. In the early years of Isaiah's life, both Judah and Israel were prosperous and wealthy nations—but also very wicked. Shortly after his ministry began, the dreaded Assyrian empire invaded Palestine. Both Israel and Judah were soon paying tribute to Assyria; and in about 721 BC the Northern Kingdom, Israel, was destroyed as a nation.

Jerusalem became an island in the midst of Assyria's conquered lands, surviving largely due to the inspired and untiring efforts of Isaiah. He constantly reminded the Jews that if they trusted in their covenants with the Lord and rejected alliances with other nations, the Assyrian threat would be averted. It was. But as Isaiah had warned them, continued wickedness would not go unpunished. Babylon later executed God's divine judgment against His rebellious people, and Isaiah witnessed much of that destruction.

GUSTAVE DORÉ, 1896

Tradition states that Isaiah met his death by being tied to a tree and sawed in half at the hands of King Manasseh.[3]

The Greatness of Isaiah

So great was Isaiah's reputation that for hundreds of years after his death he was often referred to simply as "the prophet"—much the same as we do for the Prophet Joseph Smith in our day.

Ben Sirach was a great sage who lived about 200 BC. He wrote or compiled an apocryphal book called the *Wisdom of Ben Sirach* or *Ecclesiasticus.* He wrote of the prophet Isaiah: "Isaiah [was] a great man trustworthy in his vision. … In the power of the spirit he saw the last things, he comforted the mourners of Zion, he revealed the future to the end of time, and hidden things long before they happened" (Ecclesiasticus 48:22, 24–25).

Josephus, the Jewish historian born about AD 37, described Isaiah in his history of the Jews: "Now as to this prophet [Isaiah], he was, by the confession of all, a divine and wonderful man in speaking truth; and out of the assurance that he had never written what was false, he wrote down all his prophecies, and left them behind him in books, that their accomplishment might be judged of from the events by posterity."[4]

Dr. Sydney B. Sperry wrote:

> Isaiah was one of the greatest men of all time. ... In the first place, Isaiah had great natural gifts, which were disciplined and sharpened by the best education that his time afforded. He was blessed with fine judgment and insight, together with the courage to defend to the uttermost a cause he knew to be right. Secondly, he possessed great spiritual intuition and insight, which made him a marvelous and ready instrument in the hands of Jehovah, whom he loved and served with all his heart. Isaiah thus combined earthly and heavenly wisdom to a most unusual degree. All this he of course used for the benefit of his fellow men. Valeton pays this tribute to him:

> "Never perhaps has there been another prophet like Isaiah, who stood with his head in the clouds and his feet on the solid earth, with his heart in the things of eternity and with mouth and hand in the things of time, with his spirit in the eternal counsel of God and his body in a very definite moment of history."[5]

THE IMPORTANCE OF ISAIAH

Both Nephi and the Savior emphasized the importance of Isaiah's writings. Nephi said, "I ... write more of the words of Isaiah, for my soul delighteth in his words. For I will liken his words unto my people, and I will send them forth unto all my children, for he verily saw my Redeemer, even as I have seen him" (2 Ne. 11:2). And the Savior said, "I say unto you, that ye ought to search these things. Yea, a commandment I give unto you that ye search these things diligently; for great are the words of Isaiah" (3 Ne. 23:1). We are therefore *commanded* to give diligent effort to reading and understanding Isaiah, as have prophets throughout the scriptures.

The Isaiah Barrier

Elder Bruce R. McConkie said: "If, as many suppose, Isaiah ranks with the most difficult of the prophets to understand, his words are also among the most important for us to know and ponder. ... It just may be that my salvation (and yours also!) does in fact depend upon our ability to understand the writings of Isaiah as fully and truly as Nephi [did]."[6]

This could be discouraging news to Old Testament and Book of Mormon readers, since everyone who has ever begun reading these books knows that the Isaiah chapters can be much more difficult to interpret than what precedes and follows them. But it is well worth the effort to try to understand them because of the rich understanding they provide and the beauty of their language.

Elder Boyd K. Packer said:

> Those who never move beyond the Isaiah chapters [in the Book of Mormon] miss the personal treasures to be gathered along the way. They miss the knowledge of:
>
> — The purpose of mortal life and death,
>
> — The certainty of life after death,
>
> — What happens when the spirit leaves the body,
>
> — The description of the Resurrection,
>
> — How to receive and retain a remission of sins,
>
> — What hold justice or mercy may have on you,
>
> — What to pray for,
>
> — Covenants and ordinances,
>
> — And many other jewels that make up the gospel of Jesus Christ.[7]

UNDERSTANDING ISAIAH'S WRITINGS

This chapter is provided to help you understand Isaiah's writings. Even Nephi admits: "Isaiah spake many things which were hard for many of my people to understand; for they know not concerning the manner of prophesying among the Jews" (2 Ne. 25:1).

Nevertheless, Nephi offers help, as does the Savior in His teachings to the Nephites when He visited them.

We have many other helps in this process. For the explanations provided in this chapter we are indebted to many valuable sources that can be consulted for an even deeper understanding of Isaiah's methods and sayings. A list of these sources is available at the end of this chapter.

NEPHI'S KEYS TO INTERPRETING ISAIAH

● **2 Nephi 25:1–5 Nephi provided two keys to understanding Isaiah.** Nephi chose to comment on Isaiah's writings because "Isaiah spake many things which were hard for many of my people to understand; for they know not concerning the manner of prophesying among the Jews" (v. 1). We find ourselves in the same condition today—not fully understanding the ways in which Hebrew prophets prophesied. Nevertheless, Isaiah's writings were and are crucial because they contain "the judgments of God, that [have and will] come upon all nations, according to the word which he hath spoken" (v. 3).

Nephi promises that while "the words of Isaiah are not plain unto you, nevertheless they are plain unto all those that are filled with the spirit of prophecy" (v. 4). While interpreting Isaiah's writings for us, Nephi promises to "prophesy according to the plainness which hath been with me from the time that

I came out from Jerusalem with my father; for behold, my soul delighteth in plainness unto my people, that they may learn" (v. 4). He thus becomes one of our greatest helpers in deciphering Isaiah.

Nephi was himself an Israelite, fully familiar with "the things of the Jews" (v. 5). He observed that "the Jews do understand the things of the prophets, and there is none other people that understand the things which were spoken unto the Jews like unto them, save it be that they are taught after the manner of the things of the Jews" (v. 5). Thus we see that Nephi identifies two keys to understanding Isaiah:

— The spirit of prophecy (v. 4)

— The letter of prophecy (knowing Jewish customs, language, and ways; vv. 1, 5).

The Spirit of Prophecy

The spirit of prophecy is a testimony of Christ (see Rev. 19:10). This suggests that only people with faith in and a testimony of the Savior will fully understand Isaiah. All true prophets have such a testimony, and they deliver their message by inspiration from the Holy Ghost (see 2 Pet. 1:20–21). A correct understanding of scripture (including Isaiah) comes from the same source (see D&C 50:17–22).

If we read Isaiah with a believing heart, the mysteries it contains can be unfolded to our understanding by the Spirit. This "spirit of prophecy" is obtained through fasting and prayer (see Alma 17:3), so we must approach our study of Isaiah with that kind of devotion. As Elder Packer observed, the casual reader can never hope to understand Isaiah.

The Letter of Prophecy

The letter of prophecy is "[knowing] the manner of prophesying among the Jews" (2 Ne. 25:1). To understand the writings of ancient Jewish prophets, we must be familiar with their physical and cultural circumstances, including their language conventions. An understanding of the following would be necessary to achieve this:

● **The geography of the Holy Land and surrounding regions.** Isaiah frequently referred to cities and towns of the Holy Land and other neighboring nations. If we know the geography of this area, his writings are clearer and have greater impact. Our LDS version of the scriptures contains maps for a reason—to provide a ready reference for the places and geographic features of which the prophets speak.

PHOTO COURTESY OF NASA

— **Isaiah 9:1–2** (2 Nephi 19:1-2): When Isaiah says, "The land of Zebulun and the land of Naphtali ... beyond Jordan, in Galilee ... have seen a great light ... upon them hath the light shined," it helps to pull out the maps to see that he is talking about the area of Nazareth. Knowing this, we can understand that he is predicting that the Savior will come from Nazareth.

— **Isaiah 10:24** (2 Nephi 20:24): Here Isaiah speaks of the Lord's protection of Israel in the face of the advancing armies of Assyria. It helps to refer to the maps to see that Assyria lies to the north of Israel and will be coming from that direction.

— **Isaiah 10:28–32** (2 Nephi 20:28–32): The Lord describes the advance of the Assyrian army through a series of towns. If we look at the map, we see that these towns lie in a ten-mile path north of Jerusalem, with Nob located right outside the walls of Jerusalem. Knowing this gives this passage greater significance and impact.

● **The historical setting of Isaiah's writings.** Understanding Isaiah's writings requires the reader to be at least somewhat familiar with Israel's history: their exodus from Egypt; their wanderings in the wilderness; their covenants with God; their conquest of Canaan; the reign of the judges; the reigns of King David and Solomon; the division of Israel into two kingdoms; the wicked influence of surrounding nations; and Israel's apostasies. Isaiah speaks of all of these in his prophecies.

This would put his ministry about 100–140 years before Lehi and his family left Jerusalem—approximately the same amount of time that has passed in our day since the Prophet Joseph Smith's ministry. This at least partly explains the great affection Nephi and Jacob had for Isaiah, whom they call "the prophet," just like we do the Prophet Joseph Smith (see 1 Ne. 19:24; 1 Ne. 22:1–2; 2 Ne. 6:12–14).

We can also learn from the Bible dictionary that Isaiah lived and preached during very wicked times for both Israel (the northern kingdom) and Judah (the southern kingdom). By Nephi's time, his prophecies of the destruction of Israel had all been fulfilled, and his prophecies of the destruction of Judah were about to be. Little wonder, then, that Isaiah mixed his prophecies of doom for the wicked people of his day with glorious prophecies of the birth, life, and death of the Savior and the great events of the latter days, offering hope to the righteous in Israel.

His explanations of the current and future status of the children of Israel had profound meaning to the Nephites, who had been scattered far from home. Andrew C. Skinner wrote: "[Nephi's] family [was] on the cutting edge ... of the scattering of Judah that Isaiah prophesied. [The Nephites] were alone in a strange land, bereft of their familiar surroundings and struggling to forge a new life. Nephi envisions how an understanding of Christ's redemptive power, including the specific promises made to the house of Israel of a physical, geographical redemption, could buoy up and strengthen his family as well as future generations."[8]

- **Hebrew imagery and figurative language.** This may be the most difficult part of understanding Isaiah. The manner of speaking and writing among the Jews was so very different from our own. Their parables, Isaiah's writings in Hebrew figures of speech, symbolic images, and methods of writing poetry seem completely foreign to us.

When we realize that we are reading things that were written more than 2,700 years ago, and that those writings have since been translated first into Greek and then from Greek into fifteenth-century English (which is quite different from the English we use today),

Isaiah's writings in Hebrew

little wonder that the meaning of many things was lost in the process. We need help from someone who knows the manner of speaking among the Jews and can interpret for us—someone like the Savior or one of His chosen and inspired prophets like Nephi.

Difficult as it may seem to decode these things, there are consistencies in Isaiah's writing style that are readily recognizable once readers become familiar with them. And if readers apply themselves to carefully reading, referencing, and pondering Isaiah, it all opens up into a most beautiful flower—gems of Jewish poetry that can reward us in deeply moving ways. Some of these consistent patterns include:

— **Parables drawn from the lives of the people.** If Hebrew poets had written in our generation, they would have used stories taken from our everyday lives—

Winnowing wheat from chaff

things like debt or the Internet. Writing in their own times, they focused on activities common to the people of their day—things like planting, harvesting, pruning, and burning. Sometimes Isaiah's parables seem perfectly clear, but at other times they seem confusing and obscure. To understand ancient parables, we must familiarize ourselves with the lives and times of the people to whom they were given. Nephi is very helpful in this regard because he was raised in Jewish culture.

— **Figures of speech** can be very difficult to interpret because they are so unique to the culture from which they are drawn. For example, if I were to say to you that I've had a long day today and I am "bushed," you would know exactly what I mean—that I'm very tired. But if this saying were translated into another language and then translated again into a third language, and if 2,700 years pass away in the process, it is unlikely that a future reader will have any idea of what I was trying to say. They might even think me strange to suggest that I'm a "bush." So, too, does Isaiah sound strange to us when he speaks of "the rock whence ye are hewn, and … the hole of the pit whence ye are digged" (Isa. 51:1; 2 Ne. 8:1). But if we know that this figure of speech is similar to one of our own—calling a young boy "a chip off the old block" when comparing him to his father—then it starts to make sense to us. Here again, Nephi (who came from Jewish culture) can be very helpful, as can modern scholars who have studied their culture in great depth.

— **The language of covenant**—the Hebrews used special figures of speech in connection with their covenants with the Lord. For example, in the language of covenant:

- Isaiah 1:17, 20   To "do well" is an exhortation to keep covenants with the Lord.

- Isaiah 1:18   The reward is forgiveness.

- Isaiah 1:19   "Eating the good of the land" means receiving covenant blessings.

- Isaiah 1:16, 20   "Evil" means covenant "curses," such as disasters, calamities, and misfortunes.

- **Isaiah 45:7** is an example of the language of the covenant. It says, "I make *peace,* and create *evil,*" which seems contradictory to us. But because it has to do with covenants, we know it means "I make *covenant blessings* and create *covenant curses.*"

- **Isaiah 1:17–19** is another example. "Learn to do well" (v. 17) means "learn to keep your covenants." When Isaiah writes, "[The] willing and obedient … shall eat the good of the land" (v. 19), he means if we are willing and obedient, we will receive covenant blessings.

- Examples of language that indicate the reversal of covenant curses:

  - Isaiah 5:6; 27:2–3   Barrenness turned to fertility.

  - Isaiah 3:1; 30:23   Famine to productivity.

  - Isaiah 9:2; 60:1–2   Darkness to light.

— **Synonymous parallels** are the chief feature of ancient Near Eastern poetry, and since most of Isaiah is Hebrew poetry, we need to develop some skill at interpreting them. This we can do largely on our own if we understand the format.

When writing poetry in Western culture, we normally rhyme the last word of a line with the last word of a previous line:

- **Hymn 134:** "I believe in Christ; he is my *King*. With all my heart, to him I'll *sing*."

In Hebrew poetry, instead of rhyming words, the poets rhyme concepts. An idea is stated at least twice (sometimes more), with each version of the idea clarifying its parallel counterpart:

- **Isaiah 1:27:** "Zion shall be [ransomed] with [justice], and her converts with righteousness."

By looking at the parallel counterparts in each line, we can understand that "Zion" means "her converts" and that they will be ransomed with "justice" by their "righteousness."

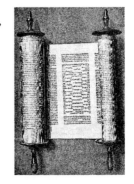

The parallel meanings become even more clearly defined when we look at what Isaiah more likely said, and not at what the King James Bible translators interpreted it to mean in their own day and time. This is an excellent example of the difficulty that arises when trying to understand a symbolic saying from one ancient culture (Isaiah's), which has then been passed through a later—but still ancient (to us)—early English culture before we finally read it in our own day.

Avraham Gileadi, in addressing ways to understand these parallels fully, wrote: "Some knowledge of Hebrew, or, alternately, the use of a translation consistently accurate against the Hebrew [is needed]. Having made my own translation of the Masoretic text of Isaiah into English, and in the process having compared every term employed in twelve of the most authoritative versions of the Bible, I retain strong reservations about depending for an interpretation on a single English translation of Isaiah, as one translation alone can never say all that the Hebrew says." Gileadi translates Isaiah 1:27 this way:

- "Zion shall be ransomed with justice
  and those of her who repent by righteousness."

Gileadi continues, "[Which] by parallelism, defines 'Zion' as 'those of her who repent,' a concept similarly stated in Isaiah 59:20."[9]

— **Chiasmus** is a special form of parallelism—an inverted parallelism—that creates a mirror image of a series of ideas over several lines of Hebrew poetry. The first series of words or thoughts is followed by a second presentation of those words or thoughts in reverse order.

- **Isaiah 6:10** (2 Nephi 16:10) is an example of chiasmus. Notice how the word *heart* is found in the two A lines, the word *ears* is found in the two B lines, and *eyes* is found in the two C lines.

  Make the heart of this people fat,
      and make their ears heavy,
          and shut their eyes;
          lest they see with their eyes,
      and hear with their ears,
  & understand with their heart, & convert, & be healed.

- **Isaiah 55:8–9** is another example of chiasmus.

  For my thoughts are not your thoughts,
      neither are your ways my ways, saith the Lord.
          For as the heavens are higher than the earth,
      so are my ways higher than your ways,
  and my thoughts than your thoughts.

Chiasmus is not limited to a few lines, as in these examples. Hebrews poets took chiasmus to great lengths, sometimes creating chiasms of many lines or over an entire chapter or book. And a smaller chiasm (perhaps several of them) can be embedded within a larger chiasm, creating a very complex structure. When we realize the great complexity of Isaiah's poetry, with its synonymous parallels within individual chiasms with even larger chiasmatic organization of chapters, we begin to fully appreciate the great talent of Isaiah as a writer, and the beauty of his writings begins to unfold for us.

Nephi admired Isaiah as a writer as well as a prophet, and he followed Isaiah's example in his own writings, as did Mormon.

George Potter writes: "The Book of Mormon contains large and extremely complex chiasms of many elements and layers, a feature which points to the ancient origins of the book since Joseph Smith would not have known about chiasms, as they were not rediscovered until the mid-nineteenth century. It was not until 1854, twenty-four years after the first publishing of the Book of Mormon, with the publication of John Forbes's *The Symmetrical Structures of Scripture*, that the complicated and sophisticated nature of biblical chiasmus was fully appreciated. ... Book of Mormon scholars have shown how Nephi's record is a complex work containing numerous parallels and chiasms."[10]

■ **2 Nephi 29:13** is an example of a chiasm written by the prophet Nephi:

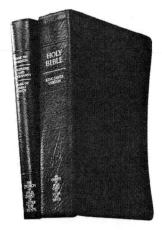

> And ... the Jews
>> Shall have the words
>>> Of the Nephites
>>> And the Nephites
>> Shall have the words
> Of the Jews
>
> And the Nephites and the Jews
>> Shall have the words
>>> Of the lost tribes of Israel
>>> And the lost tribes of Israel
>> Shall have the words of
> The Nephites and the Jews

■ Other examples of chiasmus in the Book of Mormon include Mosiah 3:18–19; 5:10–12; and the entire Book of Mosiah, to name just a few. All of these were written by Mormon.

John W. Welch wrote:

Chiasmus was first noticed by a few nineteenth century pioneer theologians in Germany and England, but the idea had to wait until the 1930s before it found an ardent exponent, Nils Lund, who was able to lay the principle before the eyes of the world in a convincing way. ... Today, articles on the subject are quite common. ... I think it would be fair to say that the discovery of this pattern, the discovery of chiasmus, has added more insights into the nature of biblical literature than has any other single discovery of a comparable kind in modern times. … Needless to say, the discovery of chiasmus has given us plenty to think about. It has led us to think about the nature of our sacred literature and to reevaluate the skill and deliberation with which it was written. By it many passages that were previously obscure have now become clear. Other places that once seemed disorganized have now regained their original orderliness.[11]

— **Metaphors and similes** make a direct comparison between two things, suggesting similarity. Similes add the words *as* or *like* to the comparison, whereas metaphors generally do not. There are many metaphors and similes in Isaiah.

■ **Isaiah 1:10** refers to Judah and Jerusalem as "Sodom" and "Gomorrah" (rather than their real names) as a metaphor to emphasize their wickedness.

Metaphors can sometimes have multiple meanings:

■ **Isaiah 13:4** (2 Nephi 23:4)**: Mountains as kingdoms.** The parallel occurrence of "mountains" and "kingdoms" makes "mountains" a metaphor for "kingdoms" in this verse.

■ **Isaiah 2:14** (2 Nephi 12:14)**: Mountains as nations.** Here "mountains" is a metaphor for "nations." Therefore, the leveling of "high mountains" in the day of the Lord's coming implies leveling of exalted kingdoms or nations (see also Isa. 64:1–3).

■ **Isaiah 2:2** (2 Nephi 12:2)**: Mountains as temples.** "Mountains" are also sometimes metaphors for temples. Sometimes a metaphor is combined with a synonymous parallel, which helps to make the meaning of the metaphor more clear:

The mountain of the Lord's house

■ **Isaiah 2:3** (2 Nephi 12:3)**:** "Let us go up to the mountain of the Lord, to the house of the God of Jacob." From this, we can see that "the mountain of the Lord" means "the house of the God of Jacob," so in this case Isaiah is using *mountain* as a metaphor for the temple.

— Royal metaphors—metaphors of kings and nations—were widely used in Isaiah's time. These metaphors are also figures of speech—phrases that were clearly understood in Isaiah's time but seem somewhat strange to us today.

- **Isaiah 5:25** (2 Nephi 15:25)**:** The "left hand of punishment" is the executioner.

- **Isaiah 11:11, 15** (2 Nephi 21:11, 15)**:** The "right hand of deliverance" is the king.

- **Isaiah 5:26; 11:10, 12** (2 Nephi 15:26; 21:10, 12)**:** An ensign or banner is a flag that rallies people. In this case it may be rallying wicked nations to punish the Lord's people for their wickedness, or rallying the righteous from among all nations to Zion—a safe place in the day of judgment.

- **Isaiah 10:5; 14:5** (2 Nephi 20:5; 24:5)**:** Kings of Assyria and Babylon are called the "rod" and "staff" of the Lord's punishment. Elsewhere they represent the Lord's anger and wrath (see Isa. 5:25; 10:5; 13:5, 9; 2 Ne. 15:25; 20:5; 23:5, 9) or "ax" or "saw" to hew down the wicked (see Isa. 10:15; 14:8; 37:24; 2 Ne. 20:15; 24:8).

- **Isaiah 8:7; 11:15** (2 Nephi 18:7; 21:15)**:** The king of Assyria and his confederation of wicked nations are further depicted as a "river" and "sea" (see Isa. 5:30; 10:26; 17:12; 2 Ne. 15:30; 20:26), well-known metaphors for chaos and evil in Isaiah's time.

- **Isaiah 41:2, 15:** Dust and chaff also represented destructive chaos in those days.

- **Isaiah 41:2, 10:** A righteous king of the Davidic line was sometimes called "the Lord's righteousness" (Isa. 51:5), a forerunner of "salvation" (Isa. 46:13; 56:1), and sometimes was a metaphor for the Lord Himself (see Isa. 12:2; 62:11; 2 Ne. 22:2).

- **Isaiah 41:10–15, 25:** Israel, when strengthened by the right hand of the Lord, will thresh mountains into dust and chaff. Interpreting this metaphor with the information presented above, we can understand that Israel and its king will make chaos of wicked nations after such nations serve the Lord's purpose in punishing Israel.

— **Rhetorical context.** Whatever literary devices are being used, they all must be understood in context. What a term means in the Hebrew dictionary or lexicon is less important than how Isaiah uses it in a particular prophecy.

- **Isaiah 1:27**   *Zion* is defined (by parallelism) as a people (those who repent and are ransomed).

- **Isaiah 35:10**   *Zion* is defined as a place (the place of return for the ransomed of the Lord).

- **Isaiah 51:11** (2 Nephi 8:11)

In Isaiah 13 *Babylon* must be understood in context, even within the same chapter.

- **Isaiah 13:9, 11** (2 Nephi 23:9, 11):   Here *Babylon* is defined as sinners, the world, and the wicked.

- **Isaiah 13:13–14** (2 Nephi 23:13–14):   But *Babylon* is defined later in the chapter as the entire earth.

- Thus, like Zion, Babylon represents both a people and a place.

THE SAVIOR'S KEYS TO INTERPRETING ISAIAH

● **3 Nephi 23:1–3 The Savior offered similar keys for the interpreting of Isaiah** when He visited the Nephites after His resurrection and commanded them to study Isaiah's words. He told them that they would gain understanding by:

— Searching Isaiah (v. 1).

— Understanding typologically (v. 3), which means to understand past events as a "type" (symbol) of future events.

Searching Isaiah's Words Diligently

● **3 Nephi 23:1 The Lord commanded the Nephites to search Isaiah diligently.** This suggests more than a casual or quick reading. It means serious and sustained study. We must:

— Read prayerfully and ponder.

— Study phrases and verses according to the "ways of the Jews."

— Analyze and relate them to our own lives.

— Compare what we read to known principles of the gospel and prophecies.

- **Isaiah 6:9–10** (2 Nephi 16:9–10): **Isaiah's words are deliberately veiled,** just as the Savior's words were veiled from the spiritually unprepared during His earthly ministry (see Matt. 13:11, 13, 15–16). "Go, and tell this people, Hear ye indeed, but understand not; and see ye indeed, but perceive not," the Lord said to Isaiah (v. 9). "Make the heart of this people fat, and make their ears heavy, and shut their eyes; lest they see with their eyes, and hear with their ears, and understand with their heart, and convert, and be healed" (v. 10). For this reason, we have to carefully discern Isaiah's meaning through prayerful and consistent study.

- **Isaiah 28:9–10 Isaiah's words are meat, not milk.** He is communicating to those who are spiritually mature (see 1 Cor. 3:1–3; Heb. 5:13–14). "Whom shall he teach knowledge? and whom shall he make to understand doctrine?" the Lord asks, and then answers, "them that are weaned from the milk, and drawn from the breasts" (v. 9). Such knowledge is learned "precept upon precept; line upon line, ... here a little, and there a little" (v. 10). Thus, we must have a sound foundation of gospel knowledge before attempting to read and understand Isaiah.

- **Jacob 4:14 Many look beyond the mark**—they misunderstand because they are looking for something other than (or more than) the intended meaning. We must not over-interpret a scripture by assigning meanings to things that are either incorrect or mistimed. For example, the Jews looked beyond the mark when they expected the Messiah (who will come in latter days) to come and free them from Roman oppression. As a result, they rejected and crucified the Savior, who did not meet their misinterpreted criteria.

  Victor L. Ludlow wrote:

  > Like the messianic prophecies, the prophecies of the last days in the writings of Isaiah are often written on many levels and find fulfillment in ages beyond those in which they were spoken or recorded. For this reason, some latter-day prophecies seem

juxtaposed or out of place against fairly mundane historical background. But Isaiah is not alone in this prophetic style. In Revelation, John repeatedly moves backward and forward in time to make his point and strengthen his rhetoric, though in doing so he often confuses those who do not have the same prophetic insight as he does.

For ... example, Isaiah launches forth in a declaration of the restoration of the gospel in chapter 5, verses 26–30 in the midst of what could be a call to repentance for any age.

Jews reading Isaiah miss the messianic references, which apply to Jesus Christ, while the traditional Christian readers usually overlook the glorious message of the Restoration. Latter–day Saints stand apart in their perspective of Isaiah because, with their fuller understanding of the gospel, they should be able to see how Isaiah's prophecies can find a full range of fulfillment and application.[12]

Understanding Typologically

To understand typologically means to understand past events as a "type" (symbol) of future events. The Savior describes "all things [Isaiah] spake" as things that "have been and shall be" (3 Ne. 23:3), meaning that things that have been in the past shall also be in the future. Here are some other examples of typological prophecy:

— **2 Nephi 25:7–10 Nephi speaks of events that have already happened, yet he speaks of their fulfillment in the latter days.** This appears to be a contradiction, until we realize that Nephi, as a Jew, viewed the words of Isaiah typologically. He used an event from Israel's past as a type or symbol of an event yet to come.

Jerusalem's first destruction is a "type" of 2 more to come

Nephi also said Isaiah's writings will seem clear in the latter days when they are fulfilled (v. 8). For example, Isaiah 29 becomes quite clear when one knows about the real historical events surrounding the coming forth of the Book of Mormon and compares them with prophecies uttered by Isaiah more than 2,700 years ago.

— **2 Nephi 6:4**	Nephi's brother Jacob describes Isaiah's writings as "things which are, and which are to come."
— **Ecclesiastes 1:9**	Solomon says "[what has] been" is a type (symbol) of what "shall be."
— **Isaiah 44:7**	The Lord uses typology to "foreshadow things to come."

● **Dualism.** Sometimes metaphors and prophecies apply to more than one time and place:

— **Isaiah 2:2–3** (2 Nephi 12:2–3): This is a metaphoric prophecy concerning the "mountain of the Lord's house ... in the top of the mountains." It was (and will be) fulfilled multiple times:

  * By the return of Judah to Jerusalem from their Babylonian captivity, and by their rebuilding of the temple around 520 BC.

  * By Mormon pioneers establishing the Church and temples in Utah in the 1800s.

  * When a new temple is built by the Jews at Jerusalem just prior to the Second Coming of Christ (see D&C 133:13).

— **Isaiah 13–14** (2 Nephi 23–24): The gathering of Israel and their eventual triumph over Babylon.

  * Babylon refers to the nation of Babylon in Isaiah's time.

  * It also refers to wickedness and dominions of Satan and the world.

  * It also refers to the premortal overthrow of Lucifer and his hosts.

ISAIAH IN THE BOOK OF MORMON

The Book of Mormon as a Guide to Understanding Isaiah

Elder Bruce R. McConkie said, "The Book of Mormon is the world's greatest commentary on the book of Isaiah."[13]

This is certainly true when we consider the following:

— The Book of Mormon prophets loved Isaiah's writings and quoted from them often.

— Large blocks of Isaiah are included with inspired commentary and explanations.

— This Isaiah material was taken from the brass plates, written before 600 BC.

— This is the oldest and most accurate available version of Isaiah's writings.

— It provides commentary by prophets who shared Isaiah's background.

● **Nephi and his brother Jacob studied, expounded upon, and loved the writings of Isaiah:**

— 1 Nephi 15:20 "Isaiah ... spake concerning the restoration of the ... house of Israel."

— 1 Nephi 19:23 "That I might more fully persuade them to believe in the Lord their Redeemer I did read unto them that which was written by the prophet Isaiah."

— 1 Nephi 19:24 "Hear ye the words of the prophet, which were written unto all the house of Israel."

— 2 Nephi 6:4 "Behold, I would speak unto you concerning things ... which are to come; wherefore, I will read you the words of Isaiah."

— 2 Nephi 6:4 "I speak [Isaiah's words] that ye may learn and glorify the name of your God."

— 2 Nephi 11:2 "[Isaiah] verily saw my Redeemer."

— 2 Nephi 11:8 "And now I write some of the words of Isaiah, that whoso of my people shall see these words may lift up their hearts and rejoice for all men."

— 2 Nephi 11:8 "And ye may liken [the words of Isaiah] unto you and unto all men."

— 2 Nephi 25:5 "Yea, and my soul delighteth in the words of Isaiah."

— 2 Nephi 25:7–8 "The prophecies of Isaiah ... shall be of great worth ... in the last days."

● **2 Nephi 6:5** Nephi's brother Jacob, who succeeded him as the Lord's prophet to the Nephites, said Isaiah's teachings apply to all of us as children of Israel.

● **Jacob 5** Jacob quoted an allegory by the Judean prophet Zenos about olive trees. We can gain a greater understanding of Isaiah's writings by studying the symbolism he used to describe the Lord's efforts to establish Israel as a righteous people.

Elder Russell M. Nelson wrote: "Isaiah is ... one of the major contributors to the Book of Mormon. ... Some 433 verses of Isaiah—roughly a third of the entire book—are quoted in the Book of Mormon. In the English language edition, more than half (about 233 verses) differ in some detail from their biblical counterpart, while about 200 verses have the same wording as [the] KJV."[14]

ISAIAH'S PROPHECIES OF THE LATTER DAYS

Isaiah spoke frequently of the latter days: 53 of the 66 chapters of Isaiah contain verses pointing to our time (those that do not are chapters 7–9, 15–16, 20–21, 23, 36–39, and 46).

— "In that day" One clue to finding Isaiah's passages about the last days is to look for the phrase "in that day." It occurs 43 times in Isaiah, almost always in conjunction with prophecies about our day.

● **2 Nephi 25:7–8** Nephi said that Isaiah's writings will seem clear in the latter days when they are fulfilled. Isaiah 29 is an example of this. Its meaning is clear to those who have read and accepted the Book of Mormon.

Monte S. Nyman wrote: "A major reason for searching Isaiah's prophecies, as declared by the Savior and confirmed by Nephi and Jacob, is that Isaiah spoke concerning all the house of Israel and the covenants unto them which were to be fulfilled in the latter days."[15]

Elder Bruce R. McConkie said: "Much of what Isaiah ... has to say is yet to be fulfilled. ... But if we are to truly comprehend the writings of Isaiah, we cannot overstate or overstress the plain, blunt reality that he is in fact the prophet of the restoration, the mighty seer of Jacob's seed who foresaw our day and who encouraged our Israelite fathers in their spiritually weary and disconsolate state, with assurances of glory and triumph ahead for those of their descendants who would return to the Lord in the last days and at that time serve Him in truth and righteousness."[16]

The Prophet Joseph Smith said: "Search the scriptures—search the revelations which [are published], and ask your Heavenly Father, in the name of His Son Jesus Christ, to manifest the truth unto you, and if you do it with an eye single to His glory, nothing doubting, He will answer you by the power of His Holy Spirit. You will then know for yourselves and not for another. You will not then be dependent on man for the knowledge of God; nor will there by any room for speculation. ... For when men receive their instruction from Him that made them, they know how He will save them. ... Again we say: Search the scriptures, search the prophets, and learn what portion of them belongs to you."[17]

Other Helpful References for Understanding Isaiah

Many of the helps and suggestions found in this chapter have been adapted from those provided by other Isaiah scholars. If you desire further help, you may profit from obtaining these works and reading them in their entirety.

* "Understanding Isaiah" and "The World of Isaiah," in *Old Testament Student Manual, 1 Kings–Malachi*, Religion 302 (Salt Lake City: The Church of Jesus Christ of Latter-day Saints, 2003), 131–37, 171–78.

* "Hebrew Literary Styles," in *Old Testament Student Manual, Genesis–2 Samuel*, Religion 301 (Salt Lake City: The Church of Jesus Christ of Latter-day Saints, 2003), 303–8.

* "Nephi's Keys to Understanding Isaiah," by Donald W. Parry, in *Isaiah in the Book of Mormon* (Provo, UT: FARMS, 1998), 47–65.

* Bruce R. McConkie, "Ten Keys to Understanding Isaiah," *Ensign*, Oct. 1973, 78–83.

* Daniel H. Ludlow, *A Companion to Your Study of the Book of Mormon* (Salt Lake City: Deseret Book, 1976), 134–45.

* Joseph Fielding McConkie and Robert L. Millet, *Doctrinal Commentary on the Book of Mormon*, 4 vols. (Salt Lake City: Deseret Book, 1987–92), 1:151–67, 232–82.

* "Nephi and Isaiah," by Kent P. Jackson, in *Studies in Scripture, Vol. 7: 1 Nephi to Alma 29* (Salt Lake City: Deseret Book, 1987), 131–45.

Notes:

1. "Ten Keys to Understanding Isaiah," *Ensign*, Oct. 1973, 81.

2. In Conference Report, Oct. 1999, p. 90, footnote 17; or *Ensign*, Nov. 1999, p. 71, footnote 17; see also Monte S. Nyman, *"Great Are the Words of Isaiah"* [1980], 7, 283–87.

3. R. H. Charles, ed., *The Apocrypha and Pseudepigrapha of the Old Testament in English*, 2 vols. [1913], 2:162; see also Hebrews 11:37.

4. *Antiquities of the Jews*, 10.2.2.

5. As quoted by G. L. Robinson, in *The Book of Isaiah* [1910], 22, in *The Voice of Israel's Prophets* [1952], 14.

6. "Ten Keys to Understanding Isaiah," 80, 78.

7. In Conference Report, Apr. 1986, 77; or *Ensign*, May 1986, 61.

8. "Nephi's Lessons to His People: The Messiah, the Land, and Isaiah 48–49 in 1 Nephi 19–22," in D. W. Perry and J. W. Welch, ed., *Isaiah in the Book of Mormon* [1998], 99.

9. "Isaiah: Four Latter-day Keys to an Ancient Book," in Monte S. Nyman, ed., *Isaiah and the Prophets: Inspired Voices from the Old Testament*, [1984], 124–25.

10. *Lehi in the Wilderness: 81 New, Documented Evidences that the Book of Mormon Is a True History* [2003], 163–64.

11. "Chiasmus in the Book of Mormon; or, the Book of Mormon Does It Again," *New Era*, Feb. 1972, 6–7.

12. *Isaiah: Prophet, Seer, and Poet* [1982], 56.

13. "Ten Keys to Understanding Isaiah," 81.

14. In Conference Report, Oct. 1999, p. 90, footnote 17; or *Ensign*, Nov. 1999, p. 71, footnote 17.

15. *"Great Are the Words of Isaiah"*, 4.

16. "Ten Keys to Understanding Isaiah," 81.

17. *History of the Church*, 1:282

CHAPTER 3

Isaiah, Pt. 1:
The Messiah, the Scattering, and Restoration
(Isaiah 1–12)

ISAIAH'S VISION OF THE LORD

(Isaiah 1; 6)

The beginning of Isaiah's ministry is not found in chapter 1 but in chapter 6. There he describes his inaugural vision of the Lord and his call to be a prophet. As was the case with Abraham, Isaac, Jacob, Moses, Samuel, Joseph Smith, and so many more, Isaiah's ministry came in response to an open visitation of the Lord. That is how the Lord calls His prophets.

● **Isaiah 1:1 Isaiah's glorious vision occurred in the Holy of Holies of the Jerusalem temple,** a fact that is not included in Isaiah 1:1, but we learn this in Isaiah 6:1 and 2 Nephi 16:1.

Isaiah saw a vision of the Lord

GIOVANNI BATTISTA TIEPOLO,1726–1729

- **Isaiah 6:1** (2 Nephi 16:1): **Isaiah sees the Lord.** The vision occurred "in the year that king Uzziah died" (approximately 740 BC), and in this vision he "saw ... the Lord sitting upon a throne, high and lifted up" (v. 1). Both John and Nephi testified that the Lord whom Isaiah saw was the premortal Jesus Christ (see John 12:41; 2 Ne. 11:2–3).

- **Isaiah 6:2** (2 Nephi 16:2): **Isaiah describes the holy beings that surround the throne of God.** The figure of speech "seraphim" is a term meaning "fiery ones" or "serpents" (see Num. 21:6, 8; Deut. 8:15; Isa. 14:29) and refers to the kind of glorious beings that the Prophet Joseph Smith said "dwell in everlasting burnings."[1]

  There are also a number of metaphors in this scripture that, if taken literally, would seem very strange, but if interpreted symbolically are quite beautiful:

  — The seraphim have wings, a Hebrew term meaning "veils" or "covers."

  — With these wings, they can veil or cover their faces—Hebrew for "presence." They can also hide their feet or legs—Hebrew for "footing" or "location."

  — They have the power to "fly about," meaning "to move freely through space." Elder Bruce R. McConkie wrote: "Seraphs are angels who reside in the presence of God, giving continual glory, honor, and adoration to Him. ... The fact that these holy beings were shown to him [Isaiah] as having wings was simply to symbolize their 'power, to move, to act, etc.' as was the case also in visions others had received (D&C 77:4)."[2]

- **Isaiah 6:3** (2 Nephi 16:3): **The seraphim shouted praise unto the Lord.** Isaiah heard them cry out to one another, "Holy, holy, holy, is the Lord of hosts: the whole earth is full of his glory." In Hebrew, the way to give emphasis to a statement is to repeat it three times. Thus, "holy, holy, holy" in their language is the equivalent of saying "most holy" in our language.

- **Isaiah 6:4** (2 Nephi 16:4): **Their praise shook the foundation of the temple.** To say that "the posts of the door moved at the voice of him that cried" was a Hebrew way of saying the foundation ("posts of the door") shook.

- **Isaiah 6:4** (2 Nephi 16:4): **The glory of the Lord filled the room.** Isaiah said "the house was filled with smoke," which is a Hebrew figure of speech meaning that the "presence and glory of God" were there. The Prophet Joseph Smith said: "God Almighty Himself dwells in eternal fire; flesh and blood cannot go there, for all corruption is devoured by the fire. 'Our God is a consuming fire' [Deut. 4:24; Heb. 12:29]. When our flesh is quickened by the Spirit, there will be no blood in this tabernacle. Some dwell in higher glory than others. … Immortality dwells in everlasting burnings."[3]

- **Isaiah 6:5–7** (2 Nephi 16:5–7): **Isaiah received a forgiveness of his sins.** Recognizing that he was in the presence of holy beings, he cried out, "Woe is me! for I am undone"—a figure of speech indicating Isaiah's overwhelming feeling of unworthiness before God. "I am a man of unclean lips, and … mine eyes have seen the King, the Lord of hosts" (v. 5).

Hot coal on Isaiah's lips

In response, one of the seraphim flew to him, "having a live coal in his hand, which he had taken with the tongs from off the altar: And he laid it upon my mouth, and said, Lo, this hath touched thy lips; and thine iniquity is taken away, and thy sin purged" (vv. 6–7). The hot coals of the altar of sacrifice symbolized "cleansing" or "purging" to the Hebrews. Thus Isaiah's "unclean lips" (sins) were forgiven.

- **Isaiah 6:8–9** (2 Nephi 16:8–9): **Isaiah accepts a call to minister to his people.** The Lord asked Isaiah, "Whom shall I send, and who will go for us?" to which Isaiah willingly said, "Here am I; send me" (v. 8). The Lord then commanded him,

"Go, and tell this people, Hear ye indeed, but understand not; and see ye indeed, but perceive not" (v. 9). This may seem like an odd mission—to tell people not to understand—but it is, again, a figurative way of saying that the people will not listen to Isaiah. He needed to know from the beginning that he was sent to a wicked and perverse people, few of whom would respond.

● **Isaiah 64:4 The inadequacy of mortal language to describe heavenly things.** Later in his writings, Isaiah described the inadequacy of words and even of the senses of mortal man to comprehend or describe heavenly things. "For since the beginning of the world men have not heard, nor perceived by the ear, neither hath the eye seen, O God, beside thee, what he hath prepared for him that waiteth for him." The glory and beauty of the celestial kingdom is, literally, indescribable.

— **1 Corinthians 2:9; D&C 76:10 Others who have experienced visions of the celestial realms** have cited Isaiah in an attempt to explain their limited ability to tell of what they had been shown.

The Prophet Joseph Smith said: "Could we read and comprehend all that has been written from the days of Adam, on the relation of man to God and angels in a future state, we should know very little about it. Reading the experience of others, or the revelation given to *them*, can never give *us* a comprehensive view of our condition and true relation to God. Knowledge of these things can only be obtained by experience through the ordinances of God set forth for that purpose. Could you gaze into heaven five minutes, you would know more than you would by reading all that ever was written on the subject."[4]

● **Isaiah 64:9–12 The Lord warns Isaiah that the people will reject his message.** He saw a vision in which the cities of Judah became a wilderness, and Jerusalem even worse—a desolation (v. 10). He saw the temple, "our holy and our beautiful house, where our fathers praised thee, … burned up with fire: and all our pleasant things … laid waste" (v. 11). Isaiah was distraught, crying out to the Lord, "We are all thy people" (v. 9), and "wilt thou hold thy peace, and afflict us very sore?" (v. 12). We will discuss the details of this destruction later on in this chapter.

Apostate Conditions in Isaiah's Day

- **Isaiah 1:1–4 Judah's wicked state.** Isaiah saw discouraging things about Judah and Jerusalem (v. 1). He quotes the Lord as saying, "I have nourished and brought up children, and they have rebelled against me. The ox knoweth his owner, and the ass his master's crib: but Israel doth not know, my people doth not consider" (vv. 2–3). They are a "sinful nation, a people laden with iniquity, a seed of evildoers, children that are corrupters: they have forsaken the Lord, they have provoked the Holy One of Israel unto anger, they are gone away backward" (v. 4). This was Isaiah's first use of the sacred title "Holy One of Israel." It would not be the last. It appears 30 times in his writings.

- **Isaiah 1:5–6 Their rebellion against the Lord is total.** Isaiah makes references to the head and heart and to the whole person from head to foot. "The whole head is sick, and the whole heart faint," he says (v. 5.) "From the sole of the foot even unto the head there is no soundness in it; but wounds, and bruises, and putrifying sores: they have not been closed, neither bound up, neither mollified with ointment" (v. 6). In other words, spiritual cancer had infested the entire body of Israel.

- **Isaiah 1:7–8 Their punishment will be total.** Looking ahead, Isaiah said, "Your country is desolate, your cities are burned with fire: your land, strangers devour it in your presence, and it is desolate, as overthrown by strangers. And the daughter of Zion is left as a cottage in a vineyard, as a lodge in a garden of cucumbers, as a besieged city" (vv. 7–8). "When the vineyard and the cucumber crops were ready to harvest, small booths, or huts, were built in the fields so the owner or his servants could watch over the harvest and protect it from thieves or

animals. These huts were generally crudely made and hastily erected. After the harvest, they were abandoned and quickly became dilapidated and forlorn relics of the harvest. Jerusalem was to be like that—once proud and useful, but now, through her own spiritual neglect, an empty and forlorn relic."[5]

● **Isaiah 1:9 The Lord will preserve "a very small remnant."** Otherwise, their destruction would have been as total as it was for the cities of Sodom and Gomorrah. The Lord will preserve a few people to continue the lineage of Judah for a future time. Paul cited this passage to explain what the Lord did to them (see Rom. 9:29; Isa. 10:22).

● **Isaiah 1:11–15 Their religious ceremonies are without meaning or faith.** "To what purpose is the multitude of your sacrifices unto me?" the Lord asked. "I am full of the burnt offerings of rams, and the fat of fed beasts; and I delight not in the blood of bullocks, or of lambs, or of he goats" (v. 11). "Bring no more vain oblations," He demands. "Incense is an abomination unto me; the new moons and sabbaths, the calling of assemblies, … it is iniquity, even the solemn meeting" (v. 13). The Lord wants no more of their religious ceremonies. "I am weary to bear them," He says (v. 14).

This does not mean that the Lord was rejecting the law of Moses or its ritual ceremonies. The condemnation is of the hypocritical misuse of these ordinances and gatherings. They fulfilled the outward requirements of the law, but they were not worshiping with full purpose of heart. "When ye spread forth your hands, I will hide mine eyes from you: yea, when ye make many prayers, I will not hear: your hands are full of blood" (v. 15).

Sins "As Red as Scarlet" Can Be "White as Snow"

● **Isaiah 1:16–20 The Lord is willing to forgive their sins, no matter how serious.** "Wash you, make you clean; put away the evil of your doings from before mine eyes; cease to do evil,"

He pleads (v. 16). "Learn to do well; seek judgment, relieve the oppressed, judge the fatherless, plead for the widow" (v. 17). These were sins of which they were seriously guilty. But they were not yet beyond redemption. "Though your sins be as scarlet, they shall be as white as snow; though they be red like crimson, they shall be as wool," the Lord and Savior promised (v. 18). But this offer was conditional: "If ye be willing and obedient, ye shall eat the good of the land: But if ye refuse and rebel, ye shall be devoured with the sword" (see also D&C 64:34–35).

THE LAST DAYS AND THE MILLENNIUM

(Isaiah 2)

As is true throughout the book of Isaiah, the prophet switches quickly from one dispensation to another. In chapter 1 the topic is his own sinful dispensation. In chapter 2, he changes to the last days and the Millennium, then compares the two dispensations with a series of dualistic prophecies.

The quickly-changing and non-chronological nature of Isaiah's prophecies leads some to believe that the book was assembled by somebody else as a collection of his thoughts and experiences. But it is equally possible that he is a visionary seer, whose visions sweep easily and quickly from one dispensation to another.

- **Isaiah 2:2–3** (2 Nephi 12:2–3): The Lord's house will be built in the "top of the mountains" and all nations will gather to it (see also Micah 4:1–2). The key elements of this prophecy are as follows:

  — "In the last days" (v. 2)—our latter day.

  — "The mountain of the Lord's house" (v. 2). This signifies a temple.

Lord's house in latter days

— "Established in the top of the mountains" (v. 2). Interestingly, the word *Utah* means "top of the mountains."

— "All nations shall flow unto it" (v. 2). "Many people shall go" (v. 3).

— "He will teach us of his ways" (v. 3). It will be a place of learning concerning God.

President Harold B. Lee said: "The coming forth of His Church in these days was the beginning of the fulfillment of the ancient prophecy when 'the mountain of the Lord's house shall be established in the top of the mountains.'"[6] "With the coming of the pioneers to establish the Church in the tops of the mountains, our early leaders declared … the beginning of the fulfillment of that prophecy."[7]

Elder LeGrand Richards said: "How literally … has [Isaiah 2:2–3] been fulfilled, in my way of thinking, in this very house of the God of Jacob right here on this block! This [Salt Lake] temple, more than any other building of which we have any record, has brought people from every land to learn of His ways and walk in His paths."[8]

● **Isaiah 2:3** (2 Nephi 12:2–3): **"Out of Zion shall go forth the law … [and] the word of the Lord from Jerusalem."** There will be two capitals of the Lord's kingdom in the Millennium. The political capital—the source of the "law"—will be the New Jerusalem built in the western hemisphere. The religious capital—"the word of the Lord"—will come from the Lord's own homeland and city: the Old Jerusalem. Both will be blessed by His presence and will serve the King of Kings.

President Joseph Fielding Smith wrote:

> We are informed in the revelation given to Joseph Smith the Prophet, that the city of Zion and the New Jerusalem is one and the same [D&C 28:9; 42:9; 45:66–67; 57:2; 58:7] . …
>
> Jerusalem of old, after the Jews have been cleansed and sanctified from all their sin, shall become a holy city where the Lord shall dwell and from whence He shall send forth His word unto all

people. Likewise, on this continent, the city of Zion, New Jerusalem, shall be built, and from it the law of God shall also go forth. There will be no conflict, for each city shall be headquarters for the Redeemer of the world, and from each He shall send forth His proclamations as occasion may require. Jerusalem shall be the gathering place of Judah and his fellows of the house of Israel, and Zion shall be the gathering place of Ephraim and his fellows, upon whose heads shall be conferred "the richer blessings."

"The Judge of Peace"

… These two cities, one in the land of Zion and one in Palestine, are to become capitals for the kingdom of God during the Millennium.[9]

● **Isaiah 2:4–5** (2 Nephi 12:4–5): **Establishment of the Millennium.** The Lord will reign over all nations and "many people" during His Millennial reign. It will be an era of peace, during which "they shall beat their swords into plowshares, and their spears into pruninghooks: nation shall not lift up sword against nation, neither shall they learn war any more" (v. 4). Isaiah rejoices over that day, saying, "O house of Jacob, come ye, and let us walk in the light of the Lord" (v. 5).

The writings of Isaiah in the Book of Mormon include an additional phrase in verse 5: "Yea, come, for ye have all gone astray, every one to his wicked ways" (2 Ne. 12:5). This verse indicates a widespread apostasy in Israel and the return of Israel to the Lord before the Second Coming.

CONDITIONS IN BOTH ISAIAH'S DAY & THE LATTER DAYS

(Dualistic Prophecies)

The Wicked Will Be Brought Low

● **Isaiah 2:5–22** (2 Nephi 12:5–22)**: The Lord warns the wicked not to trust in idols, because idols are "the work of their own hands"** (v. 8). As a result of their worship of idols, God will humble the "lofty looks of man" and the "haughtiness of men" (v. 11). We are told that "the Lord alone shall be exalted in that day" (v. 17). Following is a list of the most serious sins of which they were guilty, and which will be repeated in our own day.

— "Replenished from the east" (v. 6) means looking to the religious philosophies and the gods of the world for wisdom and guidance instead of to the gospel.

— "[Hearken unto] soothsayers" (v. 6) means following false prophets who claim to foretell the future.

— "Please themselves in the children of strangers" (v. 6) means joining the heathen nations in all their wickedness.

— "Full of silver and gold" (v. 7) means that people are wealthy and materialistic.

— "Full of horses, neither ... any end of their chariots" (v. 7) means reliance on military security instead of God. The horse was a symbol of warfare, as was the chariot.

— The land was filled with idolatry then (v. 8), and men still turn to false gods today, though their gods are no longer idols made of wood or stone.

— The "mean man boweth not down, and the great man humbleth himself not" (2 Ne. 12:9). Notice that the word *not* is absent from the phrases "mean man boweth not down" and "great man humbleth himself not" in the KJV of Isaiah 2:9. The Book of Mormon rendering of this verse shows that Isaiah was referring to men worshiping idols instead of the true God (see 2 Ne. 12:9, footnote b).

— The "cedars of Lebanon" and the "oaks of Bashan" (vv. 11–13) were the loftiest and most impressive trees in the ancient Middle East. They symbolized not only the great beauty of the land that would be destroyed but also the pride of men—which shall be brought low by the Lord.

— "Cease ye from man" (v. 22) is a warning about trusting merely in man.

- **Additional dualistic prophecies of sin in Isaiah's and our own day.** This theme recurs throughout Isaiah 3 and 5. Following is a summary of these additional sins that plagued Isaiah's dispensation and plague our own. Details of some of these prophecies follow below.

  — Oppression of other people and failing to honor older people (Isa. 3:5; 2 Ne. 13:5).

  — No shame for sin (Isa. 3:9; 2 Ne. 13:9).

  — Taking advantage of the poor; failing to care for them (Isa. 3:14–15; 2 Ne. 13:14–15).

  — Outward physical beauty but not righteousness and good character (Isa. 3:16–24; 2 Ne. 13:16–24).

  — Greedy desires to own more and more material things (Isa. 5:8; 2 Ne. 15:8).

  — Seeking worldly pleasures instead of the Lord and His work (Isa. 5:11–12; 2 Ne. 15:11–12).

  — Saying that evil things are good and good things are evil (Isa. 5:20; 2 Ne. 15:20).

  — Trusting in oneself instead of in God (Isa. 5:21; 2 Ne. 15:21).

  — Despising the commandments and word of God (Isa. 5:24; 2 Ne. 15:24).

PUNISHMENT AND RECOMPENSE

(Isaiah 3-5)

The Wickedness of Judah

● **Isaiah 3:1–9** (2 Nephi 13:1–9): **Noted officials and respected persons will fall because of their arrogance and sins.** Isaiah lists those upon whom a community depends for leadership and wisdom: "The mighty man, and the man of war, the judge, and the prophet, and the prudent, and the ancient, The captain of fifty, and the honourable man, and the counsellor, and the cunning artificer, and the eloquent orator," and says they will be taken away like needed bread and water (vv. 1–3). Instead, there will be oppression and a failure to honor older people (v. 5). There will be no shame for sin (v. 9). And "the shew of their countenance [will] witness against them," meaning that individuals will radiate the true nature of their spirit and attitude (v. 9).

President David O. McKay said: "Every man and every person who lives in this world wields an influence, whether for good or for evil. It is not what he says alone; it is not alone what he does. It is what he is. Every man, every person radiates what he or she really is. ... It is what we are and what we radiate that affects the people around us. As individuals, we must think nobler thoughts. We must not encourage vile thoughts or low aspirations. We shall radiate them if we do. If we think noble thoughts; if we encourage and cherish noble aspirations, there will be that radiation when we meet people, especially when we associate with them."[10]

● **Isaiah 3:9–12** (2 Nephi 13:9–12): **The sanctity of families is assaulted.** The sins of Sodom and Gomorrah were known among them (v. 9), and families will be undermined (v. 12). The righteous will be protected, "for they shall eat the fruit of their doings" (v. 10). But "woe unto the wicked! it shall be ill with him: for the reward of his hands shall be given him" (v. 11). This is a dualistic prophecy that applies both to ancient Israel, which was destroyed and taken captive, and modern Israel, when these sins will again appear.

Elder Ezra Taft Benson said: "And so today, the undermining of the home and family is on the increase, with the devil anxiously working to displace the father as the head of the home and create rebellion among the children. The Book of Mormon describes this condition when it states, 'And my people, children are their oppressors, and women rule over them.' And then these words follow—and consider these words seriously when you think of those political leaders who are promoting birth control and abortion: 'O my people, they who lead thee cause thee to err and destroy the way of thy paths' (2 Ne. 13:12)."[11]

● **Isaiah 3:12–15** (2 Nephi 13:12–15): **The leaders of the people will destroy the nation.** They will be oppressed by children and "women [will] rule over them" (v. 12). This would become literally true for Israel, but it is also a figure of speech suggesting the weakness of their kings and rulers who will have "eaten up the vineyard" (v. 14). The vineyard was a symbol of the chosen people in that day (see Isa. 5:7), and the rulers of Israel were called to be watchmen over it. Instead, they had oppressed the people and consumed the vineyard.

The Haughty Women of Zion

● **Isaiah 3:13–26** (2 Nephi 13:13–26): **Isaiah describes the wickedness of the daughters of Zion.** This is another dualistic prophecy, applying both to the women of Isaiah's day and also to the women in the latter days. These women were (and will be) proud, arrogant, and more concerned with their clothing, jewels, and personal appearance than with righteousness. The prophet contrasts their former beauty with the results of judgment. Because of their wickedness, the beauty, the pride, and the fashion shall become tragedy, disaster, and slavery.

- **Isaiah 3:16–23** (2 Nephi 13:16–23): **In Israel and Judah, the women were proud and arrogant,** and more concerned with their clothing, jewels, and personal appearance than with righteousness. These verses also describe women in the latter days.

— "Stretched forth necks" (v. 16) is an ancient figure of speech describing haughtiness—self-pride and scorn for others.

— "Mincing … and making a tinkling with their feet" (v. 16). The women wore costly ornamental chains connecting rings, often adorned with bells, around the ankles.

— "Discover their secret parts" (v. 17) is a figure of speech meaning that they would be put to shame. In addition to this, in our own day, women shamelessly display their literal secret parts to the world.

— "Cauls, and … round tires like the moon" (v. 18) were ornamental jewelry in the shape of suns and moons according to the fashions (and false religions) of that day.

— Other archaic terms (vv. 19–23) describe fashions that were popular among the worldly women in Isaiah's time:

- "muffler" = veil

- "bonnet" = headdress

- "tablets" = perfume boxes

- "earrings" = charms or amulets

- "nose jewels" = nose rings

- "changeable suits of apparel" = clothing used only for festivals

- "mantle" = overcloak

- "wimples" = a type of shawl or veil worn over the head.

- "crisping pins" = a mistranslation that suggests hair curling implements; the Hebrew word means a bag, like a purse or handbag.

- "glasses" = most authorities translate this as a metal mirror.

- "hoods" = turbans, head cover wrapped by hand.

- **Isaiah 3:24–26** (2 Nephi 13:24–26)**: The fruits of their transgression.** The prophet contrasts the former beauty of Israel's women with the results of their wickedness. Their beauty, pride, and fashion would turn into tragedy, disaster, and slavery. There are a number of figures of speech in this prophecy that need explaining:

  - The "girdle" will be replaced by a "rent"—the rope used to bind slaves.

  - "Sackcloth" was black goat's hair worn at times of great mourning.

  - The "burning" refers to the branding that accompanied being a slave.

  Thus Keil and Delitzsch translated this verse to say: "And instead of balmy scent there will be mouldiness, and instead of the sash, a rope, and instead of artistic ringlets a baldness, and instead of the dress cloak a frock of sackcloth, branding instead of beauty."[12]

- **Isaiah 4:1** (2 Nephi 14:1)**: There will be a scarcity of men due to war.** To be unmarried and childless in ancient Israel was a disgrace. So terrible will conditions in those times be that women will offer to share a husband with others and expect no material support from him, just so that they might have offspring.

- **Isaiah 4:4–6** (2 Nephi 14:4–6)**: Eventually, God will wash away the filth of the daughters of Zion** (v. 4) and restore the house of Israel as "a place of refuge, and … a covert from storm and from rain" (v. 6). Ed J. Pinegar wrote: "Isaiah outlined in painstaking detail the misdeeds and treachery of the wayward people of the Lord, whose prideful and idolatrous behaviors would predictably lead to their being smitten and dispersed. In stark contrast were Isaiah's visions of the coming times of restoration, when the scattered remnants would be gathered in from the four quarters of the earth and the nations would look to Zion as the only dependable source of wisdom and truth."[13]

The Consequences of Apostasy

● **Isaiah 5:1–7** (2 Nephi 15:1–7)**: Isaiah's parable of the desolate vineyard.** The first six verses of this chapter resemble the allegory of Zenos quoted in the Book of Mormon (see Jacob 5), and both of them may have been drawn from a similar or identical source.

The vineyard symbolizes the people or kingdom of our Lord ("my well beloved"). As with the prophet Zenos' allegory (as told by Jacob; see Jacob 5), the Lord "fenced [the vineyard], and gathered out the stones thereof, and planted it with the choicest vine, and built a tower in the midst of it, and also made a winepress therein: and he [hoped] that it should bring forth grapes, [but] it brought forth [instead] wild grapes" (v. 2). The Lord plaintively asks, "What could have been done more to my vineyard, that I have not done in it?" (v. 4). But finding it overrun with corruption, the Lord says He will "lay it waste: it shall not be pruned, nor digged; but there shall come up briers and thorns: I will also command the clouds that they rain no rain upon it" (v. 6). It will be left a desolate vineyard.

● **Isaiah 5:8–24** (2 Nephi 15:8–24)**: Sins that bring nations to destruction.**

— They greedily seek to own more and more material things (v. 8). "They, the insatiable, would not rest till, after every smaller piece of landed property had been swallowed by them, the whole land had come into their possession, and no one beside themselves was settled in the land [see Job 22:8]. Such covetousness was all the more reprehensible, because the law of Israel had provided so very stringently and carefully, that as far as possible there should be an equal distribution of the soil, and that hereditary family property should be inalienable."[14] And for ten acres to yield only one bath (about 5½ gallons) and a homer of seed (about 6½ bushels) only an ephah (about ⅔ bushel) shows how unproductive the land would become because of this wickedness (v. 10).

— They constantly seek worldly pleasures instead of seeking the Lord and His work (vv. 11–12). The Prophet Joseph Smith said: "The Church must be cleansed, and I proclaim against all iniquity. A man is saved no faster than he gets knowledge, for if he does not get knowledge, he will be brought into captivity by some evil power in the other world, as evil spirits will have more knowledge, and consequently more power than many men who are on the earth. Hence it needs revelation to assist us, and give us knowledge of the things of God."[15]

— "[They] draw iniquity with cords of vanity" (v. 18) is a figure of speech that means "they are tied to their sins like beasts to their burdens."

— They call evil things good and good things evil (v. 20). We see this sin manifest in our own modern society, where it seems that everything good is mocked and criticized while everything bad is celebrated and justified. By this means, the wicked seek to justify their unholy behavior.

— They are "wise in their own eyes" (v. 21)—trusting in themselves instead of in God. Though the logic of their excuses is questionable, they make them with an air of superiority and intellectual flair. Wicked men sit straight-faced and justify both murder and adultery as if these pernicious sins were logical and acceptable. Intellectualism becomes a cloak to cover gross deceptions and wickedness.

President N. Eldon Tanner said:

[When people] become learned in the worldly things such as science and philosophy, [they] become self-sufficient and are prepared to lean unto their own understanding, even to the point where they think they are independent of God; and because of their worldly learning they feel that if they cannot prove physically, mathematically, or scientifically that God lives, they can and should feel free to question and even to deny God and Jesus Christ. Then many of our professors begin to teach perverse things, to lead away disciples after them; and our youth whom we send to them for learning accept them as authority, and many are caused to lose their faith in God...

How much wiser and better it is for man to accept the simple truths of the gospel and to accept as authority God, the Creator of the world, and His Son Jesus Christ, and to accept by faith those things which he cannot disprove and for which he cannot give a better explanation. He must be prepared to acknowledge that there are certain things—many, many things—that he cannot understand.[16]

— They "justify the wicked for reward" (v. 23). Those who were guilty of crimes were declared innocent by bribed judges and other officials, whereas the innocent were found guilty so that they could be silenced or their property exploited.

— They despise the commandments and word of God (v. 24). In the eyes of the haughty, to be religious is to be superstitious and unsophisticated. Wishing to be free to practice their perversions, the proud mock anything that would question them.

● **Isaiah 5:21–25** (2 Nephi 15:21–25)**: Isaiah denounces the wickedness of Israel and Judah, prophesying destruction for both nations.** The Lord will scatter them over the earth, yet His "hand is stretched out still" (v. 25). That is, in spite of their wickedness the Lord has not forgotten them and is always willing to take them back (see also Isa. 9:8–21; 2 Ne. 19:8–21).

EVENTUAL GATHERING AND RESTITUTION OF ISRAEL

(Isaiah 4–6)

The Great Final Gathering

● **Isaiah 4:2–6** (2 Nephi 14:2–6)**: Zion will be beautified in preparation for the establishment of God's kingdom.** Isaiah says that "the branch of the Lord [will] be beautiful and glorious" (v. 2). The "Branch of the Lord" is Christ, who will dwell in the midst of Zion. For those that dwell in His midst, "the fruit of the earth shall be excellent and comely ... [and] he that is left in Zion, and he that remaineth in Jerusalem, shall be called holy, even every one that is written among the living in Jerusalem" (vv. 2–3). By that time, "the Lord shall have washed away the filth of the daughters of Zion, and shall have purged the blood of Jerusalem from the midst thereof by the spirit of judgment, and by the spirit of burning" (v. 4). Washing, purging, and burning all represent the purification of Zion in preparation for the establishment of God's kingdom in the last days (v. 4). As He did in the days of Moses, "the Lord will create upon every dwelling place of mount Zion, and upon her assemblies, a cloud and smoke by day, and the shining of a flaming fire by night," the glory of which shall be "a place of refuge, and for a covert from storm and from rain," which means a defense against all enemies (vv. 5–6).

Elder Orson Pratt said:

> The time is to come when God will meet with all the congregation of His Saints, and to show His approval, and that He does love them, He will work a miracle by covering them in the cloud of His glory. I do not mean something that is invisible, but I mean that same order of things which once existed on the earth so far as the tabernacle of Moses was concerned, which was carried in the midst of the children of Israel as they journeyed in the wilderness. …
>
> In the latter days there will be a people so pure in Mount Zion, with a house established upon the tops of the mountains, that God will manifest Himself, not only in their Temple and upon all their assemblies, with a visible cloud during the day, but when the night shall come, if they shall be assembled for worship, God will meet with them by His pillar of fire; and when they retire to their habitations, behold each habitation will be lighted up by the glory of God—a pillar of flaming fire by night.
>
> Did you ever hear of any city that was thus favored and blessed since the day that Isaiah delivered this prophecy? No, it is a latterday work, one that God must consummate in the latter times when He begins to reveal Himself, and show forth His power among the nations.[17]

An Ensign Will Be Lifted Up in the Last Days

(A Royal Metaphor)

● **Isaiah 5:25–30** (2 Nephi 15:25–30)**: Israel will be gathered in haste—with means not known in Isaiah's day.** Although the Lord would permit great destruction and death in Judah's streets, yet His hand was still offered to them in peace if they would take it (v. 25). And eventually, in the latter days, He will gather them again in peace.

He will "lift up an ensign to the nations from far, and will hiss unto them from the end of the earth: and, behold, they shall come with speed swiftly" (v. 26). An "ensign" or "banner" is a military symbol designating the place to which to gather. To "hiss" is a figure of speech from Isaiah's day which means to signal (such as with a whistle) to summon others to pay attention and to come. The place where the banner would be raised and the whistle blown would be "from the end of the earth"—literally half-way around the world from where Isaiah was speaking (v. 26). And they would come by means and with speed that must have seemed miraculous to Isaiah as he witnessed it (vv. 27–29).

Elder LeGrand Richards wrote:

In fixing the time of the great gathering, Isaiah seemed to indicate that it would take place in the day of the railroad train and the airplane: [Isaiah 5:26–29]. Since there were neither trains nor airplanes in that day, Isaiah could hardly have mentioned them by name.

Hooves of steel like a whirlwind and the roar of a lion

However, he seems to have described them in unmistakable words. How better could "their horses' hoofs be counted like flint, and their wheels like a whirlwind" than in the modern train? How better could "their roaring ... be like a lion" than in the roar of the airplane? Trains and airplanes do not stop for night. Therefore, was not Isaiah justified in saying: "none shall slumber nor sleep; neither shall the girdle of their loins be loosed, nor the latchet of their shoes be broken"? With this manner of transportation the Lord can really "hiss unto them from the end of the earth," that "they shall come with speed swiftly." Indicating that Isaiah must have foreseen the airplane, he stated: "Who are these that fly as a cloud, and as the doves to their windows?" (Isa. 60:8).[18]

All of this will occur in a day when the earth will be encompassed by the "roaring of the sea"—a well-known symbol of chaos and evil in Isaiah's day. It will come in a day when, upon the earth, there will be "darkness and sorrow" (v. 30).

The Return of a Remnant to Jerusalem

● **Isaiah 6:9–12** (2 Nephi 16:9–12): **Judah will reject Isaiah's message.** There are many figures of speech here, and without understanding them we would be hard-pressed to understand what he is saying.

— "Fat hearts" are hearts that do not feel.

— "Heavy ears" are ears that do not hear.

Though He knew they would not respond, the Lord sent Isaiah to preach repentance unto them so that they would be left without excuse. The people claimed to hear and see, but they did not want to understand the spirit of the message.

Keil and Delitzsch wrote: "[The command to] 'make the heart of this people fat, ... their ears heavy, and shut their eyes' is used to describe the process of making the people accountable. The command, of course, refers to 'their spiritual sight, spiritual hearing, and spiritual feeling.' ... There is a self-hardening in evil. ... Sin from its very nature bears its own punishment. ... An evil act in itself is the result of self-determination proceeding from a man's own will."[19]

When the prophet asked the Lord how long their hearts would be hardened, the Lord answered until the land is entirely forsaken and its inhabitants have been taken far away (vv. 11–12). In a wider sense, mankind will be like this until mortals no longer exist upon the earth (v. 11).

● **Isaiah 6:13** (2 Nephi 16:13): **Isaiah uses the metaphor of a teil tree to describe the cause and the results of Judah's captivity.**

The Lord will have removed the inhabitants of Judah "far away, and there be a great forsaking in the midst of the land" (v. 12). · But in the midst of this removal will be a remnant that will eventually bring life back to the holy land. "In it shall be a tenth, and it shall return, and shall be eaten: as a teil tree, and as an oak, whose substance is in them, when they cast their leaves: so the holy seed shall be the substance thereof."

— The Hebrew word that was translated as "eaten" has three meanings, and "eaten" is only one of them. The verb's primary meaning is "burned."

— The Hebrew word that was translated as "substance" has two meanings, and "substance" is only the secondary meaning. The primary meaning is "stump" or "that which is left standing."

— The "holy seed" are the descendants of Israel.

Hence, we can understand that the rotten teil trees (representing sinful Israel) will be burned, leaving only stumps. Israel's survivors (the "holy seed") are like stumps that remain alive when the tree is burned, cut down, or felled, and yet, because there is still life in the stumps, can grow into new trees.

The word *tenth* means "tithe" in Hebrew. The special ending the original word possesses makes it the "tithe of ya," or tithe of Jehovah, which refers to the "tithe of the tithe" that the Levites paid. Hence, we know that only 1 percent of the people will return after the tree of Israel is hewn down. The majority of them will be killed or dispersed away from Jerusalem.

PROPHECIES OF THE MESSIAH

(Isaiah 7, 9)

The Virgin Birth

- **Isaiah 7:1–13** (2 Nephi 17:1–13): King Ahaz (of Judah) **was invited to ask for a sign.** Syria had joined with Ephraim (the ten tribes) in a confederacy against Judah. Isaiah counseled Judah's king, Ahaz, "Fear not, neither be fainthearted. … It [the confederacy] shall not stand, neither shall it come to pass" (vv. 4, 7). The king did not believe Isaiah's prophecy, so Isaiah invited him to ask for a sign that Judah would be preserved despite its desperate situation. The king had so little faith in God's power to save them that he refused even this offer of reassurance (vv. 10–13).

- **Isaiah 7:14–15** (2 Nephi 17: 14–15): **The virgin birth of Christ is given as a sign.** Isaiah said that a son would be born of a virgin and would be known as Immanuel (meaning "God with us"), suggesting that He would be more than a prophet—He would be our God.

"A virgin shall conceive"

W. A. BOUGEUREAU, 1893

- **Isaiah 7:16–24** (2 Nephi 17:16– 24): **Before the child comes, Israel will be destroyed.** The kingdom of Israel (Ephraim), which the Jews despised, will be destroyed and will lose "both her kings" (Ephraim's and Syria's as well; v. 16). Verse 24 reads: "With arrows and with bows shall men come thither" [thither meaning "there"]. This prophecy was fulfilled when Assyria overran both Syria and Israel in 721 BC.

The Messiah Will Come to Galilee

● **Isaiah 9:1–3** (2 Nephi 19:1–3): **Galilee will "[see] a great light."** This area (the land of Zebulun and Naphtali beyond the Jordan River), which was previously afflicted by warfare when overrun by Assyria in 721 BC, will know the joy of the presence of the Messiah. Matthew saw the fact that the Messiah dwelt in the area of Galilee as a fulfillment of Isaiah's prophecy (see Matt. 4:12–16).

While speaking of the blessings the Messiah will bring, a verse in Isaiah says, "Thou hast multiplied the nation, and *not* increased the joy" (Isa. 9:3; emphasis added). The inconsistency of this statement is corrected in the Book of Mormon version of Isaiah, where the word not does *not* appear (see 2 Ne. 19:3).

● **Isaiah 9:4–5** (2 Nephi 19:4–5): **Eventually the Messiah will come as a conqueror.** In that day, the "yoke" of Israel's burdens and the "rod" of her oppressors will be broken (v. 4). In the midst of a great battle, with much blood, the Lord will come "with burning and fuel of fire" (v. 5), which means that Christ's Second Coming will be accompanied by cleansing and destruction by fire.

The Messiah Will Come As a Child

● **Isaiah 9:6–7** (2 Nephi 19:6–7): **The Messiah will be born.** When He comes the first time, the Messiah will not come in power as a great conqueror. Nevertheless, this little child will eventually become the King of Kings, who, after His Second Coming as a great Deliverer of His people in Jerusalem, will preside over a government and a peace that will last forever. The poetic beauty of this prophecy is unsurpassed in all of scripture:

> For unto us a child is born, unto us a son is given: and the government shall be upon his shoulder: and his name shall be called Wonderful, Counsellor, The mighty God, The everlasting Father, The Prince of Peace.

Elder Joseph Fielding Smith wrote about the Savior's titles:

> Isaiah ... speaks of Christ as "Wonderful, Counselor, the Mighty
> God, the Everlasting Father, the Prince of Peace." These titles, and
> the sayings that Jesus was the Creator and all things were made by
> Him, have proved to be a stumbling block to some who are not
> well informed. The question arises, "How could He, if He had not
> body and flesh and bones, before He was born of Mary, accomplish
> these things as a spirit?" Jesus had no body of flesh and bones until
> He was born at Bethlehem. This He fully explained to the brother
> of Jared. The answer to this question is simply that He did these
> wonderful works because of the glory His Father had given him
> before He was born (John 17:5–24) and because at that time He
> was God.[20]

JUDAH'S REJECTION OF SIGNS AND WARNINGS

(Isaiah 7–10; 13)

Writing was a major component of
Isaiah's mission. Thus, we have 66 chapters
of his prophecies and counsel. In this section
of Isaiah, the Lord commands Isaiah to "take
thee a great roll, and write in it with a man's
pen" (Isa. 8:1; see also 2 Ne. 18:1).

Obedient as always, Isaiah wrote what
the Lord commanded him to write.

Take a great roll & write

- **Isaiah 8:18, 1–4** (2 Nephi 18:18, 1–4):
  Symbolic names for Isaiah's sons. Isaiah
  said that "I and the children whom the
  Lord hath given me are for signs and for wonders in Israel" (v. 18).
  This means that they (including their names) were symbolic of
  Israel's status and eventual fate. We should recall that the Lord did a
  similar thing with the names of Hosea's children (see Hosea 1:4–9).

The name Isaiah means "Jehovah saves." The names of his two
known sons also convey a message to the people in Judah.

— Maher-shalal-hash-baz means "to speed the spoil; he hasteneth the prey."

— Shear-jashub means "the remnant shall return" (see Isa. 7:3).

— Prophetess. The expression is used here only to designate the prophet's wife, not a prophetic office or gift.

Because of these names, whenever anyone saw, heard, or spoke to Isaiah and his sons, he was reminded of the Lord's warning, as given through their names.

● **Isaiah 7:1–9** (2 Nephi 17:1–9): **A prophetic warning against Judah forming an alliance with Israel and Syria.** The kingdom of Israel (Ephraim) in the north had formed an alliance with Syria for mutual strength and protection against the conquering empire of Assyria. They were called by Isaiah "smoking firebrands"—torches that had burned out (v. 4). Isaiah warned King Ahaz of Judah against seeking political alliances in order to defend his people. The king eventually rejected the warning. Isaiah predicted that "within threescore and five [65] years," Israel (Ephraim) will be destroyed (v. 8). This indeed happened after initial invasions by both Tiglath-pileser III and Shalmaneser V, followed by the final conquest and displacement of the majority of the population under the Assyrian king Esarhaddon.

● **Isaiah 8:9–13** (2 Nephi 18:9–13): **Judah is told not to trust in foreign alliances but to trust in the Lord, because all alliances will come to naught.** If they sought to associate themselves with foreign powers, they would be "broken in pieces." And although foreign nations might "gird" themselves with armor, they also would be "broken in pieces" (v. 9). "Take counsel together, and it shall come to nought; speak the word, and it shall not stand" (v. 10).

Instead, they were to trust in God, who "is with us" (v. 10). Isaiah was to warn them away from any confederacy with another power, and to say unto them to be not afraid (vv. 11–12). "Sanctify the Lord of hosts himself," Isaiah taught, "and let him be your fear, and let him be your dread" (v. 13).

- **Isaiah 8:6–8** (2 Nephi 18:6–8): **Isaiah foresees the inevitable consequence—destruction, first in his own generation by the Assyrians and later by the Babylonians.** "Forasmuch as this people refuseth the waters of Shiloah that go softly, and rejoice in Rezin and Remaliah's son; Now therefore, behold, the Lord bringeth up upon them the waters of the river, strong and many, even the king of Assyria, and all his glory: and he shall come up over all his channels, and go over all his banks: And he shall pass through Judah; he shall overflow and go over, he shall reach even to the neck; and the stretching out of his wings shall fill the breadth of thy land, O Immanuel."

The Consequences of Rejecting the Lord

- **Isaiah 8:14** (2 Nephi 18:14): **The Lord, their refuge and Savior, was a "stone of stumbling" to them.** He could have been their "sanctuary," but instead became "a stone of stumbling" and "a rock of offence to both the houses of Israel," and "a gin and … a snare to the inhabitants of Jerusalem."

- **Isaiah 8:15–17** (2 Nephi 18:15–17): **Isaiah's witness will stand against them.** Many among them will "stumble, and fall, and be broken, and be snared, and be taken" in captivity (v. 15). They had been forewarned but did not repent, and now Isaiah's witness will be held against them. "Bind up the testimony, [and] seal the law among my disciples," he says. "I will wait upon the Lord, that hideth his face from the house of Jacob, and I will look for him" (v. 17).

- **Isaiah 8:19** (2 Nephi 18:19): **They sought after false spirits to guide them.** "Familiar spirits" (v. 19) is translated from a Hebrew word that meant "a leather bottle or bag." These bags were used by spiritual mediums, who pretended to communicate with the dead. It involved a form of ventriloquism wherein the voice or message of the "departed spirits" was supposedly called forth from the bag or sometimes from a pit. "Peeping" (chirping) like birds and "muttering" (twittering) were employed to supposedly get the departed spirits to come and deliver their message.

President Joseph Fielding Smith wrote: "To seek for information through … any way contrary to the instruction the Lord has given is a sin. The Lord gave positive instruction to Israel when they were in the land of their inheritance that they were to go to Him for revelation and to avoid the devices prevalent among the heathen nations who occupied their lands."[21]

● **Isaiah 8:20–22** (2 Nephi 18:20–22): **For rejecting the Lord, the Jews will inherit "trouble … darkness … [and] anguish."** Isaiah says, "There is no light in them" (v. 20). They will "be taken into captivity because they would not hearken" (v. 21, footnote a). Finding themselves in that condition, "they shall fret themselves, and curse their king and their God" (v. 21). They will look upward toward heaven and down toward the earth, and everywhere they will find "trouble and darkness, dimness of anguish" (v. 22).

● **Isaiah 9:8–21** (2 Nephi 19:8–21): **The Lord's "hand is stretched out still."** Although Israel refused to heed the Lord's offer of forgiveness, He was and is always ready to receive them back. This is a repeat of His offer of acceptance first stated in Isaiah 5:21–25 (see also 2 Ne. 15:21–25).

The Wicked Are Punished by the Wicked

● **Isaiah 10:5–11** (2 Nephi 20:5–11): **God used Assyria to punish Israel.** He called Assyria "the rod of mine anger, and the staff [of] mine indignation" (v. 5). He allowed them to conquer Israel ("an hypocritical nation, and … the people of my wrath") and to take them as prey and "to tread them down like the mire of the streets" (v. 6).

The Lord used Assyria to punish Israel

parents punish their children

This was not what the Lord wanted to do, but to destroy wickedness "it is in his heart to destroy and cut off nations not a few" (v. 7). The rulers of all nations are accountable unto Him (v. 8), and He will do unto Judah for her wickedness exactly what He did unto Israel (v. 11).

- **Isaiah 10:9, 24–34** (2 Nephi 20:9, 24–34): **The coming successful military campaigns of Assyria** (v. 9). Isaiah prophesies of the eventual intrusion and success of Assyria against Judah, even listing the names of many of the cities of Judah that will fall to them (vv. 28–32).

- **Isaiah 10:12–19** (2 Nephi 20:12–19): **Assyria will also be destroyed because of their own wickedness.** They are merely tools in His hands to perform His purposes, and they have no cause to boast, because the wicked are punished by the wicked (see Morm. 4:5). The destruction both of Israel and of Assyria is described as complete (vv. 15–19).

- **Isaiah 13:6–13** (2 Nephi 23:6–13): **God will destroy the wicked, but He will be merciful to the righteous.** This is a dualistic prophecy that has reference to (1) the destruction brought upon Judah by Babylon and (2) the destruction of the wicked at Christ's Second Coming.

President Joseph Fielding Smith wrote:

> When Christ comes the second time it will be in the clouds of heaven, and it shall be the day of vengeance against the ungodly, when those who have loved wickedness and have been guilty of transgression and rebellion against the laws of God will be destroyed. All during the ministry of Christ wickedness ruled and seemed to prevail, but when He comes in the clouds of glory as it is declared in this message of Malachi to the world, and which was said by Moroni to be near at hand, then Christ will appear as the refiner and purifier of both man and beast and all that pertains to this earth, for the earth itself shall undergo a change and receive its former paradisiacal glory.[22]

THE LATTER-DAY GATHERING

(Isaiah 10–14)

The Restoration of Scattered Israel

● **Isaiah 10:22–25** (2 Nephi 20:22–25)**: Israel will be consumed by the Assyrians.** Isaiah prophesied, "The Lord God of hosts shall make a consumption … in the midst of all the land" (v. 23). This consumption will occur under the hand of the Assyrians, who will "smite thee with a rod, and … lift up [their] staff against

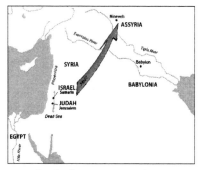

Israel taken captive into Assyria

thee, after the manner of Egypt" (v. 24). But the Lord comforts them with the knowledge that after "a very little while," their "indignation shall cease" as a result of "their [the Assyrians'] destruction" (v. 25). Not long thereafter, the children of Israel (the northern ten tribes) were set free and wandered northward toward Europe and the steppes of northern Asia.

● **Isaiah 10:20–25** (2 Nephi 20:20–25)**: A remnant of Israel will return to God and will "overflow with righteousness."** The remnant of Israel that manages to "escape" from their long captivity and dispersion "shall no more again stay [rely] upon him that smote them; but shall stay [rely] upon the Lord, the Holy One of Israel, in truth" (v. 20). This will occur when they "return … unto the mighty God" (v. 21). Although in that day the descendants of Israel shall be as numerous as the "sand of the sea," only a "remnant [of them] shall return," but they will "overflow with righteousness" (v. 22).

This scripture provides a five-point formula for salvation: seeing, hearing, understanding, returning or repenting, and being healed. This is the process converts go through as they first see [become aware of] the kingdom, then hear the message, come to understand its importance, and repent and are baptized for the remission of sins. Finally, they are "healed" from their lost condition.

The Stem, Branch, Rod, and Root of Jesse

When the angel Moroni visited Joseph Smith on 21 September 1823, "he quoted the eleventh chapter of Isaiah, saying that it was about to be fulfilled" (JS—H 1:40). The chapter was later interpreted by the Prophet Joseph Smith in March of 1838 (see D&C 113). It uses the metaphor of a tree—the family tree of Jesse (David's father)—to speak of two great events and two great descendants of Jesse who would come to help save and restore Israel.

HEINRICH HOFMANN

"Branch/Stem" of Jesse

To understand this metaphor of a tree, we must understand the meaning of certain words Isaiah uses to describe it. A "stem" is the trunk or stump of a tree. A "rod" is a small twig that grows out of a branch. And a "root" is a small shoot that grows out of a tree stump. Isaiah speaks here of a rod and a branch growing out of a tree, and he also speaks of a root growing out of the stump of the tree. A "branch" means exactly what it means today: a branch of a tree, which by definition is larger (more significant) than a rod (twig or shoot) of a tree. And "roots" also means what it does today: the roots from which a tree grows.

- **Isaiah 11:1 (2 Nephi 21:1): The "Branch" and "Stem" of Jesse.** We are told in D&C 113:1–2 that the "Stem" in this scripture is Christ. The word in Isaiah is "Branch," not "Stem," so this can be confusing. Isaiah says the "Branch" (tree) will grow out of the "roots" of Jesse. Note that the word Branch is capitalized in Isaiah but not in 2 Nephi 21:1. Thus, we can understand "stem" as both the family tree of Jesse (as Isaiah says), and also as Jesus Christ (as D&C 113 says). The metaphor works equally well with either interpretation.

Elder Bruce R. McConkie wrote: "Jesse was the father of David. Isaiah speaks of the Stem of Jesse, whom he also designates as a branch growing out of the root of that ancient worthy. He recites how the Spirit of the Lord shall rest upon Him; how He shall be mighty in judgment; how He shall smite the earth and slay the wicked; and how the lamb and the lion shall lie down together in that day—all of which has reference to the Second Coming and the millennial era thereby ushered in (Isa. 11). As to the identity of the Stem of Jesse, the revealed words says: 'Verily thus saith the Lord: It is Christ' (D&C 113:1–2). This also means that the Branch is Christ."[23]

- **Isaiah 11:1** (2 Nephi 21:1): **A "rod out of the stem of Jesse."** We are told in D&C 113: 3–4 that the rod in this scripture is "a servant in the hands of Christ, who is partly a descendant of Jesse as well as of Ephraim, or the house of Joseph, on whom there is laid much power"—an apparent reference to the Prophet Joseph Smith. If so, he is a descendant of Judah and Ephraim.

UNKNOWN ARTIST, NAUVOO, 1842

"Rod/Root" of Jesse

President Joseph Fielding Smith wrote: "It is Ephraim, today, who holds the priesthood. It is with Ephraim that the Lord has made covenant and has revealed the fulness of the everlasting gospel. It is Ephraim who is building temples and performing the ordinances in them for both the living and for the dead. When the 'lost tribes' come—and it will be a most wonderful sight and a marvelous thing when they do come to Zion—in fulfilment of the promises made through Isaiah and Jeremiah, they will have to receive the crowning blessings from their brother Ephraim, the 'firstborn' in Israel."[24]

President Brigham Young said: "It is the house of Israel we are after, and we care not whether they come from the east, the west, the north, or the south; from China, Russia, England, California, North or South America, or some other locality; and it is the very lad on whom father Jacob laid his hands, that will save the house of Israel. The Book of Mormon came to Ephraim, for Joseph Smith was a pure Ephraimite, and the Book of Mormon was revealed to him, and while he lived he made it his business to search for those who believed the gospel."[25]

● **Isaiah 11:10** (2 Nephi 21:10): **A "root" of Jesse that will stand for an ensign to the people.** We are told in D&C 113:5–6 that the "root" is "a descendant of Jesse, as well as of Joseph, unto whom rightly belongs the priesthood, and the keys of the kingdom"—another apparent reference to the Prophet Joseph Smith. Because of his heritage, he has a right to the priesthood and its keys. He is to stand as "an ensign, and for the gathering of [the Lord's] people in the last days." An ensign is a flag used in battle that, when raised, becomes a sign of where the soldiers are to gather. In this case, it is an ensign for the scattered tribes of Israel in the latter days.

Whether we see him as a rod (twig) growing out of the Branch of Christ, or as a root (shoot) emerging from the tree stump of Jesse, Joseph Smith is clearly a central figure in this prophecy of Isaiah.

The Final Gathering of Israel

● **Isaiah 11:11–12** (2 Nephi 21:11–12): **The Lord will gather His chosen people "the second time" from "the four corners of the earth."** Their first captivity and gathering was in Egypt, from which they were gathered out by Moses. The second time will be from among all the nations of the earth, even stretching to "the islands of the sea" [a figure of speech meaning the "ends of the earth"] (v. 11).

The place names in this scripture—Assyria (Syria), Egypt, Pathros (upper Egypt), Cush (Ethiopia), Elam (Iran), Shinar (Iraq), and Hamath (lower Syria and Lebanon)—are both literal and symbolic. These are nations and places that surround Israel and are today some of her most bitter enemies, yet the gospel message will apparently penetrate them before the Lord comes. After naming them, the prophet adds "the four corners of the earth" (v. 12) to the list, suggesting that the gathering will be worldwide and not just local.

- **Isaiah 11:12** (2 Nephi 21:12): **Two different groups—Israel and Judah—will be gathered.** He will do this by setting up an "ensign [a royal metaphor for a place of gathering] for the nations." And He will gather both the "outcasts of Israel" and the "dispersed of Judah" to their places of inheritance in both the old and new world (v. 12).

Elder LeGrand Richards wrote:

> From this scripture [Isaiah 11:10–12] … we learn that three important events were to transpire: (1) He shall set up an ensign for the nations; (2) He shall assemble the outcast of Israel; (3) He shall gather together the dispersed of Judah from the four corners of the earth. It is clear there are to be two gathering places—one for Israel and one for Judah.[26]

- **Isaiah 11:14** (2 Nephi 21:14): **The role of the Gentiles in the gathering of Israel.** Isaiah said that the gathered souls of Israel and Judah "shall fly upon the shoulders of the Philistines toward the west." This dualistic prophecy not only predicts the gathering of the children of Edom, Moab, and Ammon into the land of Israel to the west of them, but also the gathering of all the hosts of Israel from around the world to the western hemisphere, where the Church's headquarters and New Jerusalem will be established.

Elder Orson F. Whitney said:

> Seven hundred years before the birth of the Savior, the Prophet Isaiah, looking down the vista of time, saw the latter-day gathering

of the scattered House of Israel, and said concerning them: "They shall fly upon the shoulders of the Philistines toward the West." We recognize the fulfilment of that prophecy in the founding of this Church by Joseph Smith, a lineal descendant of Abraham, Isaac, and Jacob, who thus lifted the ensign for the gathering of their descendants from their long dispersion among the nations.

But a part of the fulfilment rests with the Gentiles. Their steamships, their railroads, their means of rapid transit and communication— these are "the shoulders of the Philistines," upon which the children of Ephraim have been and are being brought to the West, to the land of Zion, where the New Jerusalem is to rise, where the pure in heart will assemble, and the necessary preparation be made for the coming of the Lord in His glory. God works outside as well as inside His Church, and uses big things and little things for the accomplishment of His purposes.[27]

● **Isaiah 11:15–16** (2 Nephi 21:15–16): **"The Lord shall utterly destroy the tongue of the Egyptian sea ... and there shall be an highway."** Elder Parley P. Pratt wrote: "We have also presented before us, in verse 15, the marvelous power of God, which will be displayed in the destruction of a small branch of the Red Sea, called the tongue of the Egyptian Sea, and also the dividing of the seven streams of some river [perhaps the Nile], and causing men to go over dryshod; and lest any should not understand it literally, verse 16 says that 'there shall be an highway for the remnant of his people, which shall be left, from Assyria; like as it was to Israel in the day that he came up out of the land of Egypt.' Now we have only to ask whether, in the days of Moses, the Red Sea was literally divided or whether it was only a figure, for as it was then, so it shall be again."[28]

The entire chapter of Isaiah 11 is a thrilling prophecy of events in the latter days—the days in which we now live. Prophecies like these make Isaiah not only an ancient prophet but also a restoration prophet, predicting the great events of the final dispensation.

Elder Wilford Woodruff said:

Isaiah's soul seemed to be on fire, and his mind wrapt in the visions of the Almighty, while he declared, in the name of the Lord, that it should come to pass in the last days that God should set His hand again the second time to recover the remnant of His people, assemble the outcasts of Israel, gather together the dispersed of Judah, destroy the tongue of the Egyptian sea and make men go over dry-shod, gather them to Jerusalem on horses, mules, swift beasts, and in chariots, and rebuild Jerusalem upon her own heaps; while, at the same time, the destroyer of the Gentiles will be on his way; and while God was turning the captivity of Israel, He would put all their curses and afflictions upon the heads of the Gentiles, their enemies, who had not sought to recover, but to destroy them, and had trodden them under foot from generation to generation.

At the same time the standard should be lifted up, that the honest in heart, the meek of the earth among the Gentiles, should seek unto it; and that Zion should be redeemed and be built up a holy city, that the glory and power of God should rest upon her, and be seen upon her; that the watchman upon Mount Ephraim might cry—"Arise ye, and let us go up unto Zion, the city of the Lord our God;" that the Gentiles might come to her light, and kings to the brightness of her rising; that the Saints of God may have a place to flee to and stand in holy places while judgment works in the earth; that when the sword of God that is bathed in heaven falls upon Idumea, or the world— when the Lord pleads with all flesh by sword and by fire, and the slain of the Lord are many, the Saints may escape these calamities by fleeing to the places of refuge, like Lot and Noah.[29]

- **Isaiah 13:1–5** (2 Nephi 23:1–5): **God will gather His "sanctified ones ... from the end of heaven."** The synonymous parallel in verse 5 informs us that "from the end of heaven" means "from a far country." Latter-day Israel will be "a great people ... of nations gathered together" (v. 4).

- **Isaiah 14:1–3** (2 Nephi 24:1–3): **Israel will be gathered to "their own land ... the land of the Lord."** The children of Israel will be gathered to "their own land" and "strangers" (non-Israelite converts) shall be joined with them (v. 1). Isaiah makes a distinction here about where the ten tribes of Israel will gather, as opposed to Judah. They will be gathered "to their place ... from far ... to their lands of promise," where the house of Israel shall possess "the land of the Lord" (2 Ne. 24:2). It is interesting that the "land of the Lord" is designated as the place of gathering for the lost ten tribes.

George Reynolds and Janne M. Sjodahl observed that the word *America* was probably coined after indigenous American words like *Amerique* or *Marca* . These words consist of three parts: (1) *A*, which is the same as the Hebrew *the* ; (2) *malek*, or *malick*, which means king; and (3) *i* or *iah* , which means Jehovah. Put together, then, the name means "the king Jehovah." The main difference between the Book of Mormon name Amaleki and the modern name America is that there is an *R* in place of the *L* . But that can be explained by the fact that some Native American dialects lack 6 letters in the Spanish alphabet, one of which is *L*.

R, they tell us, takes its place, as it does with *Peru* for *Pelu*. They believe—and quote sources which support the idea—that America is the accepted form of the old Indian names Amerique and Marca, and not, as generally taught in our schools, in glorification of the map maker Amerigo Vespucci. "If this view is correct," they tell us, "America is, both in form and meaning, identical with the Book of Mormon names, Amaleki and Amalickiah, the meaning of which is, 'The King of Jehovah,' and, as applied to the country, 'The Land of the King Jehovah.'"[30]

It makes sense that the ten tribes will be gathered to the land of the King Jehovah.

CONDITIONS IN THE MILLENNIUM

● **Isaiah 11:2–5** (2 Nephi 21:2–5): **Christ is a righteous judge who will judge impartially.** We should take great comfort in knowing that it is Jesus Christ who will be our judge. Who better to judge the circumstances of my life than He who has experienced for and with me all of my sins, sorrows, pains, disappointments, and disabilities? In some way completely incomprehensible to us, He felt what we feel and suffered the consequences of our failures and sins. Who is better than He to judge us?

- **Isaiah 11:6–9** (2 Nephi 21: 6–9): **Great peace will exist during the Millennium.** This is the classic description of the Millennium that all Bible readers are familiar with: "The wolf also shall dwell with the lamb, and the leopard shall lie down with the kid, and the calf and the young lion and fatling together; and a little child shall lead them (v. 6). The synonymous parallels and metaphors in these verses are stunningly vivid, concluding with the great promise that "they shall not hurt nor destroy in all my holy mountain, for the earth shall be full of the knowledge of the Lord, as the waters cover the earth" (v. 9). It is in verses such as these that we are most aware of Isaiah's poetic gift, which gives rise to descriptions that are so beautiful we cannot imagine them being said in any other way.

UNKNOWN AUTHOR

Elder Orson Pratt said:

> The knowledge of God will then cover the earth as the waters cover the mighty deep. There will be no place of ignorance, no place of darkness, no place for those that will not serve God. Why? Because Jesus, the Great Creator, and also the Great Redeemer, will be Himself on the earth, and His holy angels will be on the earth, and all the resurrected Saints that have died in former dispensations will all come forth, and they will be on the earth. What a happy earth this creation will be, when this purifying process shall come, and the earth be filled with the knowledge of God as the waters cover the great deep! What a change! Travel, then, from one end of the earth to another, you can find no wicked man, no drunken man, no man to blaspheme the name of the Great Creator, no one to lay hold on his neighbor's goods, and steal them, no one to commit whoredoms—for all who commit whoredoms will be thrust down to hell, saith the Lord God Almighty, and all persons who commit sin will be speedily visited by the judgments of the Almighty![31]

- **Isaiah 11:13** (2 Nephi 21:13): **Judah and Ephraim will again live in peace with one another.** If we are familiar with the history of Judah and Israel, we know that after a brief golden age when King David and King Solomon reigned over a united nation, they split apart into two kingdoms: Israel in the north and Judah in the south, around Jerusalem. From that point forward, they were rivals and even enemies. This scripture looks forward to a day when "the envy also of Ephraim shall depart, and the adversaries of Judah shall be cut off: Ephraim shall not envy Judah, and Judah shall not vex Ephraim."

● **Isaiah 12:1–6** (2 Nephi 22:1–6): **Isaiah's hymn of praise for the great millennial era** when the Lord will reign "in the midst" of His people.

Notes:

1. *History of the Church*, 6:306.

2. *Mormon Doctrine*, 2nd ed. [1966], 702–3.

3. *History of the Church*, 6:366.

4. *History of the Church*, 6:50.

5. Edward J. Young, *The Book of Isaiah*, 3 vols. [1972], 1:55–56.

6. In Conference Report, Apr. 1973, 5; or *Ensign*, July 1973, 3–4.

7. "The Way to Eternal Life," *Ensign*, Nov. 1971, 15.

8. In Conference Report, Apr. 1971, 143; or *Ensign*, June 1971, 98.

9. *Doctrines of Salvation*, comp. Bruce R. McConkie, 3 vols. [1954–56], 3:69–71.

10. *Man May Know for Himself: Teachings of President David O. McKay*, comp. Clare Middlemiss [1967], 108.

11. In Conference Report, Oct. 1970, 21; or *Improvement Era*, Dec. 1970, 46.

12. *Commentary on the Old Testament*, 10 vols. [1996], 7:1:147.

13. *Teachings and Commentaries on the Old Testament* [2005], 589.

14. Keil and Delitzsch, *Commentary on the Old Testament*, 7:1:166.

15. *History of the Church*, 4:588.

16. In Conference Report, Oct. 1968, 48–49; or *Improvement Era*, Dec. 1968, 39.

17. In *Journal of Discourses*, 16:82.

18. *Israel! Do You Know?* [1954], 182.

19. *Commentary on the Old Testament*, 7:1:200–1.

20. *Church History and Modern Revelation*, 4 vols. [1946–49], 1:155.

21. *Answers to Gospel Questions*, comp. Joseph Fielding Smith Jr., vols. [1957–66], 4:33.

22. *Doctrines of Salvation*, 3:11.

23. *The Promised Messiah: The First Coming of Christ* [1978], 192.

24. *Doctrines of Salvation*, 3:252–53.

25. In *Journal of Discourses*, 2:268–69.

26. *A Marvelous Work and a Wonder* [1976], 202.

27. In Conference Report, Oct. 1919, 69.

28. *Key to the Science of Theology; A Voice of Warning* [1978], 23.

29. *History of the Church*, 6:26.

30. *Commentary on the Book of Mormon*, 7 vols. [1955–61], 2:330–31.

31. In *Journal of Discourses*, 21:325.

CHAPTER 4

Isaiah, Pt. 2:
A Voice of Warning and Lucifer's Fall

(Isaiah 13–23)

INTRODUCTION

The Burdens of the Wicked

"Burdens" are pronouncements of destruction or suffering. Isaiah 13–23 contains a collection of "burdens" Isaiah pronounced upon the nations of his time. Ancient Babylon, Assyria, Philistia, Moab, Damascus (Syria), Egypt, and others (ten nations in all) were all recipients of Isaiah's prophecies of Divine judgment. The timetable for their repentance had run out and they were to reap the judgments of God. The Lord revealed through these burdens how they would be brought to judgment.

Isaiah foresaw God's judgment

GUSTAVE DORÉ, 1896

These burdens provide significant insights into both the ancient and modern worlds because they are dualistic prophecies. Each nation is also a symbol of a particular type of wickedness in the latter-day world. When Isaiah uses the phrase "in that day," it signals a latter-day meaning for the prophecy. For example, ancient Babylon with all its evils is a symbol of our own present-day Babylon—the world. The following chart summarizes the symbolic meanings of each of these nations.

Nation:	Reference:	Wickedness:
Jerusalem	Isaiah 13	Pretended piety while killing the prophets
Babylon	Isaiah 13	Idolatry and worldliness
Sodom	Isaiah 14	Corruption
Philistia	Isaiah 14	Hatred of Israel
Moab	Isaiah 15–16	Hatred of Israel
Damascus (Syria)	Isaiah 17	Hatred of Israel
Ephraim (N. Israel)	Isaiah 17	Apostasy
Egypt	Isaiah 19	Tyranny
Phoenicia (Tyre)	Isaiah 23	Worldly commerce
Spain, Cyprus, Sidon	Isaiah 23	Worldly commerce

PROPHECIES CONCERNING BABYLON

The Burden of Babylon

(Isaiah 13)

Babylon at that time was not yet a world power; it was just a province of Assyria. But later, under Nebuchadnezzar, Babylonia overthrew Assyria and became the dominant world power. Nebuchadnezzar then undertook a building program which made Babylon one of the most remarkable cities of the ancient world. If he were simply guessing, a prophet in Isaiah's time would have said that Assyria would be the conquering nation. But Isaiah foresaw that it would be Babylon, not Assyria, that would destroy Judah.

● **Isaiah 13:9** (2 Nephi 23:9): **The greatness of Babylon.** Babylon was eventually believed to be indestructible and the most beautiful city in the world. Isaiah referred to Babylon as "the lady of kingdoms" (Isa. 47:5). Jeremiah called Babylon "the praise of the whole earth" (Jer. 51:41). And Daniel made reference to "this great Babylon" (Dan. 4:30).

● **The wall around Babylon was massive.** Herodotus claimed that this wall was 84 feet thick and 336 feet high. He also said that small one-story houses were built on the top of the wall on either side, with space enough between the houses to permit four chariots to drive abreast.

Restored lion gate of Babylon

Modern archaeology shows that it was even larger than he claimed. The outer retaining wall was 23 ½ feet thick.

Inside of this there was a filling of sand and gravel which extended 69 feet, and then the inner retaining wall, which was 44 feet thick. The whole structure, therefore, was 136 ½ feet thick.

The wall and its citadels were made of baked bricks laid with asphalt, many of which were beautifully colored.[1] These massive walls encircled the entire city, a square perimeter estimated to exceed 55 miles—nearly 13 ⅘ miles on each side.[2]

● **Isaiah 13:17–22** (2 Nephi 23:17–22): **Isaiah's predictions concerning Babylon.** Isaiah correctly foretold that the Medes would eventually destroy Babylon (v. 17)—a prophecy that was fulfilled 130 years later when an alliance of Medes and Persians under Cyrus the Great dammed the Euphrates River and then marched under the walls of Babylon through the riverbed. They thus overthrew the city and the empire. Isaiah said that Babylon's beauty would perish as did Sodom and Gomorrah (v. 19). He said that Babylon would never be rebuilt or inhabited again (v. 20). And he said that only wild beasts would live there after its destruction (vv. 21–22). Each of these predictions was fulfilled literally. Babylon was destroyed and never rebuilt. And today, Babylon is a sand-covered desert, occupied only by wild animals.

● **Isaiah 20:2 Isaiah is commanded to walk "naked and barefoot."** As with many of His prophets, the Lord made a visual example of Isaiah that could not be ignored. "With the great importance attached to the clothing in the East, where the feelings upon this point are peculiarly sensitive and modest, a person was looked upon as stripped and naked if he had only taken off his upper garment. What Isaiah was directed to do, therefore, was … not [a call] to moral [in]decency. He was to lay aside the dress of a mourner and preacher of repentance, and to have nothing on but his tunic (cetoneth); and in this, as well as barefooted, he was to show himself in public."[3]

Spiritual Babylon

● **Jeremiah 51:36–49 The prophets used Babylon as a symbol of the wicked,** and they used its fall as a symbol of what will eventually befall the wicked. Isaiah delivered his sharpest condemnations upon this latter-day Babylon. Just as ancient Babylon was destroyed and never rebuilt, so will all who fight against the Lord in the latter days be destroyed. This symbolic use of Babylon continued in the New Testament, in the Book of Mormon, and in our latter-day Doctrine and Covenants.

— Rev. 18:1–10, 20–21	John prophesied that the wicked (Babylon) will be destroyed.
— 1 Nephi 22:23	Nephi said that worldly churches are a part of "Babylon."
— D&C 64:24	The Lord called the proud and the wicked "Babylon."
— D&C 133:1–7, 14	He also called wickedness "spiritual Babylon."

Overcoming Babylon

● **Isaiah 13:2–5** (2 Nephi 23:2–5): A prophecy of latter-day triumph over "Babylon" (worldliness). This prophecy used a number of well-known metaphors in Isaiah's day that we discussed in the "Understanding Isaiah" chapter earlier. The "banner" to be lifted up in the last days (v. 2) will be the gospel standard, or ensign, to which the world may gather (see also Isa. 5:26). The "mountain" (v. 2) is the House of the Lord and/or the nation of the Lord. And the "multitude" (v. 4) is a great people who come together in the Lord's name. These multitudes are the Latter-day Saints who will be gathered from every nation in the last days and enlisted in the army of God to wage war against wickedness.

● **Isaiah 13:6–10** (2 Nephi 23:6–10): **The great "day of the Lord" on which the Savior will return.** It will be a day of great "destruction from the Almighty" (v. 6). It will be a day when "he shall destroy the sinners thereof out of it" (v. 9). There will be heavenly signs: the sun will be darkened, the moon will turn to blood, stars will fall from heaven (v. 10).

● **Isaiah 13:11–12** (2 Nephi 23:11–12): **A man being "more precious than fine gold."** Righteous men will become as difficult to find as precious gold and will be treasured as highly (see also Isa. 4:1–4). But then, the wicked will be cleansed from the earth, and the worthy righteous will remain to become the precious jewels in the royal diadem of the Lord (see D&C 60:4; Isa. 62:1–3). Ophir was the rich, gold-producing province of India. Isaiah says that the treasure of "the golden wedge of Ophir" (Isa. 13:12) is insignificant compared to the worth of one righteous man (see D&C 18:10).

● **Isaiah 13:13** (2 Nephi 23:13): **The "heavens ... [will] shake" and the "earth [will be] remove[d]."** To say that the heavens will shake and the earth will be removed are both figures of speech for "great calamity and disaster," suggesting that the whole political climate and circumstances of the world will be shaken. It refers to the great political upheavals of Isaiah's day. But it is a dualistic prophecy that will also be fulfilled in the latter days. The heavens will "flee" as the earth is returned to its previous paradisiacal glory (see Rev. 6:12–17 and D&C 88:87–91). This should not be confused with the celestial state that the earth will eventually enjoy. It is, rather, speaking of the Millennium, during which all life will enjoy continual peace.

● **Isaiah 13:14–22** (2 Nephi 23:14–22)**: Judgments for the wicked.** Men will "fall by the sword" and "their houses shall be spoiled" (vv. 15–16). Children and women will also suffer greatly (vv. 16, 18). The Lord declares, "I will be merciful unto [the righteous], but the wicked shall perish" (2 Ne. 23:22). This prophecy is also dualistic, with both literal and spiritual meaning. These things happened literally to the Babylonians when they fell to the Medes and Persians in 539 BC. But Babylon is also the name for Satan's kingdom or the world (see D&C 1:16), and this spiritual Babylon will be destroyed in the same manner in the latter days (see 1 Ne. 14:10; Rev. 17:1–5).

THE FALL OF LUCIFER

(Isaiah 14)

● **D&C 76:26–28 Lucifer is Satan.** In Joseph Smith and Sidney Rigdon's vision of the three degrees of glory, they learned much about the premortal status of Satan. He was eventually called *Perdition* (meaning "utter loss and destruction") because "the heavens wept over him" (v. 26).

A "son of the morning" fell

But he was originally called *Lucifer* (meaning "light bearer") because he was "a son of the morning." This would seem to indicate that he was one of our Father's first sons and a person of immense intelligence and potential and a person of light—a "light bearer."

But they testified that in their vision they "beheld, and lo, he is fallen! is fallen, even a son of the morning!" (v. 27). They referred to Satan as "that old serpent, even the devil, who rebelled against God, and sought to take the kingdom of our God and his Christ" (v. 28). Thus, envying the throne of God Himself, and desiring to thwart the plan of salvation God had laid before all His children, Lucifer sought to persuade the children of God to follow him instead of the Father.

● **Isaiah 14:4–12** (2 Nephi 24:4–12): **Isaiah taunts both Nebuchadnezzar and Lucifer.** This prophecy is dualistic. It can be interpreted as taunting words against both Satan and Israel's oppressor, Nebuchadnezzar, whose "pomp is brought down to the grave" (v. 11). By comparing Babylon's king to Lucifer, Isaiah was also telling us many things about Satan's fall in the premortal existence. The metaphor continues through verse 21.

● **Isaiah 14:12–15** (2 Nephi 24:12–15): **Isaiah describes Lucifer's downfall.** We first notice that he calls him "Lucifer, son of the morning" (v. 12), who is "fallen from heaven." Lucifer, whose name means "light bearer," is Satan (see D&C 76:25–28). He became Perdition (which means "utter loss and destruction"), but the title "son of the morning" suggests that he was once one of God's greatest sons. As a figure of speech, "son of the morning" means that he was also one of God's oldest sons. And as we know, he "fell from heaven" in the premortal existence.

The word *congregation* (v. 13) should be translated "assembly of gods." Lucifer wanted to be exalted above God the Father, but he will instead inherit hell (vv. 13–15). He is a liar and sought personal power at the expense of our agency (see Moses 4:1–4). There was a war in heaven, and Michael (Adam) prevailed over him (see Rev. 12:7–9).

Robert J. Matthews said:

> The war was severe, and it had eternal consequences. Every kind of sin (with the possible exception of sins involving death) was present in that premortal state, and there were many casualties. Repentance was in order for all who sinned; and forgiveness in that premortal life was available through faith in Jesus Christ and obedience to the plan of salvation (D&C 93:38). This was not a war just of words and debate and forensics. It was a war of misdeeds, lies, hatred, pride, jealousy, remorse, envy, cursing, blasphemy, deception, theft, cajoling, slander, anger, and sins of almost every kind that are also known in mortality. The issues were so well defined that coexistence was not possible. Those who wholeheartedly supported Lucifer's rebellion became like him; and after having sinned beyond the possibility of reclamation, they were cast out of heaven and placed (as spirits) upon the earth, never to have the opportunity to be born with a body of flesh and bone.
>
> The precise number who thus rebelled we do not know, but the scriptures speak of them as a "third part" of the spirits who were originally scheduled for birth into mortality (Rev. 12:4; D&C 29:36). If a "third part" means one-third, then there are half as many evil spirits as the remaining two-thirds who are privileged to come to earth through the birth process and obtain physical bodies. That is, there are half as many spirits who rebelled and were cast out as all the mortals who ever have been born or will be born into this world to the end of the millennium. These rebellious spirits are "the devil and his angels," and also "vessels of wrath" (D&C 29:36–37; 76:33). They are literally devils, forever miserable, and they are enemies of Christ and of all who align themselves with Christ. They are enemies of the Father's plan, and, with as many mortals as they can influence, do the devil's bidding on this earth.[4]

Christ said Satan fell "as lightning" from heaven (Luke 10:18). He was allowed to come to earth with his angels to tempt us so that we might have agency (see D&C 29:36–39). He still wishes to rule over us, but because of Christ's Atonement he "hath nothing" in the end (John 14:30).

As opposed to his arrogant plans to command the respect of all of God's children by force, people will "narrowly look upon" him—a figure of speech that means they will disrespect him despite the great evil he will cause (vv. 16–17). It is interesting to note that people will be surprised at how common he looks (no glory, no commanding features, no horns or tail or cloven foot). They will say, "Is this the man that made the earth to tremble, that did shake kingdoms? That made the world as a wilderness, and destroyed the cities thereof, that opened not the house of his prisoners?" (vv. 16–17).

Lucifer's punishment is that he will never have a body. It follows that he will never have a grave like all the honored kings of the earth (vv. 18–20). For him, there is no resurrection, no earth to inherit, and no children (v. 21).

- **Isaiah 14:20–32** (2 Nephi 24:20–32): **Nebuchadnezzar will fall from glory in the same way Lucifer did.** Though Babylon was once a mighty nation, God will cut it off (v. 22). The same is true of the Assyrians who despoiled Ephraim (v. 25). Zion will be established, "and the poor of his people shall trust in it" (v. 32).

ISRAEL'S BURDEN AND EVENTUAL REDEMPTION

(Isaiah 17–19)

- **Isaiah 17:4–14 Poetic descriptions of Israel's future.** Using the poetic language for which he is justifiably famous, Isaiah compares Israel to a garden or a bough that is largely unfruitful and to a garden in which a man plants but reaps only a few ears of corn or gleans only a few grapes from his vines (vv. 4–6). "Gleaning grapes" (v. 6) are those few missed by the harvesters.

Israel will be in need of help and find none. They will see that the groves and altars of the false gods they trusted in will not have power to deliver them (vv. 7–8). Israel's cities will resemble a bough on a tree that has been forsaken, or remained uncultivated, and is therefore desolate, unfruitful, and unproductive (v. 9). Olives were harvested by shaking the branches, which always left a few scattered berries in the top branches. This harvest of sorrow for Israel will be the result of their forgetting God (v. 11).

Nations will rush against Israel "like the rushing of mighty waters." But those same nations will eventually be "like a rolling thing before the whirlwind" (v. 13). Thus, those that over-powered and ransacked Israel would themselves be rendered destitute (v. 14).

"At evening-tide, trouble"

This prophecy was fulfilled in the captivity and scattering of Israel. A better description could hardly be found of the land of Palestine throughout the centuries after Isaiah's time. The land and its people produced neither spiritually nor physically. Only now, as the Jews are gathering from among the nations, is the land once again becoming fruitful. When the Jews begin to believe in Jesus Christ as their Lord and Savior, spirituality will also increase for Israel once again.

- **Isaiah 14:1–3** (2 Nephi 24:1–3): **Israel will be joined by individuals from other nations, find rest in their own lands, and rule over their former oppressors.** "The Lord will have mercy on Jacob, and will yet choose Israel, and set them in their own land," Isaiah says. "And … strangers [foreigners] shall be joined with them, and … shall cleave to the house of Jacob" (v. 1). They will be restored to "their place … in the land of the Lord" (see the discussion that follows below concerning America as the land of the Lord). Their "servants and handmaids" will be those "whose captives they were; and they shall rule over their oppressors" (v. 2). In that day, "the Lord shall give thee rest from thy sorrow, and from thy fear, and from the hard bondage wherein thou wast made to serve," the Lord promises through Isaiah (v. 3).

America and Israel's Gathering

(Isaiah 18)

● **Isaiah 18:1–7 The Lord's messengers will take the gospel to the world.** This short chapter (7 verses) seems to be referencing America as the location of latter-day Israel.

— Isaiah 18:1 "Woe to the land shadowing with wings ... beyond the rivers of Ethiopia." Actually, no woe was intended; it is a greeting, and the King James translators simply got it wrong. Other translations correct this. "Shadowing" is a Hebrew way of saying "in the shape of." Ethiopia is far to the west of Palestine, and this greeting is to a land far beyond Ethiopia. Thus, a more plain translation would be, "Hail to the land in the shape of wings, far to the west."

President Joseph Fielding Smith said:

> Now, do you know of any land in the shape of wings? Think of your map. About twenty–five years ago one of the current magazines printed on the cover the American continents in the shape of wings, with the body of the bird between. I have always regretted that I did not preserve this magazine. Does not this hemisphere take the shape of wings; the spread out wings of a bird?[5]

"America ... is the land 'shadowing with wings' spoken of by Isaiah that today is sending ambassadors by the sea to a nation scattered and peeled."[6]

"This chapter [Isaiah 18] is clearly a reference to the sending forth of the missionaries to the nations of the earth to gather again this people who are scattered and peeled. The ensign has been lifted upon the mountains, and the work of gathering has been going on for over one hundred years. No one understands this chapter, but the Latter-day Saints, and we can see how it is being fulfilled."[7]

President Spencer W. Kimball said: "With some of the Brethren we have just returned recently from the area conferences in São Paulo, Brazil, and in Buenos Aires, Argentina. In that southern world of Zion we reminded them that Zion was all of North and South America, like the wide, spreading wings of a great eagle, the one being North and the other South America."[8]

— **Isaiah 18:2** "That sendeth ambassadors … in vessels of bulrushes … swift messengers." These ambassadors and "swift messengers" (D&C 124:26) are our "elders of Israel," our "messengers of the kingdom," or the Lord's servants who are working to establish Zion in the last days. "Vessels of bulrushes" refers to the speed of their vessels—they are very swift.

In our previous chapter, we noted that Isaiah foresaw "an ensign to the nations from far, … from the end[s] of the earth," that will travel "with speed swiftly" (Isa. 5:26; 2 Ne. 15:26). So swiftly, in fact, that "none shall be weary nor stumble among them; none shall slumber nor sleep; neither shall the girdle of their loins be loosed, nor the latchet of their shoes be broken" (Isa. 5:27; 2 Ne. 15:26–27) as they travel across the earth. They will arrive in a matter of hours.

"Who are these that fly as a cloud, and as the doves to their windows?" Isaiah marvels as he sees the Lord's messengers flying to their destinations (Isa. 60:8).

— **Isaiah 18:2** "To a nation scattered and peeled … and trodden down." This refers to the Israelites, who for thousands of years have been scattered among the nations of the earth, oppressed, and disdained.

— **Isaiah 18:3** "All ye inhabitants of the world, … see ye [and] hear ye." Isaiah invites all nations to take notice when the Lord "lifteth up an ensign on the mountains," identifying the place of gathering, and "bloweth a trumpet," which was an Israelite signal to gather together (see Isa. 11:11–12; 2 Ne. 21:11–12).

— **Isaiah 18:4** "Like a cloud of dew in the heat of harvest." This is an analogy using a figure of speech that means "relief."

— **Isaiah 18:5–6** Like a pruner who prepares the grape vine for greater growth, the Lord will prepare His people to bring forth fruit and separate the unproductive from them.

— **Isaiah 18:7** "Scattered and peeled" and "trodden under foot" are references to the scattered and oppressed children of Israel.

— **Isaiah 18:7** In describing the place of gathering, Isaiah identifies many of its characteristics:

- "A people terrible from [the] beginning" means "a nation always feared."
- "Whose land the rivers have spoiled" means "criss-crossed with rivers."
- "The place of the name of the Lord" means a place with the Lord's name.
- "Mount Zion" means the New Jerusalem (D&C 84:2).

The only place that meets all these criteria is America, whose very name (Amalickiah) among its early inhabitants means "the land of the Lord."

The Prophet Joseph Smith said: "[We] have labored without pay, to instruct the United States [and now the world] that the gathering had commenced in the western boundaries of Missouri, to build a holy city, where, as may be seen in the eighteenth chapter of Isaiah, the present should 'be brought unto the Lord of Hosts.'"[9]

BURDENS OF OTHER NATIONS

(Isaiah 14–23)

The Burden of Philistia (Palestine)

- **Isaiah 14:28–32** (2 Nephi 24:28–32): **The Philistines were Canaanites who inhabited the land when Israel conquered it.** They were long-time enemies of Israel, and warfare between these two nations continued for centuries. Rome called Philistine territory "Palestina" (Palestine) in an effort to deny Israel's claim to it. For this reason, modern Israelis do not like the name Palestine. They view it as a continuing effort to deny their rightful claim to it. It certainly lies within the territory the Lord designated for Israel, both to Moses and to Joshua. But Israel has rarely had control of this region, either anciently or in modern times.

The Burden of Assyria

● **Isaiah 14:24–27** (2 Nephi 24:24–27): **Assyria was like Babylon.** In addition to his use of the Babylonian empire as a symbol of spiritual Babylon, Isaiah also predicted the demise of the Assyrian empire. This began when, in the days of King Hezekiah, Assyria suffered a crushing defeat on the hills outside of Jerusalem, at the hands of an angel of destruction (see Isa. 37:33–38). Assyria also served as a type or symbol of the world. In like manner, all evil nations of the latter-day world will feel the hand of God's judgments (see Isa. 14:26).

The Burden of Moab

● **Isaiah 15–16 Moab was the eldest son of Lot's eldest daughter.** He therefore came from an honorable heritage as cousins of the Israelites. His descendants settled east of the Dead Sea from the Zered River northward. They eventually fell into idolatry, worshiping the vicious god Molech, whose idol was heated red-hot and then received in its outstretched arms the living babies of the people. They also worshiped other idols such as Baal. During the Israelites' sojourn in the promised land, they had continual strife with the Moabites.

— **Isaiah 15:2–3** "Baldness" means the clipping of the hair and beard. This was an indication of great shame in ancient Israel, and to say it would happen to Moab was to say that Moab's pride and prominence would turn to shame. They will find themselves mourning on the tops of their houses.

Mourning on rooftops

— **Isaiah 15:5** "A three-year-old ox" means "in the prime of life." It was a well-known figure of speech in Isaiah's day, but is mysterious to the modern reader. Isaiah predicted Moab's destruction within 3 years.

— **Isaiah 15:8–9** The very center of Moab will be stained with blood. "Lions" is a reference to Judah.

The Burden of Damascus (Syria)

● **Isaiah 17:1–3 Damascus will become "a ruinous heap."**
Damascus was the capital city of the northern kingdom of
Israel. "Behold, Damascus is taken away from being a city, and
it shall be a ruinous heap," Isaiah prophesied. Others of its cities
will be "forsaken: they shall be for flocks, which shall lie down,
and none shall make them afraid" (v. 2). There will be no more
fortresses in "Ephraim" (another name for the northern kingdom
of Israel); instead, their glory will cease just as it will for the
children of Israel (v. 3).

The Burden of Egypt

● **Isaiah 19 Dualistic curses upon Egypt.** They had a literal
fulfillment in Isaiah's day, and will also be fulfilled in the latter
days. Elder Bruce R. McConkie shared a quotation to explain
how Egypt, Moab, and Babylon symbolize wickedness of the
latter-day world: "Babylon [symbolizes] its idolatry, Egypt its
tyranny, Sodom its … corruption, Jerusalem its pretensions
to sanctity [and] spiritual privileges, whilst all the while it [the
world] is the murderer of Christ [and] His members."[10]

● **Isaiah 19:3** "Wizards" are those who practice black magic, who
have entered into a compact with Satan, who are sorcerers or
sorceresses. Today, the term would be "witch." "Familiar spirits"
is the practice of speaking to the dead. Today, this would be the
use of seances or spiritual mediums.

Elder Bruce R. McConkie wrote: "One of the most evil
and wicked sects supported by Satan is that which practices
witchcraft, such craft involving as it does actual intercourse
with evil spirits. A witch is one who engages in this craft, who
practices the black art of magic, who has entered into a compact
with Satan, who is a sorcerer or sorceress. Modernly the term
witch has been limited in application to women. There are no
witches, of course, in the sense of old hags flying on broomsticks

through October skies; such mythology is a modernistic spoofing of a little understood practice that prevailed in all the apostate kingdoms of the past and which even now is found among many peoples."[11]

- **Isaiah 19:8–9 Egypt's wealth will cease as her industries flounder.** Fishing was one of the three major industries of Egypt. And Egypt was well known for its "fine flax" (fine twined linen) and "weaving" (the making of cloth from cotton).

- **Isaiah 19:11–14 The leaders of Egypt will be as fools and unable to save their nation.** Because of her wealth, power, and ancient origin, Egypt and its leaders were extremely proud of themselves. But Isaiah said that "the princes of Zoan [Tanis] are fools, [and] the counsel of the wise counsellors of Pharaoh is become brutish" (v. 11). "Where are they?" he asks. "Where are thy wise men?" (v. 12). "The princes of Zoan [Tanis] are become fools, [and] the princes of Noph [Memphis] are deceived" (v. 13). "They have caused Egypt to err in every work thereof, as a drunken man staggereth in his vomit" (v. 14).

- **Isaiah 19:16–17 In the latter days, Judah will strike terror in the hearts of the Egyptians.** "In that day [meaning the latter days] shall Egypt be like unto women: and it shall be afraid and fear because of the shaking of the hand of the Lord of hosts, which he shaketh

Israel has defeated Egypt twice

over it," Isaiah prophesied (v. 16). "The land of Judah shall be a terror unto Egypt, every one that maketh mention thereof shall be afraid in himself, because of the counsel of the Lord of hosts, which he hath determined against it" (v. 17). We have seen this prophecy fulfilled several times in the latter days as modern Israel has defeated and subdued the Egyptian army—something that would have been unthinkable in Isaiah's day.

- **Isaiah 19:18–22 Egypt will eventually worship the Lord.** The cities of Egypt will speak the language of Canaan and will "swear to the Lord of hosts" (v. 18). "In that day shall there be an altar to the Lord in the midst of the land of Egypt" (v. 19). "The Lord shall be known to Egypt, and the Egyptians shall know the Lord in that day, and shall do sacrifice and oblation; yea, they shall vow a vow unto the Lord, and perform it" (v. 21). The Lord will smite Egypt, causing them to "return even to the Lord, and he shall be intreated of them, and shall heal them" (v. 22).

- **Isaiah 19:23–25 Judah will be joined to Egypt and Assyria.** Isaiah foresaw "a highway out of Egypt [all the way north] to Assyria, and the Assyrian shall come into Egypt, and the Egyptian into Assyria" (v. 23). "The Egyptians shall serve with the Assyrians," and "Israel [shall] be the third [party] with Egypt and with Assyria, even a blessing in the midst of the land" (vv. 23–24). And all three will be blessed by the Lord.

Judgments on the Arabians and Edomites

- **Isaiah 21:11–17 Isaiah prophesied the destruction of even the minor nations of the east.** Dumah is located in the northern heart of the Arabian Desert; Dedanim identifies the residents of Dedan, which is southeast of the Gulf of Aqaba along the coast of the Red Sea; and Kedar is the region eastward from Mount Hermon that includes the area called Bashan.

Judgments on Tyre, Sidon, Spain, and Cyprus

- **Isaiah 23 Tyre, Zidon, Tarshish, and Chittim were four major seaports of Isaiah's day.** They represent the wealth of merchants who traded back and forth between them. Isaiah prophesied against them also.

  — Tyre was on the Mediterranean coast, perhaps the major seaport of Isaiah's day. It was "the crowning city, whose merchants are princes, whose traffickers are the honourable of the earth" (v. 8). Though Babylon would possess the military and political power of the world, Tyre had control of, and was the commercial center of, Isaiah's world. Like Babylon, Tyre represented the world and so eventually would come under the judgments of God. Isaiah said that Tyre would be "laid waste," with "no house" and "no entering in" (v. 1).

Tyre was compared by Isaiah to a harlot committing fornication (joining in wickedness) with the kingdoms of the world (see Isa. 23:15, 17–18; compare Rev. 17:1–2). After its destruction, "Tyre shall be forgotten seventy years, ... [and] after the end of seventy years shall ... sing as an harlot" (v. 15). "Take an harp, [and] go about the city, thou harlot that hast been forgotten," Isaiah says. "Make

The ancient seaport of Tyre

sweet melody, sing many songs, that thou mayest be remembered" (v. 16). Tyre will then return to her "hire" and "commit fornication with all the kingdoms of the world upon the face of the earth" (v. 17) . Nevertheless, the Lord will reestablish Tyre so that merchandise can be obtained for Israel, "to eat sufficiently, and for durable clothing" (v. 18).

— Zidon (Sidon) was the sister port to Tyre, very nearby on the same seacoast. Sidon was the older city, but the newer site of Tyre had gained supremacy during the Assyrian captivity. Sidon received her revenue from the grain (seed) of Sihor (the Nile waters of Egypt). Her merchants were so renowned that they were honored by their national associates as "great ones" (v. 8; see also Rev. 18:23). All of this would cease. "Be thou ashamed, O Zidon," said Isaiah, "for the sea hath spoken, even the strength of the sea" (which was the source of the city's wealth), "saying, I travail not, nor bring forth children, neither do I nourish up young men, nor bring up virgins" (v. 4).

— Tarshish is believed to be the ancient name for Spain, which was a sister city to Tyre in merchant shipping and trade. Isaiah predicted a time when in Tarshish "there is no more strength" (v. 10). The Lord will have "stretched out his hand over the sea, [and] shook the kingdoms," and "given a commandment against the merchant city, to destroy the strong holds thereof" (v. 11). "Howl, ye ships of Tarshish," said Isaiah, "for your strength is laid waste" (v. 14).

— Chittim was the early name for present-day Cyprus. Those traveling the Mediterranean from Tyre to Tarshish would "replenish" their ships at Chittim. "Be still, ye inhabitants of the isle [where] the merchants of Zidon, that pass over the sea, have replenished," Isaiah said (v. 2). "Howl, ye inhabitants of the isle" (v. 6). "Is this your joyous city, whose antiquity is of ancient days?" he asks. They will be "carr[ied] … afar off to sojourn" (v. 7).

THE PAINFUL FULFILLMENT OF ISAIAH'S VISIONS

(Isaiah 21–22)

The Destruction of Babylon

● **Isaiah 21:1–2 Babylon is called the "desert of the sea."** Keil and Delitzsch believe that this name for Babylon was symbolic. The city sat on a hot and dusty plain in the Euphrates valley—literally a desert. But anciently, before flood control dams were built, the whole plain was flooded each spring during the high water runoff of the Euphrates. Thus, Babylon sat both in a desert and on a sea.[12] This interpretation seems to be supported by Jeremiah's description of Babylon as she that "dwellest upon many waters" (Jer. 51:13) and his promise that her waters would be "dried up" (Jer. 50:38).

Isaiah's Reaction

The destruction of ancient Babylon was not a pleasant thing to behold. But Isaiah also saw another destruction, the destruction of the world (spiritual Babylon) before the advent of the Lord Jesus Christ in the last days. That destruction would be so intense and complete that it was probably beyond anything Isaiah had imagined could be possible.

● **Isaiah 21:3–4 The pain caused by the visions given to Isaiah** was so intense that he describes it using graphic Hebrew terms which suggest much more than mere sorrow:

— "chalchalah" Contortion from cramps.

— "tzirim" The pains of child-birth.

— "na avah" Convulsive reaction to pain.

— "ah" Feverish and irregular beating of the pulse.

Isaiah foresaw Babylon's destruction

"The darkness of evening and night, which the prophet loved so much ('cheshek,' a desire [to lie down]), ... that he might rest from ... labour, [was] changed into quaking by the horrible vision."[13]

Israel and Jerusalem's Destruction

● **Isaiah 21:10 Israel will be threshed:** mowed off its own field, beaten, and carried captive into Babylon. This verse seems to be a foreshadowing of the event that is portrayed in some detail in Isaiah 22 (especially the "threshing" language in vv. 3–4).

● **Isaiah 22 Judah and Jerusalem will be surrounded, destroyed, and laid waste.**

— **Isaiah 22:1–7** The "valley of vision" refers to Jerusalem—where Isaiah received his visions. Isaiah predicts that the inhabitants of Jerusalem and their fleeing leaders will be "bound" by their captors (vv. 2–3). This would come in a day of "the spoiling of the daughter of my people" (v. 4), a day of perplexity, the breaking down of walls, and the treading down of the city (v. 5). The city will be encompassed by chariots which will fill all of the surrounding valleys and will be at the very gates of the city (v. 7).

— **Isaiah 22:8–11** The "house of the forest" was the forest-house built by Solomon upon Mount Zion for the storing and display of valuable arms and utensils. It was given this name because of the four rows of cedar columns that ran all round the royal palace and upon which it rested. These armaments will be "discovered" by the enemy (v. 8). The citizens of the city will attempt to fortify the wall and dig trenches to defend themselves (vv. 9–11), but it will be to no avail.

— **Isaiah 22:12** "Baldness" (not natural baldness, but the shaving of the hair) was a great shame and signified great calamity (compare Isa. 3:24). Isaiah suggested that when Judah saw their impending doom they should have seen it as a call to deep repentance and clothed themselves with sackcloth and baldness.

— **Isaiah 22:13** Instead, Judah acted as if they had been called to a joyous feast, saying, "Let us eat and drink; for to morrow we shall die." Typical of the wicked in a crisis, they preferred to indulge their passions before they died, rather than repent.

SYMBOLS OF CHRIST

(Isaiah 22)

● **Isaiah 22:20–25 The Messiah will appear,** receive the key to the house of David, and stand as a nail in a sure place.

— **Isaiah 22:20–22** Eliakim was a symbol of Christ. He was the righteous son of Hilkiah the priest, and his name means "the resurrection of the Lord" or "my God, he shall arise." Thus, the hope of salvation, resurrection, and eternal life comes only through Eliakim—the resurrection of Jesus Christ from the dead.

— **Isaiah 22:22** With the "key of the house of David," the Messiah will have power to "open, and none shall shut; and ... shut, and none shall open." This is a symbolic way of saying the Savior has the power to admit or exclude any person from His kingdom (see also Rev. 3:7–8; 2 Ne. 9:41–45).

— **Isaiah 22:23–24** The "nail in a sure place" symbolizes the terrible reality of the cross. Just as the nail that was driven in the sure place secured the body of the one being crucified, so the Savior Himself is a nail in a sure place, assuring that we will not fall from grace despite our many weaknesses.

Notes:

1. Samuel Fallows, ed., *The Popular and Critical Bible Encyclopedia and Scriptural Dictionary*, 3 vols. [1920], "Babylon," 1:208–9.

2. Merrill F. Unger, *Unger's Bible Dictionary* [1972], "Babylon," 116.

3. Keil and Delitzsch, *Commentary on the Old Testament*, 10 vols. [1996], 7:1:372.

4. Robert J. Matthews, "Two Ways in the World: The Warfare Between God and Satan," in Kent P. Jackson, ed., *Studies in Scripture, Vol. 7: 1 Nephi to Alma 29* [1987], 147–48.

5. *The Signs of the Times* [1952], 51.

6. Joseph Fielding Smith, in Conference Report, Apr. 1966, 14; or *Improvement Era*, June 1966, 499.

7. *The Signs of the Times*, 54–55.

8. In Conference Report, Apr. 1975, 4; or *Ensign*, May 1975, 4.

9. *History of the Church*, 2:132.

10. Quoting Robert Jamieson and others, *Commentary on the Whole Bible* [1961], 577, in *Doctrinal New Testament Commentary*, 3 vols. [1965–73], 3:510.

11. *Mormon Doctrine*, 2nd ed. [1966], 840.

12. *Commentary on the Old Testament*, 7:1:377.

13. *Commentary on the Old Testament*, 7:1:379

CHAPTER 5

Isaiah, Pt. 3:
The Latter Days
and the Second Coming
(Isaiah 24–35)

INTRODUCTION

Isaiah the Seer

Isaiah was not only a prophet but also a seer. "A seer," said King Mosiah, "is greater than a prophet" (Mosiah 8:15). Ammon said that "a seer is a revelator and a prophet also. … A seer can know of things which are past, and also of things which are to come, and by them shall all things be revealed" (Mosiah 8:16–17).

Isaiah saw many dispensations in vision

The Prophet Joseph Smith said:

> Search the revelations of God: study the prophecies, and rejoice that God grants unto the world seers and prophets. They are they who saw the mysteries of godliness; they saw the flood before it

came; they saw angels ascending and descending upon a ladder that reached from earth to heaven: they saw the stone cut out of the mountain, which filled the whole earth; they saw the Son of God come from the regions of bliss and dwell with men on earth; they saw the deliverer come out of Zion, and turn away ungodliness from Jacob; they saw the glory of the Lord when He showed the transfiguration of the earth on the mount. They saw every mountain laid low and every valley exalted when the Lord was taking vengeance upon the wicked; they saw truth spring out of the earth, and righteousness look down from heaven in the last days, before the Lord came the second time to gather His elect; they saw the end of wickedness on earth, and the Sabbath of creation crowned with peace; they saw the end of the glorious thousand years, when Satan was loosed for a little season; they saw the day of judgment when all men received according to their works, and they saw the heaven and earth flee away to make room for the city of God, when the righteous receive an inheritance in eternity. And, fellow sojourners upon earth, it is your privilege to purify yourselves and come up to the same glory, and see for yourselves, and know for yourselves.[1]

According to this definition, Isaiah was one of the greatest seers of all time because he saw all these things long before they took place. And Isaiah's seership was dynamic and ever-changing. He could be wrapped in a vision of the Apostasy one moment and gazing upon the Millennium the next. The chapters and verses of this part of Isaiah, in particular, can be bewildering to the Western mind, which prefers a linear, subject-consistent arrangement.

We will, therefore, treat these visions and prophecies topically—gathering together all those of a particular subject regardless of which chapter they come from. The prophecies in this section of Isaiah's writings will be divided into five main categories:

— The apostasy of Israel and of the latter days.

— The Restoration, including the Book of Mormon.

— Final judgments upon the wicked.

— The Second Coming of Christ and the Millennium.

ISAIAH'S PROPHECIES OF APOSTASY

The Fruits of Apostasy

● **Isaiah 24:1–5 Describes apostasy in any day or time, but more particularly in our latter days.** "Behold, the Lord maketh the earth empty, and maketh it waste, and turneth it upside down, and scattereth abroad the inhabitants thereof" (v. 1). He who created both the earth and its inhabitants can empty any part of the earth as it suits His purposes. But He can also empty it spiritually by removing the prophets and the priesthood from a nation that rejects such things. Such was the case with the citizens of Judah and Israel in Isaiah's day, and such was the case in the long period of apostasy that followed the deaths of the Apostles.

"And it shall be, as with the people, so with the priest; as with the servant, so with his master; as with the maid, so with her mistress; as with the buyer, so with the seller; as with the lender, so with the borrower; as with the taker of usury, so with the giver of usury to him. The land shall be utterly emptied, and utterly spoiled: for the Lord hath spoken this word" (vv. 2–3). None are exempt from the effects of apostasy, great or small, wealthy or poor, educated or not, priest or parishioner. "The earth mourneth and fadeth away, the world languisheth and fadeth away, the haughty people of the earth do languish" (v. 4).

During periods of apostasy, the earth itself is "defiled under the inhabitants thereof" (v. 5). And why? "Because they have transgressed the laws, changed the ordinance[s], broken the everlasting covenant" (v. 5). From this we can see that changing ordinances is a serious sin. Ordinances are part of the specific means outlined by the Lord whereby one can overcome his natural state, receive a spiritual rebirth, and become like God. Each ordinance was designed by God to teach spiritual truths and move men toward godliness. When the ordinances are changed, their power to save is lost.

The Prophet Joseph Smith said: "If there is no change of ordinances, there is no change of priesthood. Wherever the ordinances of the gospel are administered, there is the priesthood."[2]

President Spencer W. Kimball said:

> The term *priest* is here used to denote all religious leaders of any faith. Isaiah said: "The earth also is defiled under the inhabitants thereof; because they have transgressed the laws, changed the ordinance, broken the everlasting covenant" (Isa. 24:5). From among the discordant voices we are shocked at those of many priests who encourage the defilement of men and wink at the eroding trends and who deny the omniscience of God. Certainly these men should be holding firm, yet some yield to popular clamor.
>
> I give some quotes from the press:
>
> "Many churchmen are reluctant to give a definite yes or no to marijuana." "It depends upon circumstances."[3] They have developed "situation ethics," which seem to cover all sins.
>
> Other religious leaders are saying, " … precise rules of Christian conduct should not necessarily apply to problems of sexuality."[4]
>
> In contrast hear the strong voice of a prophet. Peter prophesied: "But there were false prophets also among the people, even as there shall be false teachers among you, who privily shall bring in damnable heresies, even denying the Lord that bought them . . . . And many shall follow their pernicious ways. … (2 Pet. 2:1–2)."[5]

Such changes do not always start with a deliberate attempt to displease the Lord. Men sometimes seek to "improve" ordinances according to their own ideas of what makes sacred things special. A friend of mine once attended a family baptismal service in a stake in Salt Lake City. Apparently, that stake allowed individual families to arrange such ordinances in their own swimming pools (an unwise policy for sure).

When my friend arrived, he found the indoor pool area darkened, lit only by candlelight. Rose petals had been scattered upon the water, and incense was burning. The baptism was undertaken with great pomp and ceremony. The simplicity of the ordinance and its associated covenants was buried in a surfeit of sanctimony. When I heard this story, I thought, "This is precisely how the Great Apostasy crept into the early Church." With no priesthood leadership, the people changed the ordinances and the doctrines to suit their fancy. And I am certain that the Lord was and is not pleased when it happens.

● **Isaiah 24:6–12 The serious consequences of apostasy.**
Whenever apostasy occurs, eventually "the curse [of it] devour[s] the earth, and they that dwell therein are desolate: therefore the inhabitants of the earth are burned, and few men left" (v. 6). For the Jews this was a literal, physical result as their beautiful cities were left desolate and they were marched off into captivity in Babylon. But in a spiritual sense, they (and any dispensation that turns apostate) were also left desolate—bereft of the Spirit and of the blessings of the gospel, the priesthood, and all related blessings.

For the Jews, Isaiah predicted that the merry-hearted would sigh, the mirth of tabrets would cease, the noise of rejoicing would end, and the music of the harp would cease (vv. 7–8). Their cities would be broken down and all the houses shut up (v. 10). All joy and mirth would cease, and the city would be left desolate, with her gates destroyed (vv. 11–12). All of this resulted from their rejection of the Lord and His ordinances.

● **Isaiah 27:9–11 Jerusalem will become desolate and forsaken.**
The children of Israel were His chosen people. They could have become a Zion people and enjoyed the very presence of the Lord in their midst. Instead, they chose the wicked ways of the Canaanites that surrounded them. They defiled their lives and

their sanctuaries with the lascivious sexual rites of false religions. And they laughed at and scorned the prophets who were sent to call them to repentance. Isaiah was one of these.

Now, by means of their destruction and captivity, "the iniquity of Jacob [was] purged" (v. 9). Their false idols and groves were knocked down, their defensed city became desolate, and their land forsaken and left like a wilderness (vv. 9–10). Though He loved them, the Lord would not show mercy to this people of "no understanding," and "he that formed them will shew them no favour" (v. 11). They will be taken into captivity and scattered over the earth until the day of the great latter-day gathering (vv. 12–13).

- **Isaiah 28:1–8 The Northern Kingdom will be destroyed because of transgression.** "Woe to the crown of pride, to the drunkards of Ephraim, whose glorious beauty is a fading flower," said Isaiah (v. 1). The northern kingdom of Israel—called Ephraim here—will suffer under the attack of "a mighty and strong one, which as a tempest of hail and a destroying storm, as a flood of mighty waters overflowing, shall cast [them] down to the earth" (v. 2).

Isaiah then suddenly sees forward to the day of the gathering, a day when "the Lord of hosts [shall] be for a crown of glory, and for a diadem of beauty, unto the residue of his people. ... And ... a spirit of judgment to him that sitteth in judgment, and for strength to them that turn the battle to the gate" (vv. 5–6).

But the vision of this glorious future closes as quickly as it opened, and he returns to the present state of wicked Israel, in which "the priest and the prophet have erred through strong drink, ... they err in vision, they stumble in judgment. For all tables are full of vomit and filthiness, so that there is no place clean" (vv. 7–8). The contrast could not be more stark than this, and Isaiah tells it with the great power of his vision and poetic language.

Isaiah 28:14–20 An overflowing scourge will come—the people will be "trodden down." Turning back to the people of Judah, Isaiah warns, "Wherefore hear the word of the Lord, ye scornful men, that rule this people which is in Jerusalem. Because ye have said, We have made a covenant with death, and with hell are we at agreement; when the overflowing scourge shall pass through, it shall not come unto us: for we have made lies our refuge, and under falsehood have we hid ourselves" (vv. 14–15).

Foreign tyrants in Judah

"Death, *maweth,* [as used here is] the god of the underworld, Sheol or hell. Perhaps the Canaanite god of the underworld, Mot, is intended, or the reference may be to the Egyptian god Osiris. It was customary for the prophets to speak of the alien deities as lies and falsehood (see Amos 2:4; Jer. 10:14)."[6]

The Israelites were worshiping these false gods at the time and may have believed these gods would protect them. Some others of them believed that they were the Lord's people, with His temple in their midst, and that the Lord would never allow them to be destroyed. They could not have been more wrong.

Again, Isaiah's prophetic vision took him momentarily away from present troubles, and he spoke joyously of the day when the Lord Jesus Christ will reign as the tried and true cornerstone of the kingdom (vv. 16–17). We will discuss this prophecy later in this chapter. Isaiah's vision then returned to his own day as quickly as it left, and he finished the thought he had begun before, as explained above.

"Your covenant with death shall be disannulled, and your agreement with hell shall not stand; when the overflowing scourge shall pass through, then ye shall be trodden down by it," he warns the recalcitrant Jews (v. 18). It will be relentless, morning after morning, day and night, and it will be troubling for people to even understand the brutality and totality of it (v. 19). It would be as uncomfortable as a man trying to sleep on a too-short bed, or trying to cover himself with a blanket that is too narrow to cover him (v. 20).

● **Isaiah 30:1–7; Isaiah 31:1–8 Israel is counseled not to trust in the arm of flesh.** The people were trying to find protection from Assyria by relying on Egypt, rather than relying on the Lord. This, of course, meant that the people had to live worthily so they could receive the Lord's protection. The result of their efforts to rely on armaments rather than on righteousness would be shame and confusion, not deliverance.

As with many (if not most) of Isaiah's prophecies, these warnings are dualistic. They apply equally well to our own day, when we are surrounded on every side by threats to our peace and prosperity. Monte S. Nyman wrote: "The warning in [Isaiah 30:1–7] is ... extended to our day by the Lord's commanding Isaiah to record it as a witness for the latter days (verse 8); a marginal note in the KJV specifically identifies 'the latter day.'"[7] No amount of arms or political diplomacy will ever be sufficient to keep us safe. We must learn to be righteous and then rely on the Lord to protect and prosper us.

● **Isaiah 30:8–11 Israel's response was to rebel.** The people did not want to hear the Lord's rebukes nor His calls for them to repent. It could have seemed pointless to preach to them, knowing they would not listen. But the Lord commanded Isaiah, "Now go, write it before them in a table, and note it in a book, that it may be for the time to come for ever and ever" (v. 8). His writings and prophecies were not just for the people of his day, but for many generations and dispensations to come. We are living proof of this prophecy, studying those same words many thousands of years later for our own good.

"This is a rebellious people, lying children, children that will not hear the law of the Lord: Which say to the seers, See not; and to the prophets, Prophesy not unto us right things, speak unto us smooth things, prophesy deceits" (vv. 9–10). They wanted Isaiah to teach "smooth things" [false doctrine] rather than "right things." "Get you out of the way," they demanded, and "cause the Holy One of Israel to cease from before us" (v. 11).

RAPHAEL, 1511–1512

President Harold B. Lee said:

> Now the only safety we have as members of this Church is to do exactly what the Lord said to the Church in that day when the Church was organized. We must learn to give heed to the words and commandments that the Lord shall give through His prophet, "as he receiveth them, walking in all holiness before me; ... as if from mine own mouth, in all patience and faith" (D&C 21:4–5). There will be some things that take patience and faith. You may not like what comes from the authority of the Church. It may contradict your political views. It may contradict your social views. It may interfere with some of your social life. But if you listen to these things, as if from the mouth of the Lord Himself, with patience and faith, the promise is that "the gates of hell shall not prevail against you; yea, and the Lord God will disperse the powers of darkness from before you, and cause the heavens to shake for your good, and his name's glory" (D&C 21:6).[8]

- **Isaiah 30:12–17 As a result, their nation will be destroyed.**
The people "despise[d] this word, and trust[ed] in oppression and perverseness" (v. 12). They would, therefore, be destroyed like a wall ready to fall or a piece of pottery smashed into such small pieces that none of them could be written upon (vv. 13–14). Even now in the midst of their wickedness the Lord had promised them rest, quietness, and confidence if they would return and repent, but they would not do so (v. 15). They imagined that, even if they were attacked, they could flee upon

their horses and escape destruction, but the Lord reminded them that "they that pursue you [also] be swift" (v. 16). And their captivity will last until the latter days, when they would become "a beacon upon the top of a mountain, and as an ensign on an hill" (v. 17).

● **Isaiah 32:9–14 The land will become a wilderness for "many ... years."** The days of pleasant fields, joyous harvests, fruitful vines, and of childbirth will cease (vv. 9–13). They will be replaced by thorns and briers, empty cities, and abandoned guard towers (v. 14).

● **Isaiah 32:15–17 Their captivity will continue until the latter days.** Then the "spirit [will] be poured upon us from on high, and the wilderness be a fruitful field, and the fruitful field be counted for a forest. Then judgment shall dwell in the wilderness, and righteousness remain in the fruitful field. And the work of righteousness shall be peace; and the effect of righteousness quietness and assurance for ever." This would be the great day of the restoration of Israel from her scattered condition around the world. We turn next to the many prophecies of Isaiah concerning that happy day to come.

ISAIAH'S PROPHECIES OF THE RESTORATION

The Nephites

The Book of Mormon performs a special role in the restoration and the gathering of Israel. It is the primary evidence of the heavenly source of the Restoration, and the most effective missionary tool in the gathering. We would expect, therefore, that Isaiah would have known about it and prophesied concerning it. And he did, in Isaiah 29.

● **Isaiah 29:1–2 Isaiah speaks of a place far removed from "Ariel" (Jerusalem).** He begins his prophecy where the Nephites began—in Jerusalem. "Woe to Ariel, to Ariel, the city where

David dwelt! add ye year to year; let them kill sacrifices. Yet I will distress Ariel, and there shall be heaviness and sorrow" (vv. 1–2). The city will be destroyed and its inhabitants taken captive, as we have read in all of the prophecies discussed earlier (above).

Then, Isaiah turns suddenly (as he so often does) to another vision. "And it shall be unto me as Ariel," he proclaims (v. 2). We are left to wonder, is he talking about himself? Will he also be destroyed and taken captive? Or should we emphasize the "it" rather than the "me" in this sentence? If so, he is talking about something or someplace else, which would suffer the same fate as Ariel—"it shall be … as Ariel." We must conclude that it is a place, not a person, because none of these things happened to Isaiah personally.

- **Isaiah 29:3 Like Ariel** (Jerusalem)**, they will suffer warfare and destruction.** The Lord says, "I will camp against thee round about, and will lay siege against thee with a mount, and I will raise forts against thee."

  — **2 Nephi 26:15** The prophet Nephi said Isaiah was talking about the Nephites. "After my seed and the seed of my brethren shall have dwindled in unbelief, and shall have been smitten by the Gentiles; yea, after the Lord God shall have camped against them round about, and shall have laid siege against them with a mount, and raised forts against them; and after they shall have been brought down low in the dust, even that they are not …"

- **Isaiah 29:4 The Nephites will speak as a voice from the dust.** "And thou shalt be brought down, and shalt speak out of the ground, and thy speech shall be low out of the dust, and thy voice shall be, as of one that hath a familiar spirit, out of the ground, and thy speech shall whisper out of the dust." The people of whom Isaiah

THE PLATES OF DARIUS. PHOTOGRAPHER UNKNOWN

speaks will be destroyed and will only be known by their records, which will "whisper out of the dust" to those that read them.

— **2 Nephi 26:15–17** Nephi promised concerning the records of his people: "The words of the righteous shall be written, and the prayers of the faithful shall be heard, and all those who have dwindled in unbelief shall not be forgotten. For those who shall be destroyed shall speak unto them out of the ground, and their speech shall be low out of the dust, and their voice shall be as one that hath a familiar spirit; for the Lord God will give unto him power, that he may whisper concerning them, even as it were out of the ground; and their speech shall whisper out of the dust. For thus saith the Lord God: They shall write the things which shall be done among them, and they shall be written and sealed up in a book, and those who have dwindled in unbelief shall not have them, for they seek to destroy the things of God."

Elder LeGrand Richards said:

> If you will read [Isaiah 29:1–2] thoughtfully, you will know that he [Isaiah] not only saw the destruction of Jerusalem, but he saw the destruction of another great center like unto Jerusalem . ... He adds: "And thou shalt be brought down, and shalt speak out of the ground, and thy speech shall be low out of the dust, and thy voice shall be, as of one that hath a familiar spirit, out of the ground, and thy speech shall whisper out of the dust" (Isa. 29:4).
>
> Nobody in this world could explain that intelligently or know what people Isaiah saw like unto Jerusalem without the Book of Mormon [2 Nephi 26:15–17]. ... The Book of Mormon is the promised record that God said He would bring forth and join to the record of Judah. How could anyone understand this prophecy of Isaiah without the explanation contained in the Book of Mormon?[9]

● **Isaiah 29:5 The Nephites will be destroyed.** Though they will become very numerous, the Nephites will be destroyed, just as the Jews at Jerusalem were. "The multitude of thy strangers shall be like small dust, and the multitude of the terrible ones shall be as chaff that passeth away," Isaiah said. "Yea, it shall be at an instant suddenly."

● **Isaiah 29:6** (2 Nephi 27:2)**: The Nephites will suffer great natural disasters.** "Thou shalt be visited of the Lord of hosts with thunder, and with earthquake, and great noise, with storm and tempest, and the flame of devouring fire," said Isaiah. Of course, we know that the Lord visited them personally, but only after the most wicked among them had been cleansed from the land by incredible natural disasters— earthquakes, volcanoes, violent storms, hurricane-force winds, and raging fires, which changed the entire face of the land (see 3 Ne. 8:12). Isaiah saw all of this in vision. And note that none of these things ever happened to Jerusalem, making it even more clear that Isaiah is not talking here about the Jews. He is talking about a people who would be "as Ariel" in many (but not all) respects.

PHOTO COURTESY OF .DOCSTOC

- **Isaiah 29:7–8 (2 Nephi 27:3): The Nephites will live in a place far away from Jerusalem.** Lest anyone should think that he was talking about Jerusalem itself, Isaiah makes it plain that he is talking about a place where any mention of the difficulties at Jerusalem—its enemies, its munitions, and its distress—would be "as a dream of a night vision" to them (v. 7). They may dream concerning their homeland at Jerusalem, but it would be like dreaming of eating but waking up hungry, or dreaming of drinking and waking up thirsty; it would not be real, but only a night vision of the troubles at Mt. Zion (v. 8).

- **Isaiah 29:9–10 (2 Nephi 27:4–5): The Nephites will disappear from the land where they live.** Isaiah sees them "drunken, but not with wine," and "stagger[ing], but not with strong drink" (v. 9). They are a lost and confused people, destroyed by their own iniquity, upon whom "the Lord hath poured out ... the spirit of deep sleep, and hath closed your eyes: the prophets and your rulers, the seers hath he covered" (v. 10). In this way, they indeed were very much "as Ariel" in their ultimate fate, though their destruction was more total. The righteous Nephites descended into iniquity and were wiped out forever. Among the Jews, at least, a remnant was preserved in captivity.

The Book of Mormon

● **Isaiah 29:11 A book that is sealed.** The only thing left of the Nephite nation that Isaiah saw in vision was their records, which became "the words of a book that is sealed." This was the means by which their voices would speak out of the dust as Isaiah had predicted earlier (v. 4). And the coming forth of this book of history and scripture had been foretold since the days of Enoch.

— **Moses 7:62** Enoch foresaw truth coming out of the earth.

— **Psalm 85:11** David saw truth springing out of the earth & righteousness coming down from heaven.

— **Isaiah 45:8** Isaiah predicted that in the latter days they shall open the earth and find salvation.

● **Isaiah 29:11 The words of the book are delivered unto a learned man, who cannot read it.** The sealed book will be "deliver[ed] to one that is learned, saying, Read this, I pray thee: and he saith, I cannot; for it is sealed."

— **2 Nephi 27:10–14** Nephi tells us that "the book shall be sealed by the power of God, and the revelation which was sealed shall be kept in the book until the own due time of the Lord, that they may come forth; for behold, they reveal all things from the foundation of the world unto the end thereof. And the day cometh that the words of the book which were sealed shall be read upon the house tops; and they shall be read by the power of Christ; and all things shall be revealed unto the children of men which ever have been among the children of men, and which ever will be even unto the end of the earth." But until that day, only portions of the book would be available, and nobody would see the entire record except its translator (Joseph Smith) and certain witnesses who would be called to bear witness of its reality (vv. 12–14).

— **2 Nephi 27:15–18** Nephi prophesied that the book would be "show[n] ... unto the learned, saying: Read this, I pray thee. And the learned shall say: Bring hither the book, and I will read them. And now, because of the glory of the world and to get gain will they say this, and not for the glory of God. And the man shall say: I cannot bring the book, for it is sealed. Then shall the learned say: I cannot read it." We know that this prophecy was literally fulfilled when copies of the Book of Mormon transcript were taken by Martin Harris to Professor Charles Anthon in New York. When informed that he could not see the book, only these characters that he had been shown, Anthon responded, "I cannot read a sealed book."

● **Isaiah 29:12** (2 Nephi 27:19)**: The book is delivered to an unlearned man, who can and does read it.** Isaiah prophesied that "the book [will be] delivered to him that is not learned, saying, Read this, I pray thee: and he saith, I am not learned." This, of course, was Joseph Smith.

Elder Orson Pratt once said: "Now in regard to Joseph Smith's qualifications or attainments in learning, they were very ordinary. He had received a little education in the common country schools in the vicinity in which he had lived. He could read a little, and could write, but it was in such an ordinary hand that he did not venture to act as his own scribe, but had to employ sometimes one and sometimes another to write as he translated. This unlearned man did not make the same reply that the learned man did. For when the book was delivered to this unlearned youth and he was requested to read it, he replied, 'I am not learned.' I suppose he felt his weakness when the Lord told him to read this book; for he thought it was a great work."[10]

Elder Neal A. Maxwell said: "We have no hesitancy ... in stipulating that Joseph was, by the standards of the world, 'not learned.' Isaiah foresaw it (see Isa. 29:11–12). ... Emma Smith reportedly said that Joseph, at the time of the translation of the Book of Mormon, could not compose a 'well-worded letter, let alone dictate a book like the Book of Mormon ... [which was] marvelous to me, a marvel and a wonder, as much as to anyone else.' ... This obscure young man apparently paused while translating and dictating to Emma—probably from the fourth chapter of 1 Nephi—concerning the 'wall of Jerusalem'—and said, in effect, 'Emma, I didn't know there was a wall around Jerusalem.'"[11]

● **Isaiah 29:13–14** (2 Nephi 27:25–26): **The Restoration as a marvelous work and a wonder.** The book of which Isaiah prophesied would come forward in a day when "people draw near me [the Lord] with their mouth, and with their lips do honour me, but have removed their heart far from me, and their fear toward me is taught by the precept of men" (v. 13). That was the situation after more than 1,700 years of apostasy. The world was wrapped in spiritual darkness.

"Therefore," the Lord said, "behold, I will proceed to do a marvellous work among this people, even a marvellous work and a wonder: for the wisdom of their wise men shall perish, and the understanding of their prudent men shall be hid" (v. 14).

Elder LeGrand Richards wrote: "What would really constitute a marvelous work and a wonder? Why should not honest lovers of truth welcome the pronouncement of such a work? [Should] any generation ... reject revealed truth when ... sent from heaven? [even as they rejected the Christ when He came among men?]. Why does it seem so much easier to accept and believe in dead prophets than in living prophets? In the accomplishment of this promised marvelous work and a wonder, the Lord had in mind a 'restitution of all things' and moved upon Peter to so prophesy to those who had crucified [his Lord]: [Acts 3:19–21]."[12]

● **Isaiah 29:15–17** (2 Nephi 27:27–28): **The timing of the Restoration.** After cursing those who had sought to thwart His work, the Lord predicts that, in the latter days, "Lebanon shall be turned into a fruitful field, and the fruitful field shall be esteemed as a forest" (v. 17).

Elder Mark E. Petersen said: "The gathering of the Jews to Palestine is one of the most outstanding and significant of all the signs of the times. ... Isaiah indicated that Palestine ... was destined to be turned into a fruitful field in connection with the gathering of the Jews to their homeland. ... A sacred book was to come forth before that time. ... Where is that book? It is one of the signs of the times. ... Isaiah set a limit on the time of its publication. ... Isaiah said that the book would come forth first, and then ... in 'a very little while ... Lebanon shall be turned into a fruitful field, and the fruitful field shall be esteemed as a forest' (Isa. 29:17). The time limit has expired. This new volume of scripture must have come forth before now or Isaiah was not a true prophet, for Palestine is fruitful again."[13]

The Book of Mormon came first, just as Isaiah foresaw it would.

- **Isaiah 29:18** (2 Nephi 27:29): **The spiritually blind and deaf will understand true doctrine.** In his poetic way, Isaiah compares people who are without gospel understanding to those who are deaf and blind. But "out of obscurity, and out of darkness" would come the record of the Nephites to sweep away their spiritual deafness and blindness.

  Elder Bruce R. McConkie wrote: "Spiritual deafness [is] the state of those who are lacking in spirituality, whose spirit ears are not attuned to the whisperings of the still small voice of the Spirit. Similarly, spiritual blindness is the identifying mark which singles out those who are unable to see the hand of God manifest in the affairs of men. Such have 'unbelief and blindness of heart' (D&C 58:15); they are 'hard in their hearts, and blind in their minds' (3 Ne. 2:1)."[14]

- **Isaiah 29:19–24** (2 Nephi 27:30–35): **"They also that erred in spirit shall come to understanding."** As a result of the great restoration of truth, "the meek also shall increase their joy in the Lord, and the poor among men shall rejoice in the Holy One of Israel," while "the terrible one [Satan] is brought to nought, and the scorner is consumed, and all that watch for iniquity are cut off" (vv. 19–20).

The children of Abraham and Jacob "shall not now be ashamed, neither shall his face now wax pale" (v. 22). "They shall sanctify my name, and sanctify the Holy One of Jacob, and shall fear the God of Israel" (v. 23). "They also that erred in spirit shall come to understanding, and they that murmured shall learn doctrine" (v. 24). All this, because of the coming forth of the Nephite record of which Isaiah speaks in chapter 29 of his writings.

Elder Orson Pratt said:

> Oh, how my heart has been pained within me when I have seen the blindness of the Christian world, and I knew that many of them were sincere! I knew they desired to know the truth, but they scarcely knew whether to turn to the right or to the left, so great were the errors that were taught in their midst, and so strong the traditions which they had imbibed, the fear of the Lord being taught them by the precepts of men instead of by inspiration and the power of the Holy Ghost. "They also that erred in spirit shall come to understanding" when this book comes forth, and "they that murmur shall learn doctrine." ...
>
> But those who have read this book will bear me record that their minds have been forever set at rest in regard to doctrine, so far as the ordinances of the kingdom of God are concerned. Those who erred, and did not know whether sprinkling, pouring, or immersion was the true method of baptism, now know? Why? Because the Book of Mormon reveals the mode as it was given to the ancient Nephites on this continent. So in regard to every other principle of the doctrine of Christ—it is set forth in such great plainness that it is impossible for any two persons to form different ideas in relation to it, after reading the Book of Mormon.[15]

The Gathering

● **Isaiah 27:1–6 Israel will be restored and "fill the face of the world with fruit"—the gospel of peace.** Satan shall have long had his way with the apostate world. But in the latter days, "the Lord with his sore and great and strong sword shall punish leviathan the piercing serpent, even leviathan that crooked serpent; and he shall slay the dragon that is in the sea" (v. 1).

Both "dragon" and "serpent" are symbolic names for the enemy of all righteousness, Lucifer. Leviathan includes not only Satan personally but all who serve him (see Rev. 12:9). Isaiah saw the destruction of all these before Zion could be fully established.

In place of the destroyed and desolate "vineyard" He condemned in the days of Isaiah, the Lord will now celebrate "a vineyard of red wine" that He Himself guards and waters "every moment: lest any hurt it, … night and day" (vv. 2–3). He invites latter-day Israel: "Let him take hold of my strength, that he may make peace with me; and he shall make peace with me" (v. 5). And when they do, "Jacob [shall] take root: Israel shall blossom and bud, and fill the face of the world with fruit" (v. 6).

● **Isaiah 27:12–13 Jerusalem will "be gathered one by one."** Though they will have been conquered and scattered, the Lord will gather the Jews back to their homeland, which will stretch "from the channel of the river [Euphrates] unto the stream of Egypt" (v. 12). This will not be accomplished through the migration of an entire people, but "one by one" (v. 12). The "great trumpet" of the restoration will blow, "and they shall come which were ready to perish in the land of Assyria [captivity], and the outcasts in the land of Egypt [the world], and shall worship the Lord in the holy mount at Jerusalem" (v. 13). There is a lot of metaphoric imagery here, which can only be understood by referring back to what we learned in the previous chapter about how the nations of Isaiah's time were symbolic of things such as captivity and the world. The allegory of Zenos in the Book of Mormon (see Jacob 5) contains similar imagery.

Elder Bruce R. McConkie wrote:

> The gathering of Israel is first spiritual and second temporal. It is spiritual in that the lost sheep of Israel are first "restored to the true church and fold of God," meaning that they come to a true knowledge of the God of Israel, accept the gospel which He has restored in latter days, and join The Church of Jesus Christ of Latter-day Saints. It is temporal in that these converts are then "gathered home to the lands of their inheritance, and ... established in all their lands of promise" (2 Ne. 9:2; 25:15–18; Jer. 16:14–21), meaning that the house of Joseph will be established in America, the house of Judah in Palestine, and that the Lost Tribes will come to Ephraim in America to receive their blessings in due course (D&C 133). ...
>
> The purpose of the gathering of Israel is twofold: 1. To put the peoples of living Israel in that environment where they may the better work out their salvation, where they may have the Gentile and worldly views erased from them, and where they may be molded into that pattern of perfect righteousness which will please the Almighty; and 2. To enable the gathered remnants of the chosen lineage to build temples and perform the ordinances of salvation and exaltation for their Israelitish ancestors who lived when the gospel was not had on earth.[16]

● **Isaiah 28:5–13 Israel will learn true doctrine line upon line, precept upon precept.** Isaiah calls the Lord "a crown of glory, and ... a diadem of beauty, unto the residue of his people" (v. 5). This "residue" is the descendants of Israel that will be found on the earth in the day of restoration—the latter days. The Lord will provide "a spirit of judgment to him that sitteth in judgment, and ... strength to them that turn the battle to the gate" (v. 6). Though both the people and their prophets will have erred for many years, they will again learn correct doctrine. "Whom shall he teach knowledge? and whom shall he make to understand doctrine? them that are weaned from the milk, and drawn from the breasts" (v. 9). He will teach them "precept upon precept, ... line upon line; here a little, and there a little" until they understand the entirety of His plan for their redemption (v. 10). Isaiah is not speaking here of someone in the native land of Israel. He is speaking of a time and place when, "with stammering lips and another tongue will he speak to this people" (v. 11). There, finally, they will understand the "refreshing [that] they would not hear" in their days of apostasy.

Isaiah 35:1–7 The Lord's people will settle in a desert and it will blossom. This dualistic prophecy is a remarkably accurate description of the state of the children of Israel when the Lord gathers them again into "the wilderness." In earlier days, it might have described the refugees from Babylonian captivity when they returned to the city of Jerusalem. In our latter day, it describes the scene as the pioneers descended into their mountain refuge in the Salt Lake Valley.

Weary pioneers enter SL Valley in 1847

C.C.A. CHRISTENSEN 1800s

"The wilderness and the solitary place shall be glad for them," Isaiah predicted, "and the desert shall rejoice, and blossom as the rose" (v. 1). They will arrive worn out and discouraged. Isaiah said, "Strengthen ye the weak hands, and confirm the feeble knees. Say to them that are of a fearful heart, Be strong, fear not: behold, your God will come with vengeance, even God with a recompence; he will come and save you" (vv. 3–4). Miracles will occur there, and "in the wilderness shall waters break out, and streams in the desert" (v. 6)—a possible reference to the irrigation the pioneers used to water their crops. "The parched ground shall become a pool, and the thirsty land springs of water: in the habitation of dragons, where each lay, shall be grass with reeds and rushes" (v. 7).

Isaiah 35:8–9 A holy temple will be built there. Using the metaphor of a "highway," Isaiah then described the temple of God that would grace the wilderness where the children of Israel would settle. "And an highway shall be there ... , and it shall be called The way of holiness" (v. 8). As is true of every temple, "the unclean shall not pass over it; but it shall be for those: the wayfaring men, though fools, shall not err therein" (v. 8). "No lion shall be there, nor any ravenous beast shall go up thereon, it shall not be found there; but the redeemed shall walk there" (v. 9).

- **Isaiah 35:10 The "ransomed of the Lord"** (10 tribes) **will return to the new gathering place in America.** "And the ransomed of the Lord [the lost 10 tribes] shall return, and come to Zion with songs and everlasting joy upon their heads: they shall obtain joy and gladness, and sorrow and sighing shall flee away."

The Prophet Joseph Smith said: "Our western tribes of Indians are descendants from that Joseph who was sold into Egypt, and … the land of America is a promised land unto them, and unto it all the tribes of Israel will come, with as many of the Gentiles as shall comply with the requisitions of the new covenant. But the tribe of Judah will return to old Jerusalem. The city of Zion spoken of by David, in the one hundred and second Psalm, will be built upon the land of America, 'And the ransomed of the Lord shall return, and come to Zion with songs and everlasting joy upon their heads' (Isa. 35:10); and then they will be delivered from the overflowing scourge that shall pass through the land. But Judah shall obtain deliverance at Jerusalem" [See Joel 2:32; Isa. 26:20–21; Jer. 31:12; Ps. 1:5; Ezek. 34:11–13].[17]

- **Isaiah 33:20–24 Israel is compared to a tent with "stakes" holding it up** (see also Isa. 54:2–7; 3 Ne. 22:2–7). Isaiah describes the latter-day Zion as a "city of our solemnities: … a quiet habitation, a tabernacle that shall not be taken down; not one of the stakes thereof shall ever be removed, neither shall any of the cords thereof be broken" (v. 20). It will be a place of "broad rivers and streams," but not near the ocean with its "oars [and] gallant ship[s] pass[ing] thereby" (v. 21). It will be a place where "the Lord is our lawgiver, the Lord is our king; [and] he will save us" (v. 22), because "the people that dwell therein shall be forgiven their iniquity" (v. 24).

A bedouin tent like those Isaiah would have known, with cords and stakes holding it up

Elder Bruce R. McConkie wrote:

> In prophetic imagery, Zion is pictured as a great tent upheld by cords fastened securely to stakes. Thus Isaiah, envisioning the latter-day glory of Israel, gathered to her restored Zion, proclaimed: "Enlarge the place of thy tent, and let them stretch forth the curtains of thine habitations: spare not, lengthen thy cords, and strengthen thy stakes; For thou shalt break forth on the right hand and on the left. ... For a small moment have I forsaken thee; but with great mercies will I gather thee." (Isa. 54:2–7). And of the millennial Zion, Isaiah exulted: "Look upon Zion, the city of our solemnities: ... a tabernacle that shall not be taken down; not one of the stakes thereof shall ever be removed, neither shall any of the cords thereof be broken" (Isa. 33:20).
>
> In keeping with this symbolism, the great areas of Church population and strength, which sustain and uphold the restored Zion, are called stakes. They are the rallying points and the gathering centers for the remnants of scattered Israel.[18]

Work for the Dead

● **Isaiah 24:21–22 These "prisoners ... shut up in the prison ... shall ... be visited."** In many ages of time, stretching back to the flood of Noah and beyond, the Lord has had to punish hosts of His children for their gross wickedness. Many "high ones" and "kings of the earth" have been among them (v. 21). Having been removed from the earth, they have been "gathered together, as prisoners are gathered in the pit, and ... shut up in the prison" that God has prepared for the unrighteous in the spirit world (v. 22)—the place where the spirits of some deceased mortals go while awaiting the resurrection (see D&C 138:32). Isaiah's promise here is that "after many days shall they be visited" (v. 22). This occurred when the Savior visited the spirit world after His death and before His resurrection and organized righteous spirits to teach the gospel to the spirits in prison (see D&C 138:29–37).

The "prisoners ... gathered in the pit" and those "shut up in the prison" (Isa. 24:22) are those locked in the spirit world awaiting the preaching of the gospel.[19]

— **Isaiah 42:5–7 Our role in "bring[ing] out the prisoners from the prison."** "Thus saith God the Lord, he that created the heavens, and stretched them out; he that spread forth the earth, and that which cometh out of it; he that giveth breath unto the people upon it, and spirit to them that walk therein: I the Lord have called thee in righteousness, and will hold thine hand, and will keep thee, and give thee for a covenant of the people, for a light of the Gentiles" (v. 6). He is speaking here of us, the children of Israel in the last days. Our mission and ministry is to "open the blind eyes [of the disbelieving]," and also "to bring out the prisoners from the prison, and them that sit in darkness out of the prison house" (v. 7).

— **Isaiah 49:9–10** (1 Nephi 21:9–10): **The Savior's love and mercy for those in the spirit prison.** Though they were grossly wicked in their day, the Lord has not cast off forever His disobedient children. The people of Noah's day, the children of Israel in the wilderness, and countless others who have rejected the prophets and chosen iniquity, are still worth saving. God does not give up on them. He removes them from the earth, where their wickedness has put an end to their agency, and places them in a situation where, after many years to think about it, they might be more willing and able to hear the truth. Our merciful and forgiving Lord says "to the prisoners, Go forth; to them that are in darkness, Shew yourselves" (v. 9). He who loves all of us perfectly will "lead them, even by the springs of water shall he guide them" (v. 10).

PROPHECIES OF JUDGMENTS UPON THE WICKED

The "Apocalypse of Isaiah"

Isaiah 24–27 is commonly known as the "Apocalypse of Isaiah." In these chapters, he paid particular attention to the judgments that will be poured out upon the wicked just prior to the Second Coming of our Lord.

● **Isaiah 24:13–20, 23 Great natural destructions will attend the Second Coming of Christ.** Isaiah spoke here of those days when the final gathering has taken place— when the olive tree has been shaken to obtain the very last fruit in its upper branches, and when the very last grapes have been harvested even after the main harvest has been turned into wine (v. 13). When people have sung praises to the Lord from the "the isles of the sea" and "the uttermost part of the earth" (vv. 15–16), then the wicked will have cause to fear (v. 17).

There will be no escaping the consequences of their wicked choices. "He who fleeth from the noise of the fear shall fall into the pit; and he that cometh up out of the midst of the pit shall be taken in the snare: for the windows from on high are open, and the foundations of the earth do shake" (v. 18). "The earth is utterly broken down, the earth is clean dissolved, the earth is moved exceedingly" (v. 19). "The earth shall reel to and fro like a drunkard, and shall be removed like a cottage; and the transgression thereof shall be heavy upon it; and it shall fall, and not rise again" (v. 20).

— **D&C 88:87–91** A more detailed description of these events can be found in the Doctrine and Covenants: "For not many days hence and the earth shall tremble and reel to and fro as a drunken man; and the sun shall hide his face, and shall refuse to give light; and the moon shall be bathed in blood; and the stars shall become exceedingly angry, and shall cast themselves down as a fig that falleth from off a fig–tree" (v. 87).

Speaking to His missionaries, the Lord said, "And after your testimony cometh wrath and indignation upon the people. And after your testimony cometh the testimony of earthquakes, that shall cause groanings in the midst of her, and men shall fall upon the ground and shall not be able to stand. And also cometh the testimony of the voice of thunderings, and the voice of lightnings, and the voice of tempests, and the voice of the waves of the sea heaving themselves beyond their bounds. And all things shall be in commotion; and surely, men's hearts shall fail them; for fear shall come upon all people" (vv. 88–91).

Elder Orson Pratt said, "'The moon [will] be confounded and the sun [will be] ashamed' [Isa. 24:23] because of the superior light that will attend the presence of the Being [Jesus Christ] who is to reign in Zion and Jerusalem."[20] The brilliance of this "superior light" will make all else seem dark by comparison.

● **Isaiah 26:20–21 Hiding ourselves from the judgments poured out upon the wicked.** Isaiah counseled, "Come, my people, enter thou into thy chambers, and shut thy doors about thee: hide thyself as it were for a little moment, until the indignation be overpast" (v. 20). The place of safety, it seems, will be in our homes and other holy places. "For, behold, the Lord cometh out of his place to punish the inhabitants of the earth for their iniquity: the earth also shall disclose her blood, and shall no more cover her slain" (v. 21).

Elder Bruce R. McConkie said: "We do not say that all of the Saints will be spared and saved from the coming day of desolation. But we do say there is no promise of safety and no promise of security except for those who love the Lord and who are seeking to do all that He commands."[21]

● **Isaiah 28:17–22 Judgments will be sent against covenant breakers.** This dualistic prophecy was discussed earlier with regard to the "overflowing scourge" that would come upon

Jerusalem when they were taken into captivity. But it is also an apt description of the judgments that will overtake the wicked in the last days.

"Judgment ... and the hail shall sweep away the refuge of lies, and the waters shall overflow the hiding place. And your covenant with death shall be disannulled, and your agreement with hell shall not stand; when the overflowing scourge shall pass through, then ye shall be trodden down by it. From the time that it goeth forth it shall take you: for morning by morning shall it pass over, by day and by night: and it shall be a vexation only to understand the report. For the bed is shorter than that a man can stretch himself on it: and the covering narrower than that he can wrap himself in it" (vv. 17–20). "Now therefore be ye not mockers, ... for I have heard from the Lord God of hosts a consumption, even determined upon the whole earth" (v. 22).

● **Isaiah 30:27–30 A day of great terror for the wicked.** Using a broad variety of metaphors and similes, Isaiah described the Lord as coming "from far, burning with his anger, and the burden thereof is heavy: his lips are full of indignation, and his tongue as a devouring fire: And his breath, as an overflowing stream, shall reach to the midst of the neck, to sift the nations with the sieve of vanity: and there shall be a bridle in the jaws of the people, causing them to err" (vv. 27–28). It will be a day of great terror for all the wicked.

Yet, at the same time, "Ye [the righteous] shall have a song, as in the night when a holy solemnity is kept; and gladness of heart, as when one goeth with a pipe to come into the mountain of the Lord, to the mighty One of Israel" (v. 29). To the righteous, "the Lord shall cause his glorious voice to be heard," while to the wicked He "shall shew the lighting down of his arm, with the indignation of his anger, and with the flame of a devouring fire, with scattering, and tempest, and hailstones" (v. 30; see also Isa. 33:10–13).

- **Isaiah 34:1–10 The Lord will destroy the armies of all nations.**
The nations of the earth will proudly rely upon their armaments
to protect themselves from all enemies. But when "the indignation
of the Lord is upon all nations, and his fury upon all their armies:
he [will] utterly destroy ... them, [and] deliver ... them to the
slaughter" (v. 2). "Their slain also shall be cast out, and their
stink shall come up out of their carcases, and the mountains shall
be melted with their blood. And all the host of heaven shall be
dissolved, and the heavens shall be rolled together as a scroll: and
all their host shall fall down, as the leaf falleth off from the vine,
and as a falling fig from the fig tree. For my sword shall be bathed
in heaven: behold, it shall come down upon Idumea [the world],
and upon the people of my curse, to judgment" (vv. 3–5).

"For it is the day of the Lord's vengeance, and the year of
recompences" (v. 8). The land will be so wasted that "the streams
thereof shall be turned into pitch [tar], and the dust thereof into
brimstone [sulphur], and the land thereof shall become burning
pitch. It shall not be quenched night nor day; the smoke thereof
shall go up for ever: from generation to generation it shall lie
waste; none shall pass through it for ever and ever" (vv. 9–10).

— **D&C 87:6 The Lord will make "a full end of all nations."** "And thus, with
the sword and by bloodshed the inhabitants of the earth shall mourn; and
with famine, and plague, and earthquake, and the thunder of heaven, and
the fierce and vivid lightning also, shall the inhabitants of the earth be made
to feel the wrath, and indignation, and chastening hand of an Almighty
God, until the consumption decreed hath made a full end of all nations."

THE SAVIOR IS OUR STRENGTH AND REFUGE

Isaiah wrote of the Savior strengthening us during the storms,
tempests, deserts, and heat of our lives, as well as during the great
destructions before His Second Coming.

— He is a refuge from the storm (Isa. 25:4).

— He is a shadow from the heat (Isa. 25:4).

— He is a hiding place from wind (Isa. 32:2).

— He is a covert (cover) from the tempest (Isa. 32:2).

— He is rivers of water in a dry place (Isa. 32:2).

— He is the shadow of a great rock in a weary (thirsty) land (Isa. 32:2).

Isaiah 30:19–21 The Savior knows our trials and directs our paths. He will strengthen us when adversity comes. "For the people shall dwell in Zion [and] shalt weep no more: he will be very gracious unto thee at the voice of thy cry; when he shall hear it, he will answer thee" (v. 19). "And though the Lord give you the bread of adversity, and the water of affliction, yet shall not thy teachers be removed into a corner any more, but thine eyes shall see thy teachers" (v. 20). And we will be led of Him through the voice of the Spirit: "And thine ears shall hear a word behind thee, saying, This is the way, walk ye in it, when ye turn to the right hand, and when ye turn to the left" (v. 21).

The Savior Is Our Sure Foundation

Isaiah 28:16 Our tried and precious cornerstone is Christ. When storms and floods arise and beat upon a structure, the determining factor for whether it will continue to stand is the strength of its foundation. Isaiah spoke of the Lord as our sure foundation. "Therefore thus saith the Lord God, Behold, I lay in Zion for a foundation a stone, a tried stone, a precious corner stone, a sure foundation: he that believeth shall not make haste."

— **Ephesians 2:19–20** Paul used the same imagery when he said the foundation of the Church of Jesus Christ is Apostles and prophets, with Christ Himself being the chief cornerstone.

Isaiah 8:14–15 (2 Nephi 18:14–15)**: He is a "stone of stumbling" to the wicked.** "And he shall be for [us] a sanctuary;

but ... a stone of stumbling and for a rock of offence to [the wicked of] both the houses of Israel" (v. 14). "And many among them shall stumble, and fall, and be broken, and be snared, and be taken" (v. 15; see also Mosiah 3:17; Hel. 5:12; D&C 50:44).

Elder Bruce R. McConkie wrote: "One of Isaiah's great Messianic prophecies was that the promised Messiah would be 'for a stone of stumbling and for a rock of offence to both the houses of Israel, for a gin and for a snare to the inhabitants of Jerusalem. And many among them shall stumble, and fall, and be broken, and be snared, and be taken' (Isa. 8:14–15). Both Paul (Rom. 9:33) and Peter (1 Pet. 2:7–8) record the fulfilment of this prophecy."[22]

— **Jacob 4:15** Jacob used the same metaphor when he said that "by the stumbling of the Jews they will reject the stone upon which they might build and have safe foundation."

● **Isaiah 28:17 "Righteousness to the plummet" continues the metaphor.** "Judgment also will I lay to the line, and righteousness to the plummet: and the hail shall sweep away the refuge of lies, and the waters shall overflow the hiding place." Builders use a plumb bob to find a straight vertical line. The plumb bob is a heavy weight attached to a cord which, when dropped, falls straight down in a line that is perpendicular to its beginning point. Thus the builder knows he has a straight line. With righteousness and justice as His "plummet," the Savior starts with the chief cornerstone (Himself) and lays out a perfectly framed house of God where we can safely dwell.

EVENTS AT AND AFTER THE SECOND COMING OF CHRIST

● **Isaiah 25:6 "In this mountain."** The metaphor of a "mountain" in these verses can represent a kingdom, the Lord's kingdom, that will be established at His Second Coming. The fruits of that kingdom are compared to a sumptuous feast (v. 6; also see below concerning this feast). The same metaphor can also refer to a temple—a Millennial or heavenly temple—or a temple city like the New Jerusalem (see Ezek. 40–48). The Qumran Temple Scroll describes such a city, which requires a three-day purification just for admission. Both the city and Mount Zion (the temple) have the same sanctity as Mount Sinai.

Isaiah 25:6 A feast for the faithful. "And in this mountain shall the Lord of hosts make unto all people a feast of fat things, a feast of wines on the lees, of fat things full of marrow, of wines on the lees well refined." This feast is sometimes referred to as the "bridal feast" or the "messianic banquet." It is related to the sacred, communal meal that occurred in connection with temple sacrifices and rituals, usually at the conclusion of a covenant ceremony (see Ex. 24:7–11; 1 Kgs. 8:62–66). Having sought forgiveness through blood sacrifice of an animal, the participants then took a portion of the meat home and ate it in celebration of the occasion and as part of the symbolism of "eating" the source of their redemption.

— **Revelation 19:9** There is to be yet another messianic sacramental meal when the Lord comes again at the end of the world.

— **Revelation 7:15, 17** Those before the throne of God serve Him day and night in His temple. The Lord dwells among them, feeds them, leads them unto living fountains, and wipes away all tears from their eyes.

— **D&C 58:6–12** The same concept of the "supper of the Lord" is found in the Doctrine and Covenants.

— **D&C 27:5–14** The list of invited guests includes Moroni, Elias, John the Baptist, Elijah, Joseph, Jacob, Isaac, Abraham, Adam, Peter, James, John, and anyone else who is willing to qualify—"all those whom my Father hath given me out of the world."

— **Luke 14:15–24** Those whom the Father has given Him out of the world are the faithful Saints of all ages.

Isaiah 25:7 Righteousness and knowledge will prevail. The Lord will also "destroy in this mountain the face of the covering cast over all people, and the vail that is spread over all nations" (v. 7). Truth will prevail and ignorance and lies will be wiped away. This veil can be interpreted as the "dark veil of unbelief" (see Alma 19:6; Ether 4:15) which blinds those who reject the gospel. Or, it could be a more literal "veil of darkness," such as that described in Moses 7:61 when "the heavens shall be darkened" and "shall shake, and also the earth."

● **Isaiah 25:8, 10–11 All enemies will have been subdued,** "and the rebuke of his people shall he take away from off all the earth" (v. 8). "For in this mountain shall the hand of the Lord rest, and Moab [the world] shall be trodden down under him, even as straw is trodden down for the dunghill" (v. 10), and "he shall bring down their pride together with the spoils of their hands" (v. 11).

● **Isaiah 26 A song, or psalm, of praise to the Lord for the gathering of Israel** from its scattered condition "far unto all ends of the earth" (v. 15).

The Resurrection

● **Isaiah 25:8–9 Physical and spiritual death will be conquered.** Through the Resurrection, "He will swallow up death in victory; and the Lord God will wipe away tears from off all faces" (v. 8). And through the Atonement, "it shall be said in that day, Lo, this is our God; we have waited for him, and he will

All will arise at the Resurrection

save us ... , [and] we will be glad and rejoice in his salvation" (v. 9). Other scriptures refer to this same glorious state of existence.

— **D&C 58:3–4**	The righteous will be crowned with much glory.
— **Revelation 7:17**	God will wipe away all tears from our eyes.
— **Revelation 21:4**	There will no more sorrow, pain, or sin.

● **Isaiah 26:19 Isaiah expresses joy for the Resurrection.** "Thy dead men shall live, together with my dead body shall they arise. Awake and sing, ye that dwell in dust: for thy dew is as the dew of herbs, and the earth shall cast out the dead."

— **D&C 88:95–98 The First Resurrection will occur at Christ's coming.** "And immediately after shall the curtain of heaven be unfolded, as a scroll is unfolded after it is rolled up, and the face of the Lord shall be unveiled; And the saints that are upon the earth, who are alive, shall be quickened and be caught up to meet him. And they who have slept in their graves shall come forth, for their graves shall be opened; and they also shall be caught up to meet him in the midst of the pillar of heaven—They are Christ's, the first fruits, they who shall descend with him first, and they who are on the earth and in their graves, who are first caught up to meet him; and all this by the voice of the sounding of the trump of the angel of God."

— **D&C 88:99 The second resurrection will follow the first.** After the initial (first) resurrection that will occur at the time of Christ's return, then "another angel shall sound, which is the second trump; and then cometh the redemption of those who are Christ's at his coming; who have received their part in that prison which is prepared for them, that they might receive the gospel, and be judged according to men in the flesh."

— **D&C 76:73–75 Those of the second resurrection** will be "they who are the spirits of men kept in prison, whom the Son visited, and preached the gospel unto them, that they might be judged according to men in the flesh; Who received not the testimony of Jesus in the flesh, but afterwards received it. These are they who are honorable men of the earth, who were blinded by the craftiness of men."

President Joseph Fielding Smith wrote: "Following this great event, and after the Lord and the righteous who are caught up to meet Him have descended upon the earth, there will come to pass another resurrection. This may be considered as a part of the first, although it comes later. In this resurrection will come forth those of the terrestrial order, who were not worthy to be caught up to meet Him, but who are worthy to come forth to enjoy the millennial reign."[23]

— **Alma 11:43 The bodies of resurrected beings will be in perfect form.**
"The spirit and the body shall be reunited again in its perfect form; both·
limb and joint shall be restored to its proper frame, even as we now are at
this time; and we shall be brought to stand before God, knowing even as
we know now, and have a bright recollection of all our guilt."

— **Alma 11:44 Eventually, all of God's children who have lived on the
earth will be resurrected.** "Now, this restoration shall come to all, both
old and young, both bond and free, both male and female, both the
wicked and the righteous; and even there shall not so much as a hair of
their heads be lost; but every thing shall be restored to its perfect frame, as
it is now, or in the body, and shall be brought and be arraigned before the
bar of Christ the Son, and God the Father, and the Holy Spirit, which is
one Eternal God, to be judged according to their works, whether they be
good or whether they be evil."

● **Isaiah 25:8 The Savior will wipe away our tears,** just as
a loving parent wipes away tears from a child's face. Isaiah
prophesied, "He will swallow up death in victory; and the Lord
God will wipe away tears from off all faces; and the rebuke of
his people shall he take away from off all the earth: for the Lord
hath spoken it."

— **Revelation 21:4 The Apostle John promised the same thing.** "And God
shall wipe away all tears from their eyes; and there shall be no more death,
neither sorrow, nor crying, neither shall there be any more pain: for the
former things are passed away."

— **D&C 138:12–16, 50 The spirits in spirit prison will also rejoice.**
President Joseph F. Smith saw in vision "gathered together in one place an
innumerable company of the spirits of the just, who had been faithful in
the testimony of Jesus while they lived in mortality; And who had offered
sacrifice in the similitude of the great sacrifice of the Son of God, and had
suffered tribulation in their Redeemer's name. All these had departed the
mortal life, firm in the hope of a glorious resurrection, through the grace
of God the Father and his Only Begotten Son, Jesus Christ. ... I beheld
that they were filled with joy and gladness, and were rejoicing together
because the day of their deliverance was at hand. They were assembled
awaiting the advent of the Son of God into the spirit world, to declare
their redemption from the bands of death. ... For the dead had looked
upon the long absence of their spirits from their bodies as a bondage."

The Millennium

● **Isaiah 24:23 The Lord will reign in both Jerusalem and Zion.** The glory of Christ's presence will be such that "the moon shall be confounded, and the sun ashamed." The Lord will personally reign both "in mount Zion [America], and in Jerusalem, and before his ancients gloriously."

● **Isaiah 32:1 The Lord will reign in righteousness.** "Behold, a king shall reign in righteousness, and princes shall rule in judgment."

● **Isaiah 30:18–26 Israel will enjoy Millennial blessings.** The ever-patient and loving Lord will "wait, that he may be gracious unto you, and therefore will he be exalted, that he may have mercy upon you: for the Lord is a God of judgment [and] blessed are all they that wait for him" (v. 18). Many millennial blessings will come to Israel as a result of the Lord's patience in waiting for them to repent and gather:

— The people that dwell in Zion at Jerusalem "[shall] weep no more" (v. 19).

— "At the voice of thy cry; when [the Lord] shall hear it, he will answer thee" (v. 19).

— "Thy teachers [will not] be removed into a corner … , but thine eyes shall see [them]" (v. 20).

— The Spirit will guide them, saying, "This is the way, walk ye in it" (v. 21).

— Satan will not be among them, removing the need to say to him, "Get thee hence" (v. 22).

— They shall have an abundance of rain, the fruits of the earth, and pastures (v. 23).

— Their animals will eat plenteous and clean food of the highest quality (v. 24).

— There will be an abundance of water flowing from "every high hill" (v. 25).

— "The light of the moon shall be as the light of the sun, and the light of the sun shall be sevenfold," as if it were seven days' worth of sunshine (v. 26).

- **Isaiah 33:14–17 The righteous will dwell in "everlasting burnings."** Isaiah asked, "Who among us shall dwell with the devouring fire? who among us shall dwell with everlasting burnings?" (v. 14). Then he answered, "He that walketh righteously, and speaketh uprightly; he that despiseth the gain of oppressions, that shaketh his hands from holding of bribes, that stoppeth his ears from hearing of blood, and shutteth his eyes from seeing evil" (v. 15). "He shall dwell on high: his place of defence shall be the munitions of rocks: bread shall be given him; his waters shall be sure. Thine eyes shall see the king in his beauty: they shall behold the land that is very far off" (vv. 16–17).

Elder Bruce R. McConkie said:

> "Who among us shall dwell with everlasting burnings?" (Isa. 33:14). That is, who in the Church shall gain an inheritance in the celestial kingdom? Who will go where God and Christ and holy beings are? Who will overcome the world, work the works of righteousness, and enduring in faith and devotion to the end hear the blessed benediction, "Come, and inherit the kingdom of my Father." Isaiah answers [in Isa. 33:15–16]. ...
>
> First, "He that walketh righteously, and speaketh uprightly." That is, building on the atoning sacrifice of the Lord Jesus Christ, we must keep the commandments. We must speak the truth and work the works of righteousness. We shall be judged by our thoughts, our words, and our deeds.
>
> Second, " ... he that despiseth the gain of oppressions." That is, we must act with equity and justice toward our fellowmen. It is the Lord Himself who said that He, at the day of His coming, will be a swift witness against those that oppress the hireling in his wages.
>
> Third, " ... he that shaketh his hands from holding of bribes." That is, we must reject every effort to buy influence, and instead deal fairly and impartially with our fellowmen. God is no respecter of persons. He esteemeth all flesh alike; and those only who keep His commandments find special favor with Him. Salvation is free; it cannot be purchased with money; and those only are saved who abide the law upon which its receipt is predicated. Bribery is of the world.

Fourth, he " ... that stoppeth his ears from hearing of blood, and shutteth his eyes from seeing evil." That is, we must not center our attention on evil and wickedness. We must cease to find fault and look for good in government and in the world. We must take an affirmative, wholesome approach to all things.[24]

The Prophet Joseph Smith said, "Some [men] shall rise to the everlasting burnings of God; for God dwells in everlasting burnings, and some shall rise to the damnation of their own filthiness, which is as exquisite a torment as the lake of fire and brimstone."[25]

● **Isaiah 34:16–17 The book of the Lord.** The names of those who have kept their covenants are enrolled in a special book known as "the book of the Lord" (v. 16), "the book of the law of God" (D&C 85:5), or "the book of life" (Rev. 20:12). Records of men's works are kept on earth by the Lord's clerks, but the book of life is the record kept in heaven. Both records should agree (see D&C 128:6–9). Of those whose names are recorded in the heavenly book, "no one of these shall fail" (Isa. 34:16).

Notes:

1. *History of the Church*, 1:283–84.

2. *History of the Church*, 3:387.

3. *Time*, 16 Aug. 1968.

4. London—British Council of Churches.

5. In Conference Report, Apr. 1971, 9; or *Ensign*, June 1971, 18.

6. *The Interpreter's Bible*, 12 vols. [1952–57], 5:317.

7. *"Great Are the Words of Isaiah"* [1980], 121.

8. In Conference Report, Oct. 1970, 152.

9. In Conference Report, Apr. 1963, 118; or *Improvement Era*, June 1963, 519.

10. In *Journal of Discourses*, 15:186.

11. In Conference Report, Oct. 1983, 75; or *Ensign*, Nov. 1983, 54.

12. *A Marvelous Work and a Wonder* [1976], 33–34.

13. In Conference Report, Oct. 1965, 61; or *Improvement Era*, Dec. 1965, 1128–29.

14. *Mormon Doctrine*, 2nd ed. [1966], 184.

15. In *Journal of Discourses*, 15:188–89.

16. *Mormon Doctrine*, 305–6.

17. *History of the Church*, 1:315.

18. *Mormon Doctrine*, 764.

19. See Joseph Fielding Smith, *Doctrines of Salvation*, comp. Bruce R. McConkie, 3 vols. [1954–56], 2:155.

20. In *Journal of Discourses*, 20:12.

21. In Conference Report, Apr. 1979, 133; or *Ensign*, May 1979, 93.

22. *Mormon Doctrine*, 657.

23. *Doctrines of Salvation*, 2:296.

24. In Conference Report, Oct. 1973, 55–56; or *Ensign*, Jan. 1974, 47–48.

25. *History of the Church*, 6:317.

CHAPTER 6

Isaiah, Pt. 4:
Hezekiah, Zion's Redemption, and the God of Israel
(Isaiah 36–47)

INTRODUCTION

This section of Isaiah deals with events in Judah during the reign of King Hezekiah that were the prelude to the Babylonian captivity.

C. P. MARILLIER 1740-1808

Isaiah and King Hezekiah

- **Isaiah 36–39 Isaiah departs temporarily from his poetic writings.** These chapters cite the prophet Isaiah's counsel and prophecies to King Hezekiah. Thus, as history, they are not veiled in the symbolic language of the rest of Isaiah. They parallel the accounts recorded in 2 Kings 18:2–20:19 and 2 Chronicles 32:9–31.

Subject	Isaiah	2 Kings	2 Chron
Sennacherib/Assyrians invade Judah	36:2–22	18:2–37	32:9–17
Hezekiah prays and the Lord responds	37:1–38	19:1–37	32:20–21
Hezekiah's psalm	38:1–22	20:1–11	32:24–26
Isaiah's prophecy of Babylonian captivity	39:1–8	20:12–19	32:31

KING HEZEKIAH

(Isaiah 36–39; 2 Kings 18–20; 2 Chronicles 29–32)

Hezekiah, the son of Ahaz, became king of Judah in 726 BC. He was 25 when he began to reign, and he reigned in righteousness for 29 years. The Lord blessed him because he "trusted in the Lord God of Israel; so that after him was none like him among all the kings of Judah, nor any that were before him. For he clave to the Lord, and departed not from following him, but kept his commandments, which the Lord commanded Moses. And the Lord was with him; and he prospered whithersoever he went" (2 Kgs. 18:5–7).

● **2 Kings 18:7 Hezekiah refuses to subject Judah to Assyria.** Though his father had subjected Judah to Assyria, Hezekiah "rebelled against the king of Assyria, and served him not." He was determined to serve the Lord and not any foreign king, and he relied upon the Lord to protect him and his people.

Hezekiah Cleans and Sanctifies the Temple

● **2 Chronicles 29:3–5 In the very first year of his reign, Hezekiah "opened the doors of the house of the Lord, and repaired them"** (v. 3). Then he gathered "the priests and the Levites, … And said unto them, Hear me, ye Levites, sanctify now yourselves, and sanctify the house of the Lord God of your fathers, and carry forth the filthiness out of the holy place" (vv. 4–5).

Priests sanctified the people

— **D&C 97:15–17** In our own dispensation, the Lord has said: "Inasmuch as my people build a house unto me in the name of the Lord, and do not suffer any unclean thing to come into it, that it be not defiled, my glory shall rest upon it; Yea, and my presence shall be there, for I will come into it, and all the pure in heart that shall come into it shall see God. But if it be defiled I will not come into it, and my glory shall not be there; for I will not come into unholy temples."

— **D&C 109:20–21** The Lord later commanded "that no unclean thing shall be permitted to come into [my] house to pollute it" (v. 20). If people transgress, "they may speedily repent and return unto [God], and find favor in [His] sight, and be restored to the blessings which [He] hast ordained to be poured out upon those who shall reverence [Him] in [His] house" (v. 21).

● **2 Chronicles 29:6–7 Judah had neglected and ignored the temple.** Hezekiah said to them, "Our fathers have trespassed, and done that which was evil in the eyes of the Lord our God, and have forsaken him, and have turned away their faces from the habitation of the Lord [the temple], and turned their backs" (v. 6). Their neglect of the temple was such that they had "shut up the doors of the porch, and put out the lamps, and have not burned incense nor offered burnt offerings in the holy place unto the God of Israel" (v. 7).

● **2 Chronicles 29:8–10 Hezekiah seeks to turn away the Lord's wrath from Judah.** Because of their neglect of their covenants and of the temple, "the wrath of the Lord was upon Judah and Jerusalem, and he hath delivered them to trouble, to astonishment, and to hissing" (v. 8). "For, lo, our fathers have fallen by the sword," Hezekiah said, "and our sons and our daughters and our wives are in captivity for this" (v. 9). "Now it is in mine heart to make a covenant with the Lord God of Israel, that his fierce wrath may turn away from us" (v. 10).

● **2 Chronicles 29:20–21, 29–31, 36 The king and people offer sacrifices, seeking forgiveness and the sanctification of the temple.** Hezekiah gathered the rulers of the city at the house of the Lord, and made "a sin offering for the kingdom, and for the sanctuary, and for Judah" (vv. 20–21). "And when they had made an end of offering, the king and all that were present with him bowed themselves, and worshipped" (v. 29). Then, "the congregation brought in sacrifices and thank offerings; and as many as were of a free heart burnt offerings" (v. 31). And when all this was finished, "Hezekiah rejoiced, and all the people" (v. 36).

Hezekiah Invites All Judah and Israel to Repent

- **Israel is taken captive into Assyria.** In the fourth year of Hezekiah's reign, "Shalmaneser king of Assyria came up against Samaria [the kingdom of Israel], and besieged it. And at the end of three years they took it. ... And the king of Assyria did carry away Israel unto Assyria ... because they obeyed not the voice of the Lord their God, but transgressed his covenant, and all that Moses the servant of the Lord commanded, and would not hear them, nor do them" (2 Kgs. 18:9–12).

GUSTAVE DORÉ, 1896

- **2 Chronicles 30:1, 6–9 Hezekiah invites all the people of Judah and also Israel to come to the house of the Lord for the Passover.** Hezekiah's desire to sanctify the people of God stretched beyond his own kingdom. He invited all of Judah and also the northern kingdom of Israel (referred to here as "Ephraim and Manasseh"), "that they should come to the house of the Lord at Jerusalem, to keep the passover unto the Lord God of Israel" (v. 1).

By this time, much of the northern kingdom of Israel had already been taken captive by the Assyrians. But Hezekiah promised the remaining Israelites that if they would "turn again unto the Lord," He would bless them and would soften the hearts of the Assyrians. "Your brethren and your children shall find compassion before them that lead them captive, so that they shall come again into this land: for the Lord your God is gracious and merciful, and will not turn away his face from you, if ye return unto him" (v. 9).

- **2 Chronicles 30:10–12 Most of the people of Israel reject Hezekiah's invitation.** Unfortunately, most of the remnant of the kingdom of Israel that remained in the land "laughed [Hezekiah's letters] to scorn, and mocked them" (v. 10). But a few "humbled themselves, and came to Jerusalem" (v. 11). There, their hearts were changed and they sought "to do the commandment of the king and of the princes, by the word of the Lord" (v. 12).

- **2 Kings 18:1–4 Hezekiah seeks to eradicate idolatry in Judah.** Hezekiah then "removed the high places, and brake the images, and cut down the groves, and brake in pieces the brasen serpent that Moses had made [see Num. 21:4–9]: for [in] those days the children of Israel did burn incense to it: and he called it Nehushtan [a 'thing of brass']" (2 Kgs. 18:1–4; see also 2 Chr. 31). By this he probably meant that it was not a god to be worshiped but only a symbolic "thing of brass." To worship it was inappropriate.

Assyria Overruns Judah

Having taken the northern kingdom of Israel captive, Sennacherib, king of Assyria, next attacked "all the fenced cities of Judah, and took them" in the fourteenth year of Hezekiah's reign (2 Kgs. 18:13).

- **2 Kings 18:14–16 Hezekiah offers tribute to Assyria.** Sennacherib had not yet conquered Jerusalem. So "Hezekiah … sent to the king of Assyria [in] Lachish, saying, I have offended; return from me: that which thou puttest on me will I bear. And the king of Assyria appointed unto Hezekiah king of Judah three hundred talents of silver and thirty talents of gold."

To meet this tribute, Hezekiah gave him all the silver in the house of the Lord, and the treasures of the king's house. He also "cut off the gold from the doors of the temple of the Lord, and from the pillars which [he] had overlaid [with gold], and gave it to the king of Assyria" (vv. 15–16).

● **2 Chronicles 32:2–5 Hezekiah prepares Jerusalem to defend itself and to survive an Assyrian seige.** This account in 2 Chronicles 32 parallels the ones in 2 Kings 18:13–19:37 and Isaiah 36–37. Sennacherib's own account, written in Assyria, also verifies the essential facts of these Biblical accounts (see following pages).

● **2 Chronicles 32:1–5, 30 Hezekiah's Tunnel.** When Hezekiah saw that Sennacherib's army planned to attack Jerusalem, he diverted the water of the spring of Gihon to the pool of Siloam, inside the city walls. The spring of Gihon was in the Kidron Valley, and for centuries, even before the Israelite occupation, the inhabitants of Jerusalem went to the spring for water. Standing on an elevated platform, they would lower their buckets down a 40-foot shaft to the spring below and haul up their water. Some scholars believe that this was the "conduit of the upper pool" referenced in Isaiah 7:3, Isaiah 36:2, and 2 Kings 18:17. Located nearby was the "fuller's field."

Location of the Gihon Spring

The Gihon Spring

Hezekiah diverted the water of this spring by digging a tunnel—called Hezekiah's tunnel—through about 1,770 feet of limestone rock, so the water could flow into the city underground. He then ordered that the fountains outside the city be covered so they would not provide the Assyrians easy access to the water. Without this water inside the walls of the city, the people of Jerusalem would not have survived the siege by the Assyrians.

Hezekiah tunnel thru solid rock

- **2 Chronicles 32:6–8 The importance of preparedness and faith.** Hezekiah did all that he could do to protect his people, and then trusted absolutely in the Lord's ability to deliver them. "He set captains of war over the people, and gathered them together to him in the street of the gate of the city, and spake comfortably to them, saying, Be strong and courageous, be not afraid nor dismayed for the king of Assyria, nor for all the multitude that is with him: for there be more with us than with him: With him is an arm of flesh; but with us is the Lord our God to help us, and to fight our battles. And the people rested themselves upon the words of Hezekiah king of Judah."

- **Isaiah 37:8–13 Sennacherib sent his servants to intimidate the people of Jerusalem.** He sought to intimidate and frighten them with threats of violence and by challenging their faith. "Let not thy God, in whom thou trustest, deceive thee, saying, Jerusalem shall not be given into the hand of the king of Assyria," he said (v. 10). "Behold, thou hast heard what the kings of Assyria have done to all lands by destroying them utterly; and shalt thou be delivered? Have the gods of the nations delivered them which my fathers have destroyed … ?" (vv. 11–12). "Now therefore let not Hezekiah deceive you, nor persuade you on this manner, neither yet believe him: for no god of any nation or kingdom was able to deliver his people out of mine hand, and out of the hand of my fathers: how much less shall your God deliver you out of mine hand?" (2 Chr. 32:15).

Sennacherib wrote on a victory panel (see at right): "As for Hezekiah the Jew, who did not submit to my yoke, 46 of his strong, walled cities, as well as the small cities in their neighborhood, which were without number—by constructing a rampart out of trampled earth and by bringing up batteringrams, by the attack of infantry, by tunnels, breaches, and [the use of] axes, I besieged and took [those cities].

Panel shows victory over Judah

200,450 people, great and small, male and female, horses, mules, asses, camels, cattle, and sheep without number, I brought away from them and counted as spoil. Himself like a caged bird I shut in Jerusalem his royal city. Earthworks I threw up against him; the one coming out of the city gate I turned back to his misery."[1]

Hezekiah Seeks the Lord's Help

● **Isaiah 37:1–3 Hezekiah sent messengers to Isaiah seeking counsel.** When Hezekiah received Sennacherib's threatening letter, "he rent his clothes, and covered himself with sackcloth, and went into the house of the Lord" (v. 1). He also sent the high priest Eliakim and Shebna the scribe and the elders of the priests to Isaiah the prophet, seeking his counsel (v. 2). "And they said unto him, Thus saith Hezekiah, This day is a day of trouble, and of rebuke, and of blasphemy: for the children are come to the birth, and there is not strength to bring forth" (v. 3).

— **Isaiah 37:3; 2 Kings 19:3** "For the children are come to the birth, and there is not strength to bring forth" is "a figure [of speech] denoting extreme danger, the most desperate circumstances. If the woman in travail has not strength to bring forth the child which has come to the mouth of the womb, both the life of the child and that of the mother are exposed to the greatest danger; and this was the condition of the people here."[2]

- **Isaiah 37:14–20 Hezekiah also seeks the Lord's help in prayer** (see also 2 Chronicles 32:20; 2 Kings 19:1–5, 14–19). There, in the house of the Lord, Hezekiah spread out the letter from the Assyrians "before the Lord" (meaning before the Ark of the Covenant). Then "Hezekiah prayed unto the Lord, saying, O Lord of hosts, God of Israel, that dwellest between the cherubims, thou art the God, even thou alone, of all the kingdoms of the earth: thou hast made heaven and earth. Incline thine ear, O Lord, and hear; open thine eyes, O Lord, and see: and hear all the words of Sennacherib, which hath sent to reproach the living God" (vv. 14–17). It was a fact that the Assyrians had "laid waste all the nations, and their countries, And have cast their gods into the fire [and] destroyed them" (v. 19). "Now therefore, O Lord our God, save us from his hand, that all the kingdoms of the earth may know that thou art the Lord, even thou only" (v. 20).

Spreading it before the Lord

- **Isaiah 37:6–7 Isaiah comforts the people of Judah, promising them protection** (see also 2 Kgs. 19:6–7; 2 Chr. 32:21–22). He brought them a revelation, saying, "Thus saith the Lord, Be not afraid of the words that thou hast heard, wherewith the servants of the king of Assyria have blasphemed me. Behold, I will send a blast upon him, and he shall hear a rumour, and return to his own land; and I will cause him to fall by the sword in his own land."

- **Isaiah 37:33–38 Isaiah prophesies the destruction of the Assyrians and Sennacherib's death.** The Lord promised that the Assyrians would never enter Jerusalem and that they would go home without a fight. "He shall not come into this city," the Lord promised, "nor shoot an arrow there, nor come before it with shields, nor cast a bank against it" (v. 33). "By the way that he came, by the same shall he return, and shall not come into this city, saith the Lord. For I will defend this city to save it for mine own sake, and for my servant David's sake" (vv. 34–35).

Both of Isaiah's prophecies were literally fulfilled. That very night, a mysterious plague struck the Assyrian camp, and in the morning 185,000 Assyrians lay dead (v. 36). The remnant of Assyria's army left the scene, and Sennacherib returned to Nineveh (v. 37). And there, while "he was worshipping in the house of Nisroch his god, … Adrammelech and Sharezer his sons smote him with the sword; and they escaped into the land of Armenia: and Esar-haddon his son reigned in his stead" (v. 38).

● **Similar promises of protection in our own day.** Hezekiah and his people received the Lord's protection because of their righteousness and their worship at the temple. We have also been promised protection if we are faithful and temple worthy.

— **D&C 103:7–8** "And by hearkening to observe all the words which I, the Lord their God, shall speak unto them, they shall never cease to prevail until the kingdoms of the world are subdued under my feet, and the earth is given unto the saints, to possess it forever and ever. But inasmuch as they keep not my commandments, and hearken not to observe all my words, the kingdoms of the world shall prevail against them."

— **D&C 109:24–28** In his dedicatory prayer at the Kirtland Temple, the Prophet Joseph Smith promised, "No weapon formed against them shall prosper; that he who diggeth a pit for them shall fall into the same himself; [and] no combination of wickedness shall have power to rise up and prevail over thy people upon whom thy name shall be put in this house; And if any people shall rise against this people, [the Lord's] anger [will] be kindled against them; And if they shall smite this people [the Lord] wilt smite them; [He] wilt fight for [His] people as [He] didst in the day of battle, that they may be delivered from the hands of all their enemies."

President Howard W. Hunter said: "Let us be a temple-attending people. Attend the temple as frequently as personal circumstances allow. Keep a picture of a temple in your home that your children may see it. Teach them about the purposes of the house of the Lord. Have them plan from their earliest years to go there and to remain worthy of that blessing. If proximity to a temple does not allow frequent attendance, gather in the history of your family and prepare the names for the sacred ordinances performed only in the temple. This family research is essential to the work of the temples, and blessings surely will come to those who do that work."[3]

● **2 Kings 19:22–28 The Lord addresses Assyria through Isaiah.** Though Assyria had taken credit for all she had done, the Lord set the record straight: Assyria was but a tool in His hands, and she was at His mercy. "I know thy abode, and thy going out, and thy coming in, and thy rage against me. Because thy rage against me and thy tumult is come up into mine ears, therefore I will put my hook in thy nose, and my bridle in thy lips, and I will turn thee back by the way by which thou camest" (vv. 27–28).

Hezekiah Pleads for Longer Life

● **2 Kings 20:1–3 Hezekiah's death is announced; he pleads for mercy.** While waiting out the siege of the Assyrians, Hezekiah became "sick unto death"—so much so that the prophet Isaiah came to him and said, "Thus saith the Lord, Set thine house in order; for thou shalt die, and not live" (v. 1). Hezekiah was devastated. He "turned his face to the wall, and prayed unto the Lord, saying, I beseech thee, O Lord, remember now how I have walked before thee in truth and with a perfect heart, and have done that which is good in thy sight. And Hezekiah wept sore" (vv. 2–3).

● **2 Kings 20:4–7 Hezekiah's life is lengthened by fifteen years.** Isaiah was already gone from Hezekiah's presence, but before he could reach the "middle court," the Lord spoke to him again, saying, "Turn again, and tell Hezekiah the captain of my people, Thus saith the Lord, the God of David thy father, I have heard thy prayer, I have seen thy tears: behold, I will heal thee: on the third day thou shalt go up unto the house of the Lord. And I will add unto thy days fifteen years" (vv. 4–6).

The Lord further promised to "deliver thee and this city out of the hand of the king of Assyria; and I will defend this city for mine own sake, and for my servant David's sake" (v. 6). Isaiah then took a lump of figs and "laid it on the boil, and he recovered" (v. 7).

2 Kings 20:8–11 As a sign, the clock turns back ten degrees. Being healed of his immediate infection was one thing, but being promised 15 more years was another. Hezekiah asked for a sign from heaven that it would be so. Isaiah then asked which sign he would prefer to "have of the Lord, that the ... shadow [of the sun dial] go forward ten degrees, or go back ten degrees?" (v. 9).

Time was turned backward 10 degrees

Hezekiah thought it would be too easy for the sun dial to go forward ten degrees, so he asked, "Let the shadow return backward ten degrees" (v. 10). The prophet Isaiah "cried unto the Lord: and he brought the shadow ten degrees backward, by which it had gone down in the dial of Ahaz" (v. 11).

The "dial of Ahaz" was a special mechanism for telling time. The instrument appears to have consisted of a series of graduated lines, or steps, over which a column towered. As the earth moved, the sun would cast a shadow at a certain angle and thus roughly measure the passing of the hours.[4]

President Spencer W. Kimball said:

> I am confident that there is a time to die, but I believe also that many people die before "their time" because they are careless, abuse their bodies, take unnecessary chances, or expose themselves to hazards, accidents, and sickness. ... In Ecclesiastes 7:17 we find this statement: "Be not over much wicked, neither be thou foolish: why shouldest thou die before thy time?" I believe we may die prematurely but seldom exceed our time very much.

One exception was Hezekiah, 25–year-old king of Judah who was far more godly than his successors or predecessors. ...

A modern illustration of this exceptional extension of life took place in November, 1881.

My uncle, David Patten Kimball, left his home in Arizona on a trip across the Salt River desert. He had fixed up his books and settled accounts and had told his wife of a premonition that he would not return. He was lost on the desert for two days and three nights, suffering untold agonies of thirst and pain. He passed into the spirit world and described later, in a letter of January 8, 1882, to his sister, what happened there. He had seen his parents. "My father ... told me I could remain there if I chose to do so, but I pled with him that I might stay with my family long enough to make them comfortable, to repent of my sins, and more fully prepare myself for the change. Had it not been for this, I never should have returned home, except as a corpse. Father finally told me I could remain two years and to do all the good I could during that time, after which he would come for me. ... He mentioned four others that he would come for also. ..." Two years to the day from that experience on the desert he died easily and apparently without pain. Shortly before he died he looked up and called, "Father, Father." Within approximately a year of his death the other four men named were also dead.[5]

The Last Days of Hezekiah

● **2 Kings 20:12–13 Hezekiah unwisely shows off his treasures to messengers from Babylon.** The king of Babylon had heard that Hezekiah was sick, so he sent his son with presents and a letter to wish him well (v. 12). At least, that's how it looked to Hezekiah. Thus encouraged by this act of kindness, Hezekiah responded to their rather strange request to see "all the house of his precious things, the silver, and the gold, and the spices, and the precious ointment, and all the house of his armour, and all that was found in his treasures." Indeed, "there was nothing in his house, nor in all his dominion, that Hezekiah shewed them not" (v. 13). He did not fully comprehend that this might be a prelude to an attack upon Judah by the king of Babylon.

- **2 Kings 20:14–21 Isaiah prophesies Judah's captivity in Babylon.** When Isaiah heard of it, he came "unto king Hezekiah, and said unto him, What said these men? and from whence came they unto thee? And Hezekiah said, They are come from a far country, even from Babylon" (v. 14). Isaiah then asked, "What have they seen in thine house? And Hezekiah answered, All the things that are in mine house have they seen: there is nothing among my treasures that I have not shewed them" (v. 15). This unwise action would certainly lead to disaster.

Isaiah prophesied unto Hezekiah, "Behold, the days come, that all that is in thine house, and that which thy fathers have laid up in store unto this day, shall be carried into Babylon: nothing shall be left, saith the Lord. And of thy sons that shall issue from thee, which thou shalt beget, shall they take away; and they shall be eunuchs in the palace of the king of Babylon" (vv. 17–18).

ISAIAH RETURNS TO POETIC PROPHECY

- **Isaiah 40–66 Isaiah changes his style back to prophetic poetry.** At the end of his promised 15 years of additional life, Hezekiah died and was replaced on the throne by his son Manasseh (2 Kgs. 20:21). With that transition, the book of Isaiah ceases with its historical narrative (chapters 36–39), and shifts back to his beautiful poetic writing style for the remaining chapters of Isaiah, with the brief exception of Isaiah 44:9–20. Although reference is made to Isaiah's immediate future, the main theme of this section of chapters is prophecies for the latter days. Lacking perspective, some non-LDS Bible scholars believe that these chapters were written by different authors. They simply do not believe that Isaiah could predict the future with such accuracy—and hence, they must have been written after the fact by a later author. Latter-day scriptures show that they were indeed written by Isaiah.

THE REDEMPTION OF ZION

(Isaiah 40–41)

The Second Coming of Christ

Isaiah turns next to a vision of the latter days, when the punishment of Judah and Israel will end. At that time, the days of Jerusalem's days of trial and sadness will be over.

● **Isaiah 40:1–2 "Comfort ye my people."** Isaiah declares that Jerusalem's days of trial and sadness are over because the Lord has come (spoken as if it had already occurred). "Comfort ye, comfort ye my people, saith your God. Speak ye comfortably to Jerusalem, and cry unto her, that her warfare is accomplished, that her iniquity is pardoned: for she hath received of the Lord's hand double for all her sins."

Monte S. Nyman wrote: "The message of comfort to Jerusalem, 'that her warfare is accomplished, that her iniquity is pardoned,' clearly refers to the latter days. The Anchor Bible translates this line 'that her sentence is served, her penalty is paid.' Judah was to be sent through the 'furnace of affliction' (see Isa. 48:10), so the message given here is to be fulfilled after she has been through that furnace. A look at history and at present-day circumstances shows her still to be going through that furnace. The rest of the chapter also supports a Second Coming time period."[6]

— **Ether 13:5, 11** Ether described Jerusalem as a redeemed city in the latter days—that "after it should be destroyed it should be built up again, a holy city unto the Lord; wherefore, it could not be a new Jerusalem for it had been in a time of old; but it should be built up again, and become a holy city of the Lord; and it should be built unto the house of Israel" (v. 5). "And then also cometh the Jerusalem of old; and the inhabitants thereof, blessed are they, for they have been washed in the blood of the Lamb; and they are they who were scattered and gathered in from the four quarters of the earth, and from the north countries, and are partakers of the fulfilling of the covenant which God made with their father, Abraham" (v. 11).

- **Isaiah 40:3 "The voice of him that crieth in the wilderness, prepare ye the way of the Lord."** Isaiah sees and hears "the voice of him that crieth in the wilderness, Prepare ye the way of the Lord, make straight in the desert a highway for our God" (v. 3). This verse refers to John the Baptist, but, as with so many other Old Testament prophecies, it is dualistic. The Savior clearly identified the "voice in the wilderness" as John the Baptist (see Matt. 3:3; John 1:23; 1 Ne. 10:8–9). But if this forerunner was to prepare the way for the person who was to tell Jerusalem that her times of trial were over (see Isa. 40:1–3), then the prophet clearly could not be referring only to John the Baptist's mortal ministry but to one or more Eliases of the latter days who would also prepare the way.

  — **Matthew 3:1–3 This prophecy was fulfilled in Christ's day.** "In those days came John the Baptist, preaching in the wilderness of Judea, And saying, Repent ye: for the kingdom of heaven is at hand. For this is he that was spoken of by the prophet Esaias, saying, The voice of one crying in the wilderness, Prepare ye the way of the Lord, make his paths straight."

  — **D&C 88:66 The prophecy was fulfilled again in our day.** "Behold, that which you hear is as the voice of one crying in the wilderness—in the wilderness, because you cannot see him—my voice, because my voice is Spirit; my Spirit is truth; truth abideth and hath no end; and if it be in you it shall abound."

  Elder George Teasdale said: "Instead of speaking comforting words to Jerusalem, He [Christ] exclaimed: 'O Jerusalem, Jerusalem, thou that killest the prophets, and stonest them which are sent unto thee, how often would I have gathered thy children together, even as a hen gathereth her chickens under her wings, and ye would not! Behold, your house is left unto you desolate.' Were these comforting words to Jerusalem? I think not. It is very evident that John the Baptist was not only the forerunner of His [Christ's] first coming, but also of His second advent. The scriptures are plain on this matter."[7]

- **Isaiah 40:4–5 Earthquakes will change the face of the land, and all flesh will see together the Lord's Second Coming.**

Isaiah declared, "Every valley shall be exalted, and every mountain and hill shall be made low: and the crooked shall be made straight, and the rough places plain" (v. 4). Clearly the entire geography of the earth will be altered. Then, "the glory of the Lord shall be revealed, and all flesh shall see it together" (v. 5). That will be the day of the Second Coming of our Lord Jesus Christ.

> — **Ether 13:9 There will be "a new heaven and a new earth."** "And there shall be a new heaven and a new earth; and they shall be like unto the old save the old have passed away, and all things have become new."

Isaiah 40:6–8 "All flesh is grass, … but the word of our God shall stand for ever." "All flesh is grass," Isaiah declared, "and all the goodliness thereof is as the flower of the field: The grass withereth, the flower fadeth: because the spirit of the Lord bloweth upon it: surely the people is grass. The grass withereth, the flower fadeth: but the word of our God shall stand for ever."

The spring rains in Canaan, which fall in April and May, are called the "latter rain[s]" (Jer. 3:3). When these rains are falling, the grass springs up in a glorious carpet of green all over Israel. But within a very short time the rains stop and the summer heat turns the grass brown very quickly. This withered, lifeless grass was used by Isaiah here as a metaphor for the wicked. Their ways may temporarily seem attractive to the world, but they will not endure, and will eventually be like dried grass before a blazing fire (see also D&C 101:24–25).

President Joseph Fielding Smith said that before the Second Coming of the Lord Jesus Christ in His glory, there will be a mighty earthquake, so destructive that mountains will be made low, valleys will be elevated, and rough places made as a plain. It will be so violent that the sun will be darkened and the moon will be turned to blood. The waters will be driven back into the north countries and the lands joined as they were before the days of Peleg.[8] (See also D&C 49:23; 88:87; 109:74; 133:17–25, 44; Isa. 54:10; 64:1; Ezek. 38:20; Rev. 6:14; 16:15–20).

- **Isaiah 40:9 "Zion" in the high mountain.** Speaking to those "that bringest good tidings" in the latter days, whom he calls "Zion," Isaiah says, "Get thee up into the high mountain." He also said, "O Jerusalem, that bringest good tidings, lift up thy voice with strength; lift it up, be not afraid; say unto the cities of Judah, Behold your God!" Elder Orson Pratt said that this scripture was a prophecy concerning the Lord's Zion that would be built up upon the earth before He comes in His glory. The prophecy indicated that "the people called Zion" would go to the high mountain territory (the mountain valleys of Utah and nearby areas). He further said that Joseph Smith had predicted the same thing and concluded: "Thus the prophecy was uttered—thus it has been fulfilled."[9]

God's Great Wisdom and Power

- **Isaiah 40:10–11 God is mighty and yet still tender.** Isaiah speaks first concerning the Lord's strength and power. "Behold, the Lord God will come with strong hand, and his arm shall rule for him: behold, his reward is with him, and his work before him" (v. 10). Then Isaiah speaks of the Lord's merciful nature: "He shall feed his flock like a shepherd: he shall gather the lambs with his arm, and carry them in his bosom, and shall gently lead those that are with young" (v. 11).

Readers of Isaiah chapter 40 who are familiar with George Frideric Handel's *Messiah* will notice many of Isaiah's prophecies were the inspiration for major portions of Handel's oratorio. These are the most well-known portions:

— "Comfort Ye My People" (Isa. 40:1-3)

— "Every Valley Shall Be Exalted" (Isa. 40:4)

— "And the Glory of the Lord" (Isa. 40:5)

— "O Thou That Tellest Good Tidings to Zion" (Isa. 40:9; 60:1)

— "He Shall Feed His Flock like a Shepherd" (Isa. 40:11)

Other portions of the oratorio are also taken from Isaiah:

— "Behold! A Virgin Shall Conceive" (Isaiah 7:14)

— "For Behold Darkness Shall Cover the Earth" (Isaiah 60:2-3)

— "The People That Walked in Darkness" (Isaiah 9:2)

— "For unto Us a Child Is Born" (Isaiah 9:6)

— "Then Shall the Eyes of the Blind Be Opened" (Isaiah 35:5-6)

— "He Was Despised" (Isaiah 53:3; Isaiah 50:6)

— "Surely He Hath Borne Our Griefs". (Isaiah 53:4-5)

— "And with His Stripes We Are Healed" (Isaiah 53:5)

— "All We like Sheep Have Gone Astray" (Isaiah 53:6)

— "He Was Cut Off Out of the Land of the Living" (Isaiah 53:8)

- **Isaiah 40:12–27 "Measured ... waters ... and ... comprehended ... dust."** This is Isaiah's poetic way of saying that God knows the world so intimately that He knows even the measure of the waters of the ocean and the dust of the earth. He emphasizes through the use of contrasts the greatness of God and the nothingness of nations and their gods.

- **Isaiah 40:28 One of the names of God.** Isaiah asks, "Hast thou not known? hast thou not heard, that the everlasting God, the Lord, the Creator of the ends of the earth, fainteth not, neither is weary? there is no searching of his understanding."

Elder Bruce R. McConkie wrote: "In the same sense in which one of the Lord's names is Endless and another Eternal, so Everlasting is also an appellation of Deity (Moses 1:3; 7:35; D&C 19:10). He is called the Everlasting God (Gen. 21:33; Isa. 9:6; 40:28; Jer. 10:10; Rom. 16:26; D&C 133:34), signifying that He endures forever, for 'his years never fail' (D&C 76:4)."[10]

- **Isaiah 40:28–31 The blessings of the Word of Wisdom are foretold.** Having first noted that "the everlasting God, the Lord, the Creator of the ends of the earth, fainteth not, neither is weary [and that] there is no searching of his understanding" (v. 28), Isaiah declares that "he giveth power to the faint; and to them that have no might he increaseth strength" (v. 29). In other words, the Lord's physical, emotional, and spiritual strength is unquestioned.

However, in the latter days, Isaiah says, "Even the youths shall faint and be weary, and the young men shall utterly fall" (v. 30). This would seem strange in Isaiah's day. The young were the most vibrant and healthy among them. But in the latter days it would be the youths who would faint and fall. We have seen  this prophecy fulfilled in so many ways, with drunkenness, drug use, and a lazy, unhealthy lifestyle.

Among the Lord's people, however, Isaiah predicted that in the latter days "the Lord shall renew their strength; they shall mount up with wings as eagles; they shall run, and not be weary; and they shall walk, and not faint" (v. 31).

- **Isaiah 41:1, 5 Israel in the "isles."** From time to time the Lord has led away remnants of Israel to "isles" from which He will eventually gather them before the second advent of the Lord Jesus Christ. "Isles" was a figure of speech in Old Testament times that suggested "the ends of the earth." The Americas are one of these isles to which the Israelites would be scattered.

A more literal interpretation of the idea of the American continent being "isles of the sea" can be found in Venice Priddis' book *The Book and the Map*

VENICE PRIDDIS, THE BOOK AND THE MAP 1975

[1975], which offers a map (see at page 156) based on what some scientists say South America looked like before the massive upheavals that occurred at the time of the Savior's crucifixion.

— **2 Nephi 10:20–21** Nephi's brother Jacob said, "We have been driven out of the land of our inheritance; but we have been led to a better land, for the Lord has made the sea our path, and we are upon an isle of the sea. But great are the promises of the Lord unto them who are upon the isles of the sea; wherefore as it says isles, there must needs be more than this, and they are inhabited also by our brethren."

— **1 Nephi 19:10, 16** Nephi quoted the prophet Zenock concerning the signs of Christ's death that would be given "unto those who should inhabit the isles of the sea, more especially given unto those who are of the house of Israel. … Yea, then will he remember the isles of the sea; yea, and all the people who are of the house of Israel, will I gather in, saith the Lord, according to the words of the prophet Zenos, from the four quarters of the earth."

— **1 Nephi 22:3–4** Nephi declared that "the house of Israel, sooner or later, will be scattered upon all the face of the earth, and also among all nations. And behold, there are many who are already lost from the knowledge of those who are at Jerusalem. Yea, the more part of all the tribes have been led away; and they are scattered to and fro upon the isles of the sea; and whither they are none of us knoweth, save that we know that they have been led away." Nephi refers to their location as "the isles of the sea," which they may indeed have been in his day, before the great changes that occurred at the time of the great destructions that accompanied the crucifixion of the Savior.

— **2 Nephi 10:8** Jacob declared, "And it shall come to pass that they shall be gathered in from their long dispersion, from the isles of the sea, and from the four parts of the earth; and the nations of the Gentiles shall be great in the eyes of me, saith God, in carrying them forth to the lands of their inheritance."

Israel Will Be Restored and Blessed

● **Isaiah 41:2 The righteous man from the east.** "Who raised up the righteous man from the east, called him to his foot, gave the nations before him, and made him rule over kings? he gave them as the dust to his sword, and as driven stubble to his bow."

John saw a vision similar to Isaiah's and spoke of this righteous man of the east as an "angel ascending from the east, having the seal of the living God" (Rev. 7:2). The Lord revealed to Joseph Smith that this angel of the east was "Elias which was to come to gather together the tribes of Israel and restore all things" (D&C 77:9).

Elder Bruce R. McConkie wrote: "Who has restored all things? Was it one man? Certainly not. Many angelic ministrants have been sent from the courts of glory to confer keys and powers, to commit their dispensations and glories again to men on earth. At least the following have come: Moroni, John the Baptist, Peter, James, and John, Moses, Elijah, Elias, Gabriel, Raphael, and Michael. ... Since it is apparent that no one messenger has carried the whole burden of the Restoration, but rather that each has come with a specific endowment from on high, it becomes clear that Elias is a composite personage. The expression must be understood to be a name and a title for those whose mission it was to commit keys and powers to men in this final dispensation."[11]

- **Isaiah 41:10 The Lord's comforting assurance to Israel—He will not forsake us.** "Fear thou not; for I am with thee: be not dismayed; for I am thy God: I will strengthen thee; yea, I will help thee; yea, I will uphold thee with the right hand of my righteousness." The popular hymn, "How Firm a Foundation,"[12] is written about this wonderful promise to the Saints.

- **Isaiah 41:21–29 The wisdom of the wicked is futile.** The Lord challenged the wisest of the world to produce the smallest insight into the future (vv. 21–23) and reminded them that the greatest of their works are "nothing" (v. 24), and that in the end their values "are all vanity" and will only bring "confusion" (v. 29).

THE FUTILITY OF WORSHIPING IDOLS

● **Isaiah 41:29 The folly of idol worship.** How absurd to worship something made by man's hands out of wood and stone! This is true of those who called them "gods" in Isaiah's day. It is also true of those who covet material possessions in our own day. "Behold, they are all vanity; their works are nothing: their molten images are wind and confusion," said Isaiah.

Isaiah said worshiping idols is futile

— **Psalm 115:4–8** David also spoke of the futility of worshiping dumb idols. "Their idols are silver and gold, the work of men's hands. They have mouths, but they speak not: eyes have they, but they see not: They have ears, but they hear not: noses have they, but they smell not: They have hands, but they handle not: feet have they, but they walk not: neither speak they through their throat. They that make them are like unto them; so is every one that trusteth in them."

— **D&C 1:16** A modern reminder of the futility of worshiping the things of this world: "They seek not the Lord to establish his righteousness, but every man walketh in his own way, and after the image of his own god, whose image is in the likeness of the world, and whose substance is that of an idol, which waxeth old and shall perish in Babylon, even Babylon the great, which shall fall."

● **Isaiah 42:17–18 Those who pay homage at the feet of idols are deaf and blind to the gospel message and its light.** The day will come when people who trusted in such dumb objects "shall be greatly ashamed" (v. 17). Not only are the idols deaf and dumb, but so also are the people who worship them. To these fools, Isaiah declares, "Hear, ye deaf; and look, ye blind, that ye may see" (v. 18).

● **Isaiah 42:19–23 A confusing mistranslation about blindness.** These verses speak of a servant of God who is blind—"Seeing many things, but thou observest not; opening the ears, but he heareth not. The Lord is well pleased for his righteousness' sake; he will magnify the law, and make it honourable" (vv. 20–21). How could it be that a righteous servant of God, with whom the Lord is "well pleased," could be blind and deaf to the truth? It makes no sense.

— **JST Isaiah 42:19–23** The Prophet Joseph Smith corrected verses 19–23 to show that it is not the servant who is blind, but scattered Israel, who have adopted the idols of their neighbors. With this key, the entire scripture makes much more sense.

Isaiah says of Israel, "This is a people robbed and spoiled; they are all of them snared in holes, and they are hid in prison houses: they are for a prey, and none delivereth; for a spoil, and none saith, Restore. Who among [Israel in his day] will give ear to this? who will hearken and hear for the time to come [in the latter days]?" (vv. 22–23).

● **Isaiah 44:13–20 The prophet poetically describes the idolatry of Israel.** Wood from some source was regularly used for domestic purposes. Men cut down trees to build houses, to burn in fires, and to cook food (vv. 13–16). And then, with "the residue thereof he maketh a god, even his graven image: he falleth down unto it, and worshippeth it, and prayeth unto it, and saith, Deliver me; for thou art my god" (v. 17). How much sense does this make? It makes none. But people engaged in idol worship "hath shut their eyes, that they cannot see; and their hearts, that they cannot understand. And none considereth in his heart, neither is there knowledge nor understanding" to question why they would even think of worshiping "the stock of a tree" (vv. 18–19). "He feedeth on ashes: a deceived heart hath turned him aside, that he cannot deliver his soul, nor say, Is there not a lie in my right hand?" (v. 20).

Since the right hand is the covenant hand, the phrase "Is there not a lie in my right hand?" implies that one who continues to seek treasures, or to worship false gods, becomes blinded to the truth and cannot recognize that his covenants are broken and that his lies will condemn him at the last day.

● **Isaiah 46 Idols are just idols, but Christ is God.** The poetry of this chapter is typical of Hebrew verses in Isaiah's time. The same theme is repeated again and again with only slight variations. Each retelling adds light to the interpretation of all other similar phrases. And in the end, by reading them all, the reader comes to a full understanding of Isaiah's meaning. That is what makes Isaiah difficult to understand without some serious effort to compare and contrast his phrases. But once understood, the most beautiful concepts are revealed to the mind in a majestic and memorable fashion. Isaiah was a master of this kind of writing.

In verse 9, Isaiah lists the ways in which the Lord had blessed and worked with Israel, leaving the nation with only one conclusion: "I am God, and there is none like me."

THE REDEEMER OF ISRAEL

(Isaiah 42–44)

The Mission of Jehovah

● **Isaiah 42:1–4 "The Servant" is given power of judgment** (v. 1), and is the One whose law for which the isles shall wait (v. 4). He is the Mediator of Israel and the Savior of the Gentiles. Matthew cited this passage to show why Christ did not seek an earthly kingdom (see Matt. 12:15–21). The Lord's spirit of judgment was to be withheld until the Day of Judgment.

— The imagery of the bruised reed and smoking flax (v. 3) means that even though He comes in judgment, it is not to destroy souls but to save them. The phrase "smoking flax" is translated by Keil and Delitzsch as a "glimmering wick" and explained as follows: "He does not completely break or extinguish. ... He [will] not destroy the life that is dying out, but He will actually save it; His course is not to destroy, but to save."[13]

— The phrase "he shall bring forth judgment unto truth" (v. 3) was interpreted by Keil and Delitzsch as "such a knowledge, and acknowledgment of the true facts in the complicated affairs of men, as will promote both equity and kindness."[14]

● **Isaiah 42:5–6 The Savior is the Light of the world and "of the Gentiles."** The Savior's hand is extended to strengthen, support, and protect covenant Israel. Then, each covenant person becomes a light to the world by holding up the light of the Savior through faithfully living His commandments and preaching His gospel (v. 6).

HEINRICH HOFFMAN

● **Isaiah 42:7 The Savior is also the One who will open the spirit prison.** This prison and its prisoners are dualistic metaphors. They can refer to those who respond to the gospel and are exalted (both living and dead). But with the benefit of other scriptural explanations, we realize that Isaiah is at least partially referencing the world of spirits where men go after death.

— Isaiah 24:22 The prisoners shut up in spirit prison shall be visited by the Lord.

— Isaiah 61:1–3 Christ was sent to open the spirit prison.

— 1 Peter 3:18–20 Christ preached to the spirits in prison after His crucifixion.

— D&C 76:72–74 Christ preached to those who did not hear of Him during mortality.

— D&C 138:35–46 He did not go to them personally, but organized and sent others.

The Prophet Joseph Smith said: "Here then we have an account of our Savior preaching to the spirits in prison, to spirits that had been imprisoned from the days of Noah; and what did He preach to them? That they were to stay there? Certainly not! Let His own declaration testify [Luke 4:18; Isa. 42:7]. It is very evident from this that He not only went to preach to them, but to deliver, or bring them out of the prison house. ... Thus we find that God will deal with all the human family equally, and that as the antediluvians [those who lived before the Flood] had their day of visitation, so will those characters referred to by Isaiah, have their time of visitation and deliverance, after having been many days in prison."[15]

● **Isaiah 42:9–16 The gospel light will go forth to the Gentiles.** There are many images and prophecies in these few verses. We can summarize them as follows.

— Truths and keys of former days will be restored in the dispensation of the fulness of times (v. 9)

— Isaiah describes the singing of a "new song" after the restoration of the gospel. The song is called the "song of the Lamb" (v. 10; see also D&C 133:56–57).

— Using the metaphor of childbirth he described the restoration of the earthly kingdom following a long period of apostasy (v. 14; see also Rev. 12:1–2, 13, 17).

— The Church will be restored in the last days, before the destruction that will make the mountains as plains and dry up the waters, and before the return of the scattered tribes of Israel. The light of the gospel will dispel the darkness of the Apostasy (vv. 15–16).

— The gospel will not be taken again from the earth; the Lord will never again forsake His people (v. 16; see also Isa. 2:2–3; 11:11–16; 29:14–15, 18–19; Dan. 2:44–45; Joel 2:25–29).

● **Isaiah 43:18–21 "A new thing" in the wilderness.** After recalling the destruction of the Egyptians before his day (see Isa. 43:3), and predicting the destruction of Babylon in his own future (vv. 14–17), Isaiah spoke of a miraculous time when the destruction would be reversed and the desert would "blossom as the rose" (Isa. 35:1). "Behold, I will do a new thing; now it shall spring forth ... I will even make a way in the wilderness, and rivers in the desert" (v. 19). "The beast of the field shall honour me, the dragons and the owls: because I give waters in the wilderness, and rivers in the desert, to give drink to my people, my chosen" (v. 20). This will be a people that the Lord "formed for [Himself, and] they shall shew forth [His] praise" (v. 21).

Bishop LeGrand Richards said:

Pioneers made streams in the desert

Isaiah said: "Behold, I will do a new thing," and as far as my understanding of this scripture is concerned, that new thing was the great principle of irrigation. It is true the Saints had to make the canals, they had to make the ditches, they had to put in the damns, but the land might have remained arid had not the Lord put into their minds the inspiration to do this very thing, and that is what Isaiah saw that the Lord would do [Isaiah 43:19–20].

If you want to see the rivers in the desert, just go up through Idaho and see the great canals that come out of the Snake River. They are greater than many of the rivers of the land [Isaiah 43:20–21; 41:18, 20].

So as you brethren gather in your crops by day in the harvest time, remember that it was the Lord God of Israel who did this new thing in this great wilderness to make it to prosper as a rose and to be a land that would attract the attention of all the world.[16]

● **Isaiah 43:4–9 The gathering of Israel is a worldwide event.**
The children of Abraham are "precious" in the Lord's sight, and He will keep His promises concerning them—to rejuvenate and repopulate their nations (v. 4). "Fear not: for I am with thee: I will bring thy seed from the east, and gather thee from the west; I will say to the north, Give up; and to the south, Keep not back: bring my sons from far, and my daughters from the ends of the earth" (vv. 5–6). Isaiah uses east, west, north, and south to symbolize "every one that is called by my name" (v. 7) in "all the nations" (v. 9) throughout the world to which Israel was scattered and from which she will gather.

- **Isaiah 43:14–17 Israel was delivered into bondage for her own good.** The Lord declared through Isaiah, "For your sake I have sent [you] to Babylon" (v. 14). Had they remained in their wicked state in the land of Canaan they would have never become the righteous and noble people He intended them to be. They needed a time of testing and humbling before they would be ready to be His people.

However, their captivity would not be permanent. God will overrule their captors and bring "down all their nobles, and the Chaldeans, whose cry is in the ships" (v. 14). The God of Israel, "the Lord, your Holy One, the creator of Israel, your King" (v. 15), who commands and controls all the elements of the earth, declares flatly that their enemies "shall lie down together, they shall not rise: they are extinct, they are quenched as tow" (v. 17).

Jehovah Is Our Savior

- **Isaiah 43:10–13 Jehovah is the Savior.** There is only one God of this earth, who, under the Father's direction, performs all of the mighty works that have been done in every dispensation. We are called to be His witnesses— "that I am he: before me there was no God formed, neither shall there be after me"(v. 10). "I, even I, am the Lord; and beside me there is no saviour" (v. 11). We need not be confused about the variety of "gods" that the world has imagined and/or created. There is only one God, and He is the Lord and Savior Jesus Christ, who in Old Testament times was the God of Israel, Jehovah. This set of verses makes that fact very clear. "Yea, before the day was [before creation] I am he [Jehovah was]; and there is none that can deliver out of my hand: I will work, and who shall let it [hinder it or turn it back]?" (v. 13).

HEINRICH HOFFMAN

- **Isaiah 44:1–2 Jesurun.** The Lord called this faithful servant "Jesurun" (or Jeshurun), which is the Hebrew word for "upright" or "righteous."

- **Isaiah 44:21–22 Isaiah speaks in past tense of the Atonement.** He had already seen it in vision, although it had not yet occurred. He declares that the Atonement had been made, and that Israel's redemption was predicated upon her return to Him.

HEINRICH HOFFMANN, 1890

- **Isaiah 45:5–7, 9–12 There is no God or Creator but the Lord.** "I am the Lord, and there is none else, there is no God beside me" (v. 5). "I form the light, and create darkness: I make peace, and create evil: I the Lord do all these things" (v. 7). "Shall the clay say to him that fashioneth it, What makest thou? or thy work, He hath no hands?" (v. 9). "Thus saith the Lord, the Holy One of Israel, and his Maker, Ask me of things to come concerning my sons, and concerning the work of my hands" (v. 11). "I have made the earth, and created man upon it: I, even my hands, have stretched out the heavens, and all their host have I commanded" (v. 12).

- **Isaiah 45:8 A poetic reference to the Restoration in the latter days,** when revelation would come down from heaven and the Book of Mormon would be taken out of the earth. "Drop down, ye heavens, from above, and let the skies pour down righteousness: let the earth open, and let them bring forth salvation, and let righteousness spring up together; I the Lord have created it."

PROPHECIES CONCERNING CYRUS

(Isaiah 44–45)

Cyrus, King of Persia

At the time Isaiah prophesied, Babylon had not yet come to power. More than 100 years would pass before Babylon would carry Judah into captivity. Another 70 years would pass while Judah languished in captivity. But well before all those events, Isaiah revealed the Lord's plan for Judah's restoration to their homeland under a king called Cyrus—a remarkable prediction since at the time Isaiah spoke his name, Cyrus was not yet born.

Monument to Cyrus

- **Isaiah 44:21–28 Cyrus would be the Lord's shepherd, doing His will in setting the Israelites free.** We can imagine the peace of mind these verses must have provided to the captive people of Judah. Before they were even taken captive, Isaiah was speaking to them words of comfort concerning their future. The Lord says through Isaiah, "O Jacob and Israel … thou art my servant: I have formed thee; thou art my servant: O Israel, thou shalt not be forgotten of me" (v. 21). "I have blotted out, as a thick cloud, thy transgressions, and, as a cloud, thy sins: return unto me; for I have redeemed thee" (v. 22). He who created the heavens and the earth and controls and subjects all things to His will, promised to captive Judah, "Thou shalt be inhabited; and to the cities of Judah, Ye shall be built, and I will raise up the decayed places thereof" (v. 26). And this will be accomplished through a man named Cyrus, who "shall perform all my pleasure: even saying to Jerusalem, Thou shalt be built; and to the temple, Thy foundation shall be laid" (v. 28).

Dr. Sidney B. Sperry wrote:

> Numerous commentators deny that Isaiah could foresee Cyrus so
> clearly as to be able to call him by name. They commonly claim,
> therefore, that this part of Isaiah was written by someone during
> the Exile and after Cyrus had given Israel help … —in other words,
> after the event. Nevertheless, it is of great interest to find that the
> Jewish historian Josephus accepted Isaiah's words and even quotes
> letters from Cyrus confirming the prophet's predictions. Part of the
> account of Josephus is quoted herewith:

> … He [God] stirred up the mind of Cyrus, and made him write this
> throughout all Asia:

> "Thus saith Cyrus the king: Since God Almighty hath appointed
> me to be king of the habitable earth, I believe that He is that God
> which the nation of the Israelites worship; for indeed He foretold
> my name by the prophets, and that I should build Him a house at
> Jerusalem, in the country of Judea."

> This was known to Cyrus by his reading the book which Isaiah left
> behind him of his prophecies; for this prophet said that God had
> spoken thus to him in a secret vision:

> "My will is, that Cyrus, whom I have appointed to be king over
> many and great nations, send back my people to their own land,
> and build my temple."

> This was foretold by Isaiah one hundred and forty years before the
> temple was demolished. Accordingly, when Cyrus read this, and
> admired the Divine power, an earnest desire and ambition seized
> upon him to fulfill what was so written; so he called for the most
> eminent Jews that were in Babylon, and said to them, that he gave
> them leave to go back to their own country, and to rebuild their city
> Jerusalem, and the temple of God, for that he would be their
> assistant and that he would write to the rulers and governors that
> were in the neighborhood of their country of Judea, that they
> should contribute to them gold and silver for the building of the
> temple, and, besides that, beasts for their sacrifices.[17]

● **Isaiah 45:1–4 Cyrus, a Persian King, is called the Lord's
"anointed."** We must remember that, initially, Judah was taken
captive by Babylon. It was only later, when Babylon fell to the
forces of Persia, that they became captives of the Persian kings.

Isaiah saw through all of that, his seeric vision penetrating to the day, nearly 200 years later, when "Cyrus, whose right hand I have holden," would "subdue nations before him; and I will loose the loins of kings, to open before him the two leaved gates; and the gates shall not be shut" (v. 1). God will prosper his way, breaking down all enemies before him and providing him with treasures, so that he might "know that I, the Lord, which call thee by thy name, am the God of Israel. For Jacob my servant's sake, and Israel mine elect, I have even called thee by thy name: I have surnamed thee, though thou hast not known me" (vv. 3–4).

Cyrus restored temple vessels

Alfred Martin wrote:

> Cyrus is the only Gentile king who is called God's "anointed." Since this is the translation of the Hebrew word which we spell in English as *Messiah,* Cyrus is in a sense a type of the Anointed One, the Lord Jesus Christ. Typology is often misunderstood and abused. A type is a divinely appointed prophetic symbol, usually of Christ. When a person or a thing is called a type, that does not alter its literal meaning or deny its historical reality. Cyrus was a Persian king, and we have no evidence that he ever really knew the true God, although the Persian religion was relatively free from the gross idolatries of the Babylonians.
>
> Consequently when it is asserted that Cyrus is a type of Christ, it is not said that he was like the Lord Jesus Christ in every respect. The only intended resemblance is in the fact that Cyrus was the anointed one who delivered the people of Israel from their captivity. As such he points us to the greater Anointed One who saves His people from their sins.[18]

- **Isaiah 46:11 The "ravenous bird from the east" refers to Cyrus,** who Isaiah prophesied would conquer Babylon swiftly and decisively.

● **Isaiah 45:12 What is the Lord's and what is man's own?** The Lord said to Isaiah, "I have made the earth, and created man upon it: I, even my hands, have stretched out the heavens, and all their host have I commanded." What then can we call our own upon this earth? How hollow the claim "It's my body, and I'll do what I want with it" sounds when one realizes that even the very elements of our creation were made by Him. We are not our own in any sense of the word.

Elder Spencer W. Kimball asked:

> Do you feel generous when you pay your tithes? Boastful when the amount is large? Has the child been generous to his parents when he washes the car, makes his bed? Are you liberal when you pay your rent, or pay off notes at banks? You are not generous [or] liberal … but merely honest when you pay your tithes. … Perhaps your attitudes are the product of your misconceptions.
>
> Would you steal a dollar from your friend? A tire from your neighbor's car? Would you borrow a widow's insurance money with no intent to pay? Do you rob banks? You are shocked at such suggestions. Then, would you rob your God, your Lord, who has made such generous arrangements with you?
>
> Do you have a right to appropriate the funds of your employer with which to pay your debts, to buy a car, to clothe your family, to feed your children, to build your home? Would you take from your neighbor's funds to send your children to college, or on a mission? Would you help relatives or friends with funds not your own?
>
> Some people get their standards mixed, their ideals out of line. Would you take tithes to pay your building fund, or ward maintenance? Would you supply gifts to the poor with someone else's money? The Lord's money?[19]

Elder Neal A. Maxwell said: "The submission of one's will is really the only uniquely personal thing we have to place on God's altar. The many other things we 'give,' brothers and sisters, are actually the things He has already given or loaned to us. However, when you and I finally submit ourselves, by letting our individual wills be swallowed up in God's will, then we are really giving something to Him! It is the only possession which is truly ours to give!"[20]

ISAIAH'S TESTIMONY AND WARNING

"Every Knee Shall Bow"

● **Isaiah 45:14–25 Isaiah testifies concerning the identity of the God of the Old Testament.** There is no place in the Old Testament where the identify of the God of Israel is made more clear than it is here. In just twelve verses we learn that:

— He is the Messiah, the Savior of the world (v. 15).

— He shall save Israel with an everlasting salvation (v. 17).

— He is the Creator (v. 18).

— He is just and is mighty to save (v. 21).

— No other name by which we may be saved (vv. 21–22).

— His words are truth and righteousness (v. 23).

— Every knee shall bow and every tongue confess that Jesus is the Christ (v. 23).

— He is the mediator for all the seed of Israel (v. 25).

President Joseph Fielding Smith wrote:

> I want to call attention to something that is stated frequently in the scriptures, and I think very often misunderstood, and that is the statement that, "every knee shall bow, and every tongue shall confess" [Isa. 45:23; Rom. 14:10–11; Philip. 2:9–11; D&C 76:110; 88:104]. I wonder how many of us have an idea that if a knee bows and a tongue confesses, that is a sign of forgiveness of sin and freedom from sin, and that the candidate is prepared for exaltation? If you do, you make a mistake. It does not mean that at all.
>
> The time will come when "every knee shall bow, and every tongue shall confess," and yet the vast majority of mankind will go into the telestial kingdom eternally. Let me read [Mosiah 16:1]: 'The time shall come when all shall see the salvation of the Lord; when every nation, kindred, tongue, and people shall see eye to eye and shall confess before God that his judgments are just."[21]

"Go Ye out from Babylon"

● **D&C 133:14 The Lord warns in our own day: "Go ye out ... from Babylon, from the midst of wickedness, which is spiritual Babylon."** Spiritual Babylon is the perverted counterfeit of the proper worship of Jehovah. This metaphor demonstrates as well as any in the Old Testament the extent to which Satan has gone to achieve his eternal lie.

● **Isaiah 47 Both the Babylonian Empire and Spiritual Babylon will be destroyed.**

— Babylon will be brought down to the dust (v. 1).

— Babylon will be damned as a slave of her own evil (vv. 2–3).

— Babylon will fall from her favored place among men (v. 5).

— Babylon will be denied the very thing she boasted of possessing— children (subjects) and marriage (that which saved a woman from disgrace in their society) (v. 9).

— Babylon will be destroyed by sources she knows not (v. 11).

— Babylon will be cleansed from the earth by fire (v. 14).

Notes:

1. In Madeleine S. Miller and J. Lane Miller, *Harper's Bible Dictionary*, 8th ed. [1973], "Sennacherib."

2. Keil and Delitzsch, *Commentary on the Old Testament*, 10 vols. [1996], 1:3:442.

3. In Conference Report, Oct. 1994, 8; or *Ensign*, Nov. 1994, 8.

4. William Smith and others, *A Dictionary of the Bible* [1987], "Dial."

5. *Faith Precedes the Miracle* [1972], 103–5.

6. *"Great Are the Words of Isaiah"* [1980], 141–42.

7. In *Journal of Discourses*, 25:16.

8. See *Doctrines of Salvation*, comp. Bruce R. McConkie, 3 vols. [1954–56], 1:85; 2:317.

9. In *Journal of Discourses*, 15:48.

10. *Mormon Doctrine*, 2nd ed. [1966], 243.

11. *Mormon Doctrine*, 221.

12. *Hymns* [1985], no. 85.

13. *Commentary on the Old Testament*, 7:2:176.

14. Ibid.

15. *History of the Church*, 4:596–97.

16. In Conference Report, Oct. 1948, 44–45.

17. *Antiquities of the Jews*. 11.1.1–2, quoted in *The Voice of Israel's Prophets* [1952], 107–8.

18. *Isaiah: "The Salvation of Jehovah"* [1956], 77–78.

19. In Conference Report, Apr. 1968, 77; or *Improvement Era*, June 1968, 83–84.

20. In Conference Report, Oct. 1995, 30; or *Ensign*, Nov. 1995, 24.

21. *Doctrines of Salvation*, 2:30.

CHAPTER 7

Isaiah, Pt. 5: The Gathering and the Messiah

(Isaiah 48–54)

INTRODUCTION

The Importance of Isaiah 48–54

Isaiah 48–54 includes some of Isaiah's greatest work. Six of these seven chapters are also found in the Book of Mormon. The other chapter (Isaiah 52) is found quoted throughout the Book of Mormon. And many of the passages found in Isaiah 48–54 are also explained in the Doctrine and Covenants.

The Book of Mormon prophet Nephi loved to quote Isaiah, just as we love to quote the Prophet Joseph Smith today. He referred to Isaiah simply as "the prophet" (1 Ne. 19:24; 1 Ne. 22:1–2; 2 Ne. 6:12, 14), just as we do with "the Prophet" Joseph Smith today.

1/3 of the book of Isaiah is in the Book of Mormon

Nephi lived just a little more than 100 years after Isaiah's time, placing him in approximately the same time frame with regard to Isaiah's ministry as we are today to the ministry of Joseph Smith.

Isaiah 48 is the first chapter of Isaiah quoted in the Book of Mormon and is found there as 1 Nephi 20. It appears that Nephi possessed a purer text of Isaiah than the one in the Bible. Every verse of this chapter reads differently in the Book of Mormon from the way it reads in the King James Bible, and many of the differences are significant. It can be assumed that the Book of Mormon text is more correct. Compare verses 1–2, 6–7, 11, 14, 16–17, and 22 in both versions to see the significant changes.

Of the 55 chapters that comprise 1 Nephi and 2 Nephi, 19 of them are entirely from Isaiah. Nephi quoted parts of other chapters of Isaiah as well. And all in all, one-third of Isaiah's 66 chapters are discussed in the Book of Mormon.

GOD'S FOREKNOWLEDGE

(Isaiah 48)

We read in the previous chapter how Isaiah predicted that the Babylonian empire would be destroyed (see Isa. 47). This prophecy was given by Isaiah more than 140 years before it occurred (see Isa. 44:28–45:5, 13). And when the time came, Cyrus fulfilled Isaiah's prophecy with exactness (see 2 Chr. 36:22–23; Ezra 1:1–8). From this we can see that men cannot hinder the Lord from accomplishing His will. "As well might man stretch forth his puny arm to stop the Missouri river in its decreed course, or to turn it up stream, as to hinder the Almighty from pouring down knowledge from heaven" upon His prophets and Saints (D&C 121:33).

Metaphors of Israel's Scattering and Gathering

- **Isaiah 48:3, 5–8** (1 Nephi 20:3, 5–8): **God's foreknowledge of the children of Israel's fate.** "I have declared the former things from the beginning," said the Lord, "and they went forth out of my mouth, and I shewed them; I did them suddenly, and they came to pass" (v. 3). The Lord declared these things unto the children of Israel before they came to pass "lest thou shouldest say, Mine idol hath done them, and my graven image, and my molten image, hath commanded them" (v. 5). Also, because He did not want them to claim after the fact that they already knew them, the Lord declared "new things … , even hidden things, and thou didst not know them" (vv. 6–7). The Lord knew their treacherous hearts and left them with no excuse by means of His prophecies concerning their future.

● **Isaiah 48:4** (1 Nephi 20:4)**: Apostate Israel is called hard-headed and stiff-necked by the Lord.** "And I did it because I knew that thou art obstinate, and thy neck is an iron sinew, and thy brow brass" (1 Ne. 20:4). Isaiah uses some figures of speech in this scripture:

— "Thy neck is an iron sinew"   Means you are "stiff-necked."

— "Thy brow [is] brass"   Means you are "hard-headed."

Hence the Lord is saying: You are stiff-necked, and you are hard-headed.

● **Isaiah 48:9–11** (1 Nephi 20:9–11)**: Israel will become chosen through "the furnace of affliction."** The Lord could have chosen to destroy them, as He had done their predecessors in the land of Canaan. However, He said, "For my name's sake will I defer mine anger, and for my praise will I refrain for thee, that I cut thee not off" (v. 9). Instead, He will "refine … thee, but not with silver; I have chosen thee in the furnace of affliction" (v. 10). This is a way of saying that He will purify them like silver is purified in a furnace. By this process, the Lord will avoid His name (or His people) from being polluted (v. 11).

● **Isaiah 48:18–19** (1 Nephi 20:18–19)**: The Lord reminds them of the blessings they might have enjoyed if they had chosen to be obedient.** "O that thou hadst hearkened to my commandments! then had thy peace been as a river, and thy righteousness as the waves of the sea: Thy seed also had been as the sand, and the offspring of thy bowels like the gravel thereof." Isaiah uses both similes and figures of speech in this scripture:

— Peace "as a river" means peace that is "deep and continuous."

— Righteousness "as the waves of the sea" means "strong and continuous."

— Seed "as the sand" means seed "as numerous as grains of sand."

> Hence this scripture means, "O that you had hearkened to my commandments—then would your peace have been deep and continuous. Your seed also would have been as numerous as grains of sand."

THE MISSION OF THE LATTER-DAY SAINTS

(Isaiah 49)

Monte S. Nyman wrote: "[Isaiah] chapter 49 is one of the most important chapters in the whole book of Isaiah, because it also clearly foretells the mission of the Latter-day Saints and the destiny of the land of America in connection with the house of Israel. Nephi interpreted the chapter as foretelling that the land of America would receive some of scattered Israel, while his brother Jacob applied it both to the Jews in Jerusalem and to the Gentiles. Chapter 49 is of such importance that it ought to be studied diligently by every member of the Church."[1]

The entire chapter of Isaiah 49 is quoted in 1 Nephi 21. Half of verse one is missing from the King James text—the statement that the scattering of Israel was a direct result of the wickedness of their religious leaders.

Israel's Scattering and Gathering

● **Isaiah 49:1** (1 Nephi 21:1): **"Listen, O isles, unto me; and hearken, ye people, from far."** In this scripture, Isaiah uses a synonymous parallel to identify the meaning of a metaphor. We know that "isles" in this case is a metaphor for "ye people from far," and not literally people who are living on an island.

It also helps to follow the references at the bottom of the page to more clearly understand how the metaphor of "isles" has been used by the prophets. In 1 Nephi 22:4, Nephi explains what people Isaiah is talking about, and in 2 Nephi 10:20–22, Jacob calls their land "an isle of the sea" and speaks of other "isles of the sea" where other scattered Israelites are located.

● **Isaiah 49:2** (1 Nephi 21:2): **The polished shaft hidden in the shadow of the Lord's hand.** Isaiah uses three more metaphors in this verse:

— "Mouth like a sharp sword" (v. 2) is a simile that compares His mouth to a sword, suggesting that what He says "cuts like a knife" through error and obstacles.

— Hiding Israel in "the shadow of his hand" (v. 2) is a figure of speech that means that He has covered Israel with His hand so nobody can see her (D&C 86:8–9).

— The metaphor of a "polished shaft [arrow]" hidden in the Lord's quiver [bag that hold arrows] (v. 2) compares Israel to a hidden secret weapon.

Hence this means, "And what I say shall cut through all obstacles; I will hide my people Israel from sight until the latter days and they will be my hidden secret weapon in the gathering of Israel, by which I will be glorified."

— **D&C 86:8–9** Clarifies the meaning of a "hidden" people. "Therefore, thus saith the Lord unto you, with whom the priesthood hath continued through the lineage of your fathers—For ye are lawful heirs, according to the flesh, and have been hid from the world with Christ in God."

The Prophet Joseph Smith said: "I am like a huge, rough stone rolling down from a high mountain; and the only polishing I get is when some corner gets rubbed off by coming in contact with something else, striking with accelerated force against religious bigotry, priestcraft, lawyer-craft, doctor craft, lying editors, suborned judges and jurors, and the authority of perjured executives, backed by mobs, blasphemers, licentious and corrupt men and women—all hell knocking off a corner here and a corner there. Thus I will become a smooth and polished shaft in the quiver of the Almighty, who will give me dominion over all and every one of them, when their refuge of lies shall fail, and their hiding place shall be destroyed, while these smooth-polished stones with which I come in contact become marred."[2]

Monte S. Nyman wrote: "The arrow shaft is polished that it might fly truer and faster, and the shaft that is polished is generally reserved for one's most important shot. The last dispensation, when all things are gathered in one, is the Lord's most important 'shot,' so He saved His 'polished shaft' for this latter-day work. Joseph was called to give this generation the word of God (see D&C 5:10), which recalls also the sharp sword analogy mentioned in verse 2."[3]

MAUDSLEY PORTRAIT, NAUVOO, 1844

The Prophet Joseph Smith said: "Every man who has a calling to minister to the inhabitants of the world was ordained to that very purpose in the Grand Council of heaven before this world was. I suppose I was ordained to this very office in that Grand Council. It is the testimony that I want that I am God's servant, and this people His people."[4]

- **Isaiah 49:3–13 (1 Nephi 21:3–13): Latter-day Israel will also be a light unto the Gentiles and to the spirits in prison.** In figurative language, latter-day Israel has a conversation with the Lord here. The Lord begins by saying, "Thou art my servant, O Israel, in whom I will be glorified" (v. 3). Israel responds that she has "laboured in vain" to gather her children but takes solace in the Lord's promise that "though Israel be not gathered, yet shall I be glorious in the eyes of the Lord, and my God shall be my strength" (vv. 4–5).

The Lord then says, "It is a light thing that thou shouldest be my servant to raise up the tribes of Jacob, and to restore the preserved of Israel" (v. 6). "It is a light thing" is a figure of speech meaning "it is not enough." The Lord is saying that gathering Israel is not enough—that He "will also give [them] for a light to the Gentiles, that [they] mayest be [His] salvation unto the ends of the earth" (v. 6). As a result of this gathering of Gentiles, "kings shall see and arise, princes also shall worship, because of the Lord that is faithful" (v. 7).

The Lord then lists others who will be gathered, including the "isles of the sea" (1 Ne. 21:8), which you will remember from previous chapters is also a figure of speech meaning "far flung places." Also, the gathering will include "the prisoners" to whom it will be said: "Go forth; to them that are in darkness, Shew yourselves" (v. 9). This has multiple meanings, one of which is a reference to missionary work that will be done among the dead in spirit prison. Subsequently, the Lord makes mention of His "mountains" and His "highways," both of which are metaphors for temples (v. 11). And finally, the Lord says that those who are gathered "shall come from far: and, lo, these from the north and from the west; and these from the land of Sinim" (v. 12). This gathering will be permanent, because those who are gathered "shall be smitten no more; for the Lord hath comforted his people, and will have mercy upon his afflicted" (1 Ne. 21:13).

● **Isaiah 49:14–23** (1 Nephi 21:14–23): **Metaphors of the gathering.** The Lord uses a series of metaphors and figures of speech to describe what the gathering of Israel will be like in the last days.

— Attentive Mother metaphor. Verse 15 asks if mothers can forget their nursing children while they are feeding at their breasts. Perhaps. But the Lord will not forget us.

— Attentive Savior metaphor. Verse 16 says that He has "graven [us] upon the palms of [His] hands"—a figure of speech about making it impossible to forget, but also a metaphor for the Lord's crucifixion. Can He forget what He did for us? No, He can't. Verse 16 also talks about our "walls"—a metaphor for our circumstances—that are continually before (within the view of) Him.

— Growing Family metaphor. Verse 20 reads: "The place is too strait for me: give place to me"—a figure of speech that says so many people will come that it will seem too crowded.

Verse 21 reads: "Who hath begotten me these. ... Where had they been?"—a figure of speech for "Where in the world did all these people come from?"

— Nurturing Parents metaphor. In verse 22 we read how the Lord will set up His "standard"—a military flag that is raised to indicate where soldiers should gather. Verse 22 also tells of the Gentiles that will carry you "upon their shoulders"—a figure of speech meaning "help you get there." Verse 23 describes the Gentiles as nursing fathers and nursing mothers unto Israel—a metaphor of nurturing parents protecting a child.

President Spencer W. Kimball saw a partial fulfillment of these verses in the Church's modern missionary efforts with the Lamanites. Also, in 1917, Great Britain established a protectorate in Jerusalem administered by a Jew—the first Jewish government there since AD 70. Also, in 1949, the United Nations, including Russia and many other countries now hostile to Israel, voted to partition Palestine and create a Jewish state in the land for the first time in nearly two thousand years.

● **1 Nephi 22:15–17 Additions to Isaiah in the Book of Mormon.** Monte S. Nyman wrote: "As Nephi commented on Isaiah 49 in 1 Nephi 22, he quoted or paraphrased three verses from 'the prophet,' obviously Isaiah. We do not have these verses in the present Bible text, but they fit very well into the context of Isaiah 49 and 50. We can illustrate this by placing [1 Nephi 22:15–17] between the last verse of chapter 49 and the first verse of chapter 50."[5]

ZION'S FUTURE REDEMPTION

(Isaiah 50–52)

● **Isaiah 50:1 (2 Nephi 7:1): The Lord uses the metaphor of divorce to emphasize how He has not abandoned Israel and never will.** "Thus saith the Lord, Where is the bill of your mother's divorcement, whom I have put away? or which of my creditors is it to whom I have sold you? Behold, for your iniquities have ye sold yourselves, and for your transgressions is your mother put away."

— "Put thee away" (2 Ne. 7:1) is a figure of speech that means "divorced you."

— "Where is the bill of your mother's divorcement?" Under Mosaic law, a man who divorced his wife had to give her a written bill of divorce. She was then free to marry again. But if a man refused to give her such a bill, then she was considered still bound to him until he died. The Lord makes it clear that He has not given a bill of divorce to Israel, despite her unfaithfulness.

— "To which of my creditors have I sold you?" Under the same laws, a man could sell himself or his children into slavery to satisfy his creditors. The Lord has not done this, although Israel has "sold herself" (like a harlot).

Throughout the scriptures, the Lord uses marriage as a metaphor for His relationship to Israel and to each of us personally. This is a deeply moving comparison, showing how sacred the Lord considers His covenants with us—like those between a husband and a wife.

He will always be faithful to His promises to us, and He expects us to keep ours to Him. When He speaks here about divorce, He does so to show that He has not given up on Israel, even though they have proven to be unfaithful to Him.

● **Isaiah 50:2–6** (2 Nephi 7:2–6): **Isaiah uses typology concerning our Lord's Atonement.** Typology is speaking of the future as if it were already past. Speaking as if he were the Lord, he says concerning the Atonement, "Wherefore, when I came, was there no man? when I called, was there none to answer? Is my hand shortened at all, that it cannot redeem? or have I no power to deliver?" (v. 2).

The obvious answer is "no" because He is the all-powerful Creator of heaven and earth: "Behold, at my rebuke I dry up the sea, I make the rivers a wilderness: their fish stinketh, because there is no water, and died for thirst. I clothe the heavens with blackness, and I make sackcloth their covering" (vv. 2–3).

The coming Redeemer will have "the tongue of the learned, that I should know how to speak a word in season to him that is weary" (v. 4) and a listening ear (v. 5). He will not be rebellious concerning His redeeming role, nor will He give up and turn back (v. 5).

As part of His redeeming sacrifice, He will "[give] my back to the smiters, and my cheeks to them that plucked off the hair: I hid not my face from shame and spitting" (v. 6). All of these things He endured for our sakes (see Matt. 27:26; 26:67).

A. GIOACCHINO, 1640s

Christ was severely scourged

- **Isaiah 50:7–9** (2 Nephi 7:7–9): **Israel says "the Lord … will help me; … I shall not be ashamed."** This is a poetic way of speaking for latter-day Israel, who will have the Lord's help and "not be confounded" nor "ashamed" (v. 7). "He is near that justifieth me," and if the Lord is on Israel's side, "who will contend with me? let us stand together: who is mine adversary?" (v. 8). With the Lord's help, "who is he that shall condemn me? lo, they all shall wax old as a garment; the moth shall eat them up" (v. 9).

- **Isaiah 50:10–11** (2 Nephi 7:10–11): **The Lord speaks of the futility of walking by our own light** rather than the Light of Christ.

  — "Who is among you that feareth the Lord, that obeyeth the voice of his servant, that walketh in darkness, and hath no light?" (v. 10) means that those who listen to the Lord's servants are never left in spiritual darkness.

  — To "stay upon his God" (v. 10) means to trust in God.

  — "Behold, all ye that kindle [your own] fire, that compass yourselves about with sparks … that ye have kindled. This shall ye have of mine hand; ye shall lie down in sorrow" (v. 11). We can read this scripture as: "Those who walk in their own light (by their own understanding) rather than trusting in the Lord will, in the end, reap only sorrow."

● **Isaiah 51:1–3** (2 Nephi 8:1–3): **Israel must remember who they are—descendants of Abraham and Sarah.** "Hearken to me, ye that follow after righteousness, ye that seek the Lord: look unto the rock whence ye are hewn, and to the hole of the pit whence ye are digged" (v. 1).

"Look unto Abraham your father, and unto Sarah" (v. 2).

— "The rock from whence ye are hewn" and "the hole of the pit from whence ye are digged" are figures of speech similar to one in our own day—you are "chips off the old block" of Abraham.

Because of the promises made to Abraham and Sarah, "the Lord shall comfort Zion: he will comfort all her waste places; and he will make her wilderness like Eden, and her desert like the garden of the Lord; joy and gladness shall be found therein, thanksgiving, and the voice of melody" (v. 3).

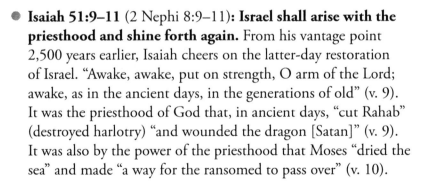

Our father Abraham

● **Isaiah 51:9–11** (2 Nephi 8:9–11): **Israel shall arise with the priesthood and shine forth again.** From his vantage point 2,500 years earlier, Isaiah cheers on the latter-day restoration of Israel. "Awake, awake, put on strength, O arm of the Lord; awake, as in the ancient days, in the generations of old" (v. 9). It was the priesthood of God that, in ancient days, "cut Rahab" (destroyed harlotry) "and wounded the dragon [Satan]" (v. 9). It was also by the power of the priesthood that Moses "dried the sea" and made "a way for the ransomed to pass over" (v. 10).

"The redeemed of the Lord shall return," Isaiah predicts, "and come with singing unto Zion; and everlasting joy shall be upon their head: they shall obtain gladness and joy; and sorrow and mourning shall flee away" (v. 11). The long days of their dispersal will be over.

There is a suggested typology here—the creation of a highway in the sea for the children of Israel to pass over. It happened anciently by the power of the priesthood and it will happen again. Isaiah says flatly in a later prophecy that "thy land shall be married" (Isa. 62:4). And in the latter days, the "ransomed" and the "the redeemed" (the lost ten tribes of Israel) will return to Zion (the New Jerusalem) on the highway the Lord will create for them in the ocean (see D&C 133:23–27).

Elder Bruce R. McConkie wrote:

> As the Lord provided a highway through the Red Sea for His people anciently, as they traveled to their promised land, so will He provide a way for them to travel in the latter days.
>
> Our latter-day revelation, after stating that the great deep shall be driven back into the north countries and that the continents shall become one land, states that "they who are in the north countries," meaning the Ten tribes, shall return. "And an highway shall be cast up in the midst of the great deep" for them (D&C 133:23–27) .
>
> Would we go too far astray if we were to suggest that the highway is created by the joined landmasses, and that as ancient Israel found a dry path through the Red Sea, so latter-day Israel will find a dry path where the Atlantic Ocean once was? It is at least a thought to ponder, for surely we are expected to seek for interpretations relative to all that has been revealed concerning the Lord and His coming.[6]

- **Isaiah 51:12–16 (2 Nephi 8:12–16): The Lord will be with Israel's leaders and speak to them.** Through His prophet Isaiah, the Lord declares, "I, even I, am he that comforteth you," and reminds them that they should not "be afraid of a man that shall die, and ... be made as grass" (v. 12). Rather, they should follow "the Lord thy maker, that hath stretched forth the heavens, and laid the foundations of the earth" (v. 13). Israel will have long "feared ... because of the fury of the oppressor," but "where [now] is the fury of the oppressor?" (v. 13). The Lord promises further that He will put words in their mouths (revelation) (v. 16) and claim them as His people and protect them.

Isaiah 51:17–23 (2 Nephi 8:17–23): **Two witnesses who will rescue Jerusalem.** The Holy City will suffer greatly in the latter days and then be rescued and suffer no more. In the midst of the fury of the war of Armageddon, there will be no one from among the men of Jerusalem to rescue Jerusalem (vv. 17–18). However, two other men will come to them and have compassion on them.

The streets of Old Jerusalem

We know from other scriptures that these are two latter-day Apostles—special witnesses to the Jews (see Rev. 11:1–6)—who will have much power (see D&C 77:15). These two witnesses will "faint" (be martyred) at Jerusalem and lie in the streets for a time. We know from other scriptures that they will then rise from the dead when the Savior descends to save Jerusalem and usher in the Millennium (v. 20).

Elder Bruce R. McConkie wrote:

> Their ministry will take place after the latter-day temple has been built in Old Jerusalem, after some of the Jews who dwell there have been converted, and just before Armageddon and the return of the Lord Jesus. How long will they minister in Jerusalem and in the Holy Land? For three and a half years, the precise time spent by the Lord in His ministry to the ancient Jews. The Jews, as an assembled people, will hear again the testimony of legal administrators bearing record that salvation is in Christ and in His gospel.
>
> Who will these witnesses be? We do not know, except that they will be followers of Joseph Smith; they will hold the holy Melchizedek priesthood; they will be members of The Church of Jesus Christ of Latter-day Saints. It is reasonable to suppose, knowing how the Lord has always dealt with His people in all ages, that they will be two members of the Council of the Twelve or of the First Presidency of the Church.[7]

Priesthood Messengers

● **Isaiah 52:1–2** (2 Nephi 8:24–25): **Isaiah implores latter-day Israel to rise up and take the priesthood upon them.** "Awake, awake; put on thy strength, O Zion; put on thy beautiful garments, O Jerusalem, the holy city: for henceforth there shall no more come into thee the uncircumcised and the unclean" (v. 1).

When Elias Higbee asked the Prophet Joseph Smith for an interpretation of verse 1 of this scripture, he responded, "[Isaiah] had reference to those whom God should call in the last days, who should hold the power of priesthood to bring again Zion, and the redemption of Israel; and to put on her strength is to put on the authority of the priesthood, which she, Zion, has a right to by lineage; also to return to that power which she had lost" (D&C 113:7–8). "Put on thy beautiful garments" is a metaphor meaning the same thing as "put on thy strength."

Isaiah continues his prophecy by saying, "Shake thyself from the dust; arise, and sit down, O Jerusalem: loose thyself from the bands of thy neck, O captive daughter of Zion" (v. 2). Regarding this verse, the Prophet Joseph Smith said, "We are to understand that the scattered remnants are exhorted to return to the Lord from whence they have fallen; which if they do, the promise of the Lord is that he will speak to them, or give them revelation. …

The bands of her neck are the curses of God upon her, or the remnants of Israel in their scattered condition among the Gentiles" (D&C 113:9–10).

● **Isaiah 52:7–10** (Mosiah 12:21–24): "How beautiful upon the mountains are the feet of him that bringeth good tidings, that publisheth peace; that bringeth good tidings of good, that publisheth salvation; that saith unto Zion, Thy God reigneth!" (v. 7). This is partly a Messianic prophecy, since the bringer of "good tidings" is Christ, the "founder of peace" (Mosiah 15:18).

But it is also a prophecy concerning missionary work, as the next verse shows: "Thy watchmen shall lift up the voice; with the voice together shall they sing: for they shall see eye to eye, when the Lord shall bring again Zion" (v. 8). These "watchmen" are those who preach the gospel—who publish peace by spreading His word.

The Prophet Joseph Smith said Jackson County was the Zion of verse 8:

> I received, by a heavenly vision, a commandment in June following, to take my journey to the western boundaries of the State of Missouri, and there designate the very spot which was to be the central place for the commencement of the gathering together of those who embrace the fulness of the everlasting gospel. Accordingly I undertook the journey, with certain ones of my brethren, and after a long and tedious journey, suffering many privations and hardships, arrived in Jackson County, Missouri, and after viewing the country, seeking diligently at the hand of God, He manifested Himself unto us, and designated, to me and others, the very spot upon which He designed to commence the work of the gathering, and the upbuilding of an "holy city," which should be called Zion—Zion, because it is a place of righteousness, and all who build thereon are to worship the true and living God, and all believe in one doctrine, even the doctrine of our Lord and Savior Jesus Christ. "Thy watchmen shall lift up the voice; with the voice together shall they sing: for they shall see eye to eye, when the Lord shall bring again Zion" (Isa. 52:8). ...

> After having ascertained the very spot, and having the happiness of seeing quite a number of the families of my brethren comfortably situated upon the land, I took leave of them and journeyed back to Ohio, and used every influence and argument that lay in my power to get those who believed in the everlasting covenant, whose circumstances would admit, and whose families were willing, to remove to the place which I had designated to be the land of Zion."[8]

Isaiah praises the day when these things shall be: "Break forth into joy, sing together, ye waste places of Jerusalem: for the Lord hath comforted his people, he hath redeemed Jerusalem. The Lord hath made bare his holy arm in the eyes of all the nations; and all the ends of the earth shall see the salvation of our God" (vv. 9–10). We are living in the day when these wonderful promises have been, and are being, fulfilled.

The last three of these verses are quoted four times in the Book of Mormon—in Mosiah 12:20–24 (where King Noah's priests asked Abinadi about its meaning); Mosiah 15:28–31 (where Abinadi explained its meaning); 3 Nephi 16:10–20 (where the Savior explained it); and 3 Nephi 20:29–35 (where the Savior explained it again).

- **Isaiah 52:11–12** (3 Nephi 20:41–42): **Departing from Babylon.** Speaking to latter-day Israel, Isaiah declares, "Depart ye, depart ye, go ye out from thence, touch no unclean thing; go ye out of the midst of her; be ye clean, that bear the vessels of the Lord" (v. 11). We learn from the Doctrine and Covenants that the Lord is speaking here of departing from Babylon—the world with all its wickedness (see D&C 133:5, 14).

UNKNOWN PHOTOGRAPHER

In a world where gross impropriety has become the norm, it is crucial that those who "bear the vessels of the Lord" (the priesthood) maintain a standard of moral cleanliness.

Nevertheless, those who gather to Zion to escape worldly influences should not be unwise or act impulsively. The Lord also says in this scripture, "Ye shall not go out with haste, nor go by flight: for the Lord will go before you; and the God of Israel will be your rereward" (v. 12). Thus, we are to depart from wickedness, but in an orderly manner and under the Lord's direction. In the Doctrine and Covenants we are counseled, "Let all things be prepared before you" and "not look back" (D&C 133:15).

The Presiding Elders in Missouri said in July of 1833:

> For the disciples to suppose that they can come to this land without ought to eat, or to drink, or to wear, or anything to purchase these necessaries with, is a vain thought. For them to suppose that the Lord will open the windows of heaven, and rain down angel's food for them by the way, when their whole journey lies through a fertile country, stored with the blessings of life from His own hand for them to subsist upon, is also vain. For them to suppose that their clothes and shoes will not wear out upon the journey ... is just as vain. ...
>
> Do not conclude from these remarks, brethren, that we doubt in the least, that the Lord will provide for His Saints in these last days; or think that we would extend our hands to steady the ark; for this is not the case. We know that the Saints have the unchangeable word of God that they shall be provided for; yet we know, if any are imprudent, or lavish, or negligent, or indolent, in taking that proper care, and making that proper use of what the Lord has made them stewards over, they are not counted wise; for a strict account of every one's stewardship is required, not only in time, but will be in eternity. ... Relative to [your] coming to Zion, ... the experience of almost two years' gathering has taught us to revere that sacred word from heaven, "Let not your flight be in haste, but let all things be prepared before you."[9]

● **Isaiah 52:13–15** (3 Nephi 20:43–45): **The Servant.** This is a Messianic prophecy. Isaiah predicts that the Savior will "deal prudently, he shall be exalted and extolled, and be very high" (v. 13). That is clearly the case with our Lord and Savior Jesus Christ. Yet, despite His high position in the eternities, the people will be "astonied [astonished]" because "his visage was so marred more than any man, and his form more than the sons of men" (v. 14). No mortal man has been (or even could be) abused as He was in the flesh and yet continue to live (see the discussion of Isaiah 53:4–7 below). But by that suffering, He will "sprinkle many nations"—atone for all mankind.

— **3 Nephi 21:7–10** Yet, this prophecy is also dualistic. The Savior Himself interpreted it also to mean the Prophet Joseph Smith: "And when these things come to pass that thy seed shall begin to know these things—it shall be a sign unto them, that they may know that the work of the Father hath already commenced unto the fulfilling of the covenant which he hath made unto the people who are of the house of Israel" (v. 7).

"And when that day shall come, it shall come to pass that kings shall shut their mouths; for that which had not been told them shall they see; and that which they had not heard shall they consider. For in that day, for my sake shall the Father work a work, which shall be a great and a marvelous work among them; and there shall be among them those who will not believe it, although a man shall declare it unto them" (vv. 8–9).

"But behold, the life of my servant shall be in my hand; therefore they shall not hurt him, although he shall be marred because of them. Yet I will heal him, for I will show unto them that my wisdom is greater than the cunning of the devil" (v. 10).

THE BRIDE AND BRIDEGROOM

(Isaiah 54)

The Metaphor of Marriage

Christ considers His relationship with us to be sacred—like a marriage. He uses the metaphor of marriage when discussing covenants and blessings, and those who seek after other gods are called "unfaithful." Christ is always faithful to His promises to us, and He expects us to do the same. If we are faithful we become joint-heirs with Him of all things.

Isaiah 54 centers around the metaphor of marriage. The Savior read and explained this chapter of Isaiah to the Nephites when He visited them (see 3 Ne. 22), making it all the more poignant as an explanation of the sacredness of our covenants with Him. He considers it a very personal bond between Himself and us.

Elder Jeffrey R. Holland taught: "The imagery of Jehovah as bridegroom and Israel as bride is among the most commonly used metaphors in scripture, being used by the Lord and His prophets to describe the relationship between Deity and the children of the covenant. ... Christ has, on occasion, been rightfully angry with backsliding Israel, but that has always been brief and temporary—'a small moment.' Compassion and mercy always return and prevail in a most reassuring

Traditional 19ᵗʰ-century Jewish wedding

way. ... The Lord's kindness and peace will never be taken from His covenant people."[10]

● **Isaiah 54:1–3** (3 Nephi 22:1–3): **The "barren wife" will become fruitful.** Israel is called a barren wife—unable to produce spiritual offspring. "Sing, O barren, thou that didst not bear; break forth into singing, and cry aloud, thou that didst not travail with child" (v. 1). This barrenness is symbolic of Israel's few scattered descendants. But the promise is that "more are the children of the desolate than the children of the married wife" (v. 1), meaning that Israel will have many children in the latter days.

A bedouin tent's curtains are held up by its stakes

"Enlarge the place of thy tent, and let them stretch forth the curtains of thine habitations: spare not, lengthen thy cords, and strengthen thy stakes" (v. 2). The numbers of them will grow to the point where the tent of Israel will have to expand to accommodate them all. This scripture, and others like it, is the basis for calling our regional membership divisions "stakes." They are the units that hold up the tent of Israel and they must be continually strengthened.

"For thou shalt break forth on the right hand and on the left; and thy seed shall inherit the Gentiles, and make the desolate cities to be inhabited" (v. 3).

Bishop Merrill J. Bateman said: "The tent … represents the gospel of Christ. He states that in the last days the cords of the tent would be stretched across the earth and stakes would be planted in every land (see Isa. 54:1–2; 3 Ne. 22:1–2). We … are seeing that fulfilled today."[11]

President Ezra Taft Benson said: "The prophets likened latter-day Zion to a great tent encompassing the earth. That tent was supported by cords fastened to stakes.

Those stakes, of course, are various geographical organizations spread out over the earth. Presently, Israel is being gathered to the various stakes of Zion. … Stakes are a defense for the Saints from enemies both seen and unseen. The defense is direction provided through priesthood channels that strengthens testimony and promotes family solidarity and individual righteousness."[12]

- **Isaiah 54:4–13 (3 Nephi 22:4–13): As the "waters of Noah."** In the Middle East in ancient times, the inability to bear children was considered a great curse. But Isaiah prophesied that in the latter days Israel will forget the shame of her "childless" years and, as her children are gathered, she will rejoice in her new and prosperous condition.

"Fear not," Isaiah said, "for thou shalt not be ashamed: neither be thou confounded; for thou shalt not be put to shame: for thou shalt forget the shame of thy youth, and shalt not remember the reproach of thy widowhood any more. For thy

Maker is thine husband; the Lord of hosts is his name; and thy Redeemer the Holy One of Israel; The God of the whole earth shall he be called," and He "hath called thee as a woman forsaken and grieved in spirit, and a wife of youth, when thou wast refused, saith thy God" (vv. 4–6). "For a small moment have I forsaken thee; but with great mercies will I gather thee. In a little wrath I hid my face from thee for a moment; but with everlasting kindness will I have mercy on thee, saith the Lord thy Redeemer" (vv. 7–8).

This promise was of the same certainty as the one made to Noah concerning the waters of the flood. "For this [the promise of gathering in the last days] is as the waters of Noah unto me," said the Lord. "For as I have sworn that the waters of Noah should no more go over the earth; so have I sworn that I would not be wroth with thee, nor rebuke thee [forever]" (v. 9). Though the mountains might depart, and the hills be removed, the Lord's promised "kindness shall not depart from thee, neither shall the covenant of my peace be removed, saith the Lord that hath mercy on thee" (v. 10).

Instead of being "afflicted, tossed with tempest, and not comforted," the Lord said He would "lay thy stones with fair colours, and lay thy foundations with sapphires. And I will make thy windows of agates, and thy gates of carbuncles, and all thy borders of pleasant stones" (vv. 11–12). These are promises of material wealth and peaceful security. Perhaps even more important, the Lord promised that "all thy children shall be taught of the Lord; and great shall be the peace of thy children" (v. 13).

— **Revelation 21:19–21** The Apostle John on the Isle of Patmos gave a similar description of the City of Zion: "And the foundations of the wall of the city were garnished with all manner of

The beautiful celestial City of Zion

JOHN MARTIN, 1841

precious stones. The first foundation was jasper; the second, sapphire; the third, a chalcedony; the fourth, an emerald; The fifth, sardonyx; the sixth, sardius; the seventh, chrysolite; the eighth, beryl; the ninth, a topaz; the tenth, a chrysoprasus; the eleventh, a jacinth; the twelfth, an amethyst. And the twelve gates were twelve pearls; every several gate was of one pearl: and the street of the city was pure gold, as it were transparent glass."

● **Isaiah 54:14–17** (3 Nephi 22:14–17): **Zion will be protected.** "In righteousness shalt thou be established: thou shalt be far from oppression; for thou shalt not fear: and from terror; for it shall not come near thee" (v. 14). True enough, Israel's enemies will gather together against her, but "whosoever shall gather together against thee shall fall for thy sake" (v. 15). "No weapon that is formed against thee shall prosper; and every tongue that shall rise against thee in judgment thou shalt condemn" (v. 17).

— **D&C 71:9–10** A similar promise was made to Joseph Smith and Sidney Rigdon in our own dispensation: "Verily, thus saith the Lord unto you— there is no weapon that is formed against you shall prosper; And if any man lift his voice against you he shall be confounded in mine own due time."

The Prophet Joseph Smith explained, "No unhallowed hand can stop the work from progressing; persecutions may rage, mobs may combine, armies may assemble, calumny may defame, but the truth of God will go forth boldly, nobly, and independent, till it has penetrated every continent, visited every clime, swept every country, and sounded in every ear, till the purposes of God shall be accomplished, and the Great Jehovah shall say the work is done."[13]

Elder Wilford Woodruff said:

> There never was a dispensation on the earth when prophets and Apostles, the inspiration, revelation, and power of God, the holy priesthood and the keys of the kingdom were needed more than they are in this generation. There never has been a dispensation when the friends of God and righteousness among the children of men needed more faith in the promises and prophecies than they do today; and there certainly never has been a generation of people on the earth that has had a greater work to perform than the inhabitants of the earth in the latter days.

That is one reason why this Church and kingdom has progressed from its commencement until today, in the midst of all the opposition, oppression, and warfare which have been waged against it by men inspired by the evil one. If this had not been the dispensation of the fulness of times—the dispensation in which God has declared that He will establish His kingdom on the earth never more to be thrown down, the inhabitants of the earth would have been enabled to overcome the kingdom and Zion of God in this as well as in any former dispensation.

But the set time has come to favor Zion, and the Lord Almighty has decreed in the heavens that every weapon formed against her shall be broken.[14]

President George Q. Cannon said: "I cannot lift my hand against this people and be prospered in it, nor can any other man. No man can join with the enemies of this people and hope to succeed; for God will desert him no matter how high his standing may be, and all who follow in his footsteps will find themselves dreadfully deceived."[15]

President George Albert Smith was about to close one of our general conferences, which happened to be at the time of the furor caused by the book *No Man Knows My History,* one of the scurrilous things published against the Church, and there had been different speakers who had said something about these apostate writings with which the Church was being flooded.

Just as President Smith was about to finish, he paused—and it was wholly unrelated to what he had been talking about—and he said: "There have been some who have belittled [Joseph Smith], but I would like to say that those who have done so will be forgotten and their remains will go back to mother earth, ... and the odor of their infamy will never die, while the glory and honor and majesty and courage and fidelity manifested by the Prophet Joseph Smith will attach to his name forever."[16]

President Harold B. Lee said: "When we see some of our own today doing similar things, some who have been recognized and honored in the past as teachers and leaders who later fall by the wayside, our hearts are made sore and tender. But sometimes we have to say just like the Master said, 'The devil must have entered into them.'... He will take care of our enemies if we continue to keep the commandments.

So, you Saints of the Most High God, when these things come, and they will come—this has been prophesied—you just say, 'No weapon formed against the work of the Lord will ever prosper, but all glory and majesty of this work that the Lord gave will long be remembered after those who have tried to befoul their names and the name of the Church will be forgotten, and their works will follow after them.'"[17]

CHRIST'S MISSION AND ATONEMENT

(Isaiah 53)

Isaiah's Witness of Christ

One of Isaiah's most important purposes was to bear witness of Christ. And nowhere in all of his writings is that witness more powerful than in Isaiah 53, which is commonly called "The Suffering Servant" by Biblical scholars. Some Bible minimalists try to discount the connection between these prophecies and the ministry of

Isaiah saw events of Jesus' ministry

Jesus Christ. But to the believing ear, this is unmistakable proof that Isaiah saw the day of our Savior's mortal ministry. He describes it here with unmistakable clarity.

Nephi said that one of the reasons he quoted Isaiah so extensively was to "more fully persuade [his people] to believe in the Lord their Redeemer" (1 Ne. 19:23). Nephi loved the Lord in a very

personal way, and therefore his "soul delighteth" in Isaiah's words—
"for he [Isaiah] verily saw my Redeemer, even as I have seen him" (2
Ne. 11:2).

Abinadi said that all the prophets have testified of Christ. "For
behold, did not Moses prophesy unto them concerning the coming
of the Messiah, and that God should redeem his people? Yea, and
even all the prophets who have prophesied ever since the world
began—have they not spoken more or less concerning these things?
Have they not said that God himself should come down among the
children of men, and take upon him the form of man, and go forth
in mighty power upon the face of the earth? Yea, and have they not
said also that he should bring to pass the resurrection of the dead,
and that he, himself, should be oppressed and afflicted?" (Mosiah
13:33–35). Abinadi then quoted Isaiah 53.

Christ's Mission and Atonement

W. A. BOUGEUREAU, 1893

● **Isaiah 53:2** (Mosiah 14:2)**: "A tender
plant."** Isaiah prophesied that the
Savior would "grow up before [the
world] as a tender plant, and as a root
out of a dry ground: he hath no form
nor comeliness; and when we shall
see him, there is no beauty that we
should desire him." In other words,
just like the rest of us, He would be
born as a small, helpless infant and
grow to maturity without attracting the
particular notice of the world.

President Joseph Fielding Smith said:
"Did not Christ grow up as a tender
plant? There was nothing about Him to
cause people to single Him out. In appearance He was like men;
and so it is expressed here by the prophet that He had no form
or comeliness, that is, He was not so distinctive, so different

from others that people would recognize Him as the Son of God. He appeared as a mortal man."[18]

● **Isaiah 53:3** (Mosiah 14:3): **"A man of sorrows, and acquainted with grief."** Isaiah predicted that the Savior would be "despised and rejected of men; a man of sorrows, and acquainted with grief." He also predicted that men would "hid[e] as it were [their] faces from him," consider Him "despised," and "esteem … him not." All of these predictions were literally fulfilled.

— John 1:11	His people—the Jews—rejected Him as the Messiah.
— John 7:5	Members of His own family rejected Him as the Messiah.
— Luke 4:16–30	People in His hometown sought to kill Him.
— Luke 22:48, 54–62	One friend betrayed Him; another denied knowing Him.
— Matthew 26:56	All the disciples forsook Him, and fled.
— Matthew 27:22–23	His enemies demanded His crucifixion.

President Joseph Fielding Smith wrote: "Was not Christ a man of sorrows? Was He not rejected of men? Was He not acquainted with grief? Did not the people (figuratively) hide their faces from Him? Did not the people esteem Him not? Surely He knew our griefs and carried our sorrows, but He was thought to be stricken of God and forsaken by Him. Did not the people say that? How true all these things are!"[19]

● **Isaiah 53:4–7** (Mosiah 14:4–7): **"Wounded for our transgressions."** Speaking as if it had already happened, Isaiah declared, "Surely he hath borne our griefs, and carried our sorrows," though the world would consider Him a vagabond: "stricken, smitten of God, and afflicted" (v. 4).

HEINRICH HOFFMANN 1890

Yet, though they had no idea what they were doing (see Luke 23:34) as they tortured and crucified Him, "he was wounded for our transgressions, he was bruised for our iniquities: the chastisement of our peace was upon him; and with his stripes we are healed" (v. 5).

Notice that He suffered for our "griefs" and "sorrows" (v. 4), but also for our iniquities (vv. 5–6). Every one of us has sinned and is in need of redemption (see 1 Jn. 1:8–10), and "like sheep [that] have gone astray; we have turned every one to his own way" (v. 6); thus, in order to save us and provide an opportunity for redemption, "the [Father] hath laid on him the iniquity of us all" (v. 6). We cannot comprehend the immensity of this burden.

Elder James E. Talmage wrote:

> Christ's agony in the garden is unfathomable by the finite mind, both as to intensity and cause. The thought that He suffered through fear of death is untenable. Death to Him was preliminary to resurrection and triumphal return to the Father from whom He had come, and to a state of glory even beyond what He had before possessed; and, moreover, it was within His power to lay down His life voluntarily.
>
> He struggled and groaned under a burden such as no other being who has lived on earth might even conceive as possible. It was not physical pain, nor mental anguish alone, that caused Him to suffer such torture as to produce an extrusion of blood from every pore; but a spiritual agony of soul such as only God was capable of experiencing.
>
> No other man, however great his powers of physical or mental endurance, could have suffered so; for his human organism would have succumbed, and syncope would have produced unconsciousness and welcome oblivion. In that hour of anguish Christ met and overcame all the horrors that Satan, "the prince of this world," could inflict. The frightful struggle incident to the temptations immediately following the Lord's baptism was surpassed and overshadowed by this supreme contest with the powers of evil.
>
> In some manner, actual and terribly real though to man incomprehensible, the Savior took upon Himself the burden of the sins of mankind from Adam to the end of the world.[20]

Isaiah further predicted that although He would be "oppressed, and ... afflicted, yet he opened not his mouth" (v. 7)—He would remain silent before His accusers (see Matt. 27:12–14). There was no reviling or retribution from the Lord, only redemption.

● **Isaiah 53:7** (Mosiah 14:7): **A sacrificial Lamb of God.** Making the metaphor of sacrifice crystal clear, Isaiah predicted that our Lord would be "brought as a lamb to the slaughter." To the Hebrew mind, this image was well known—a helpless and pure lamb brought to the altar and slain for the sins of the people.

The "suffering servant" of Isaiah is here clearly described as such a lamb, slain for the sins of the world. The imagery is unmistakable, and we know why John the Baptist referred to Him at the very beginning of His ministry as "the Lamb of God" (John 1:29).

● **Isaiah 53:8–9** (Mosiah 14:8–9): **Christ's death and burial.** Though "he had done no violence, neither was any deceit in his mouth" (v. 9), yet "he was taken from prison and from judgment ... [and] cut off out of the land of the living" (v. 8). And though He Himself would be guilty of no crime, He would "[make] his grave [die] with the wicked" (v. 9).

GUSTAVE DORÉ, 1896

This was accomplished when the Savior was placed between two thieves while being crucified (see Luke 23:33). Yet, He would be "with the rich in his death" (v. 9)— fulfilled when His lifeless body was laid in Joseph of Arimathea's tomb (see Matt. 27:60).

● **Isaiah 53:10–11** (Mosiah 14:10–11): **It "pleased" the Father to "bruise" His Son because it saved the rest of us** (v. 10). The Father allowed Him to be "put ... to grief," making "his soul an offering for sin" (v. 10). The Father will "see of the travail of his soul, and [justice] shall be satisfied" (v. 11). Indeed, "by his knowledge shall my righteous servant justify many; for he shall bear their iniquities" (v. 11).

Elder Melvin J. Ballard said:

> In that hour I think I can see our dear Father behind the veil looking upon these dying struggles until even He could not endure it any longer; and, like the mother who bids farewell to her dying child, has to be taken out of the room, so as not to look upon the last struggles, so He bowed His head, and hid in some part of His universe, His great heart almost breaking for the love that He had for His Son.
>
> Oh, in that moment when He might have saved His Son, I thank Him and praise Him that He did not fail us, for He had not only the love of His Son in mind, but He also had love for us. I rejoice that He did not interfere, and that His love for us made it possible for Him to endure to look upon the sufferings of His Son and give Him finally to us, our Savior and our Redeemer. Without Him, without His sacrifice, we would have remained, and we would never have come glorified into His presence. And so this is what it cost, in part, for our Father in Heaven to give the gift of His Son unto men. [21]

● **Isaiah 53:10** (Mosiah 14:10): **Those whom Christ redeems become His "seed."** Elder Bruce R. McConkie wrote: "The seed of Christ are those who are adopted into His family, who by faith have become His sons and His daughters (Mosiah 5:7). They are the children of Christ in that they are His followers and disciples and keep His commandments. (4 Ne. 1:17; Morm. 9:26; Moro. 7:19)."[22]

HEINRICH HOFFMANN, 1890

● **Isaiah 53:10** (Mosiah 14:10): **Though He will die, He will yet live.** Speaking of events after His death, Isaiah predicts that "he shall see his seed, he shall prolong his days, and the pleasure of the Lord shall prosper in his hand." How can this be possible for a dead man? It cannot. The implication that He will live again is quite clear to the spiritual mind.

- **Isaiah 53:12 (Mosiah 14:12): Jesus' "portion with the great."** He willingly "poured out his soul unto death" after being "numbered with the transgressors" (living among them on earth). And by so doing, He "bare the sin of many, and made intercession for the transgressors." And because of His willing sacrifice for all of us, the Father "will ... divide him a portion with the great, and he shall divide the spoil with the strong." He will inherit all that the Father has to give (see John 16:15) and reign with Him through all eternity.

- **Isaiah 53:12 (Mosiah 14:12): He will "divide the spoil with the strong."** Using a military metaphor of "dividing the spoil" after a victory has been won, Isaiah said that the Savior would divide His eternal blessings "with the strong." This implies that all those who follow Him faithfully will be joint-heirs with Him of the blessings the Father will give Him.

  — **Romans 8:17** The Apostle Paul verified this promise when he said the great (righteous) will become "joint-heirs" with Christ. "And if [we are God's] children, then [we are] heirs; heirs of God, and joint-heirs with Christ; if so be that we suffer with him, that we may be also glorified together."

The "First Testament" of Christ

Chapter 53 of Isaiah is one of the most profound testimonies found anywhere in scripture concerning the ministry of Jesus Christ. Little wonder that Nephi cherished the words of Isaiah so much, and little wonder that the Savior Himself read and explained Isaiah's words to the Nephites when He visited them.

The Old Testament is exactly that—a testament, and it is the First Testament concerning Christ. The Savior said: "Search the scriptures; for in them ye think ye have eternal life: and they are they which testify of me" (John 5:39). Clearly, when He said "the scriptures," He meant the Old Testament, since that was the only volume of scripture available to them. And He plainly said that the Old Testament testified of Him—the Savior. Thus, the Old Testament could more properly be thought of as the "First Testament of Jesus Christ." For that reason alone, it is worth serious study.

Elder Mark E. Petersen wrote: "[Jesus] never would have said that if the scriptures available to the people of that day did not testify of Him. He urged them to read the scriptures that they might see how the prophets whom they adored, but now long since dead, actually did foretell His coming. They testified of Him. ... The Lord quoted ... Moses and the other prophets ... 'in all the scriptures the things concerning himself.'"[23]

Again and again throughout the Old Testament, the Messiah's coming is predicted through profound symbols, compelling stories, and remarkably accurate prophecies. The major purpose of all testaments, old or new, is to bear witness of Christ. As a result, to the spiritual eye and ear, the Old Testament (more accurately, the "First Testament") is like a giant hand pointing forward to the coming of the Lord Jesus Christ. If we are led by the Holy Spirit we will see the unmistakable mark of the Messiah in every book we read in these scriptures.

President Brigham Young said: "The Old and New Testaments, the Book of Mormon, and the Book of Doctrine and Covenants ... are like a lighthouse in the ocean, or a finger-post which points out the road we should travel. Where do they point? To the fountain of light. ... That is what these books are for. They are of God; they are valuable and necessary: by them we can establish the doctrine of Christ."[24]

Notes:

1. *"Great Are the Words of Isaiah"* [1980], 173–74.

2. *History of the Church*, 5:401.

3. *"Great Are the Words of Isaiah"*, 177.

4. *History of the Church*, 6:364.

5. "*Great Are the Words of Isaiah*", 191.

6. *The Millennial Messiah: The Second Coming of the Son of Man* [1982], 624–25.

7. Ibid., 390.

8. *History of the Church*, 2:254–55.

9. Ibid., 1:382–83.

10. *Christ and the New Covenant: The Messianic Message of the Book of Mormon* [1997], 290.

11. In Conference Report, Apr. 1994, 84–85; or *Ensign*, May 1994, 65.

12. "Strengthen Thy Stakes," *Ensign*, Jan. 1991, 2, 4.

13. *History of the Church*, 4:540.

14. In *Journal of Discourses*, 15:8–9.

15. *Gospel Truth: Discourses and Writings of President George Q. Cannon*, comp. Jerreld L. Newquist [1957], 210.

16. In Conference Report, Apr. 1946, 181–82.

17. In Conference Report, Oct. 1973, 166–67; or *Ensign*, Jan. 1974, 126.

18. *Doctrines of Salvation*, comp. Bruce R. McConkie, 3 vols. [1954–56], 1:23.

19. *Doctrines of Salvation*, 1:24.

20. *Jesus the Christ*, 3rd ed. [1916], 613.

21. *Sermons and Missionary Services of Melvin Joseph Ballard*, comp. Bryant S. Hinckley [1949], 154–55.

22. *Mormon Doctrine*, 2nd ed. [1966], 700.

23. *Moses: Man of Miracles* [1977], 148–49.

24. In *Journal of Discourses*, 8:129.

Chapter 8

Isaiah, Pt. 6:
The Last Days
and the Millennium
(Isaiah 55–66)

INTRODUCTION

Elder Wilford Woodruff said concerning the last days and the Millennium:

Isaiah prophesied of our day

THEBIBLEREVIVAL.COM, #12

> The whole history of this people has been foretold by the prophet Isaiah, thousands of years ago; and it has been a steady growth from the commencement to the present. And will the Lord stop here? No; whether men believe or not, this Zion so often spoken of in holy writ, has got to arise and put on her beautiful garments; these mountain vales have got to be filled with the Saints of God and temples reared to His holy name, preparatory to the time when "the Gentiles shall come [to] thy light, and kings to the brightness of thy rising."

> And this time will come when the nations are fully warned by the preaching of the servant of God, and His judgments commence to be poured out upon the world, in fulfilment of the revelations of St. John. Faith then is what the unbelieving world needs to exercise

in God and in His revelations to man; but as I have said, whether we do it or not, our unbelief will never turn the hand of God to the right or the left.[1]

INVITATIONS TO RIGHTEOUSNESS

Look to Christ for Eternal Life

● **Isaiah 55:1–7 Israel is invited to come unto the Lord and live.** Isaiah invites all who thirst spiritually to "come ye to the waters" (v. 1). Christ identified Himself as the Source of such living water (see John 4:10–14) and also the bread of life (see John 6:35, 47–51). From this Source, we can "buy, and eat; yea … without money and without price" (v. 1). It can be had without cost—but not without effort. He questions why men labor and spend money for things that are not "bread" to their souls and "which satisfieth not" (v. 2) when they could instead "eat … that which is good, and let your soul delight itself in fatness" (a figure of speech suggesting full satisfaction).

C. SCHOENHERR, THE BIBLE AND ITS STORY, 1908

Isaiah identifies the Source of this living water and bread as "the sure mercies of David" (v. 3), another figure of speech suggesting the coming King and Messiah who would be a descendant of David. Isaiah calls the same Being "the Lord thy God, and … the Holy One of Israel" who would eventually glorify them (v. 5). "Seek ye the Lord while he may be found, call ye upon him while he is near: Let the wicked forsake his way, and the unrighteous man his thoughts: and let him return unto the

Lord, and he will have mercy upon him; and to our God, for he will abundantly pardon" (vv. 6–7).

Elder Joseph Fielding Smith said: "If at times we have been requested to seek the help of the Lord in this great struggle which has deluged the world, have we prayed in the true spirit of prayer? What good does it do for us to petition the Lord, if we have no intention of keeping His commandments? Such praying is hollow mockery and an insult before the throne of grace. How dare we presume to expect a favorable answer if such is the case? 'Seek ye the Lord while he may be found, call ye upon him while he is near' [Isa. 55:6]. But is not the Lord always near when we petition Him? Verily no! [D&C 101:7–8]. If we draw near unto Him, He will draw near unto us, and we will not be forsaken; but if we do not draw near to Him, we have no promise that He will answer us in our rebellion."[2]

Elder Marion G. Romney said:

> When earth life is over and things appear in their true perspective, we shall more clearly see and realize what the Lord and His prophets have repeatedly told us, that the fruits of the gospel are the only objectives worthy of life's full efforts. Their possessor obtains true wealth—wealth in the Lord's view of values. ...
>
> I conceive the blessings of the gospel to be of such inestimable worth that the price for them must be very exacting, and if I correctly understand what the Lord has said on the subject, it is. The price, however, is within the reach of us all, because it is not to be paid in money nor in any of this world's goods but in righteous living. What is required is wholehearted devotion to the gospel and unreserved allegiance to The Church of Jesus Christ of Latter-day Saints. ...
>
> A half-hearted performance is not enough. We cannot obtain these blessings and be like the rich young man who protested that he had kept the commandments from his youth up but who went away sorrowful when, in answer to the question, "What lack I yet?" Jesus said unto him, "If thou wilt be perfect, go and sell that thou hast, and give to the poor ... and come and follow me" (Matt. 19:21). Evidently he could live everything but the welfare program.

There can be no such reservation. We must be willing to sacrifice everything. Through self-discipline and devotion we must demonstrate to the Lord that we are willing to serve Him under all circumstances. When we have done this, we shall receive an assurance that we shall have eternal life in the world to come. Then we shall have peace in this world.[3]

God's Higher Knowledge and Intelligence

Isaiah 55:8–11 God's "thoughts" (intelligence) **are higher than ours.** I wonder, sometimes, if we truly appreciate the greatness of the God we worship. This Being who holds the entire universe in His control, and creates and destroys worlds with the word of His command and by virtue of the faith that He possesses, is no ordinary Being.

He is God of the entire universe

Men try to "bring Him down to earth" by professing a special "friendship" with Him that is easier to relate with. And, after all, the Father *is* our father and He loves us with all the tender feelings of an Eternal Parent. He invites us to call him "Father" rather than some title such as "King of the Universe" or "the Greatest of All Beings." No, He prefers that we fully understand that we are His children—His literal offspring—and invites us to call Him by the most noble of all titles possible: Father. But in doing so, we must not forget how great, how good, how knowledgeable, and how powerful He is.

Through Isaiah, the Lord reminds us that "my thoughts are not your thoughts, neither are your ways my ways, saith the Lord. For as the heavens are higher than the earth, so are my ways higher than your ways, and my thoughts than your thoughts" (vv. 8–9).

We cannot explain all that He does with earthly logic or known rules of physics. Much more is possible than we can even imagine. We can only wait for the day when we might begin to understand it all. Like rain falling from heaven, the Lord's commands fulfill their purposes, and do not return to Him unfulfilled (vv. 10–11). All things that He wills are done and will inevitably prosper in the process (v. 11).

Elder John Taylor said: "We know in part, and see in part, and comprehend in part; [but] many of the things of God are hid from our view. ... The wisdom of this world is foolishness with God [and] no man in and of himself is competent to unravel the designs and know the purposes of Jehovah. ... The wisdom and intelligence of God ... are as far above [man's] wisdom and intelligence as the heavens are above the earth."[4]

● **Isaiah 55:12–13 The Lord's word will be fulfilled and Israel will one day prosper.** Though ancient Israel was destroyed as a nation and scattered all over the earth, yet the Lord declared that, in the latter days, "ye shall go out with joy, and be led forth with peace: the mountains and the hills shall break forth before you into singing, and all the trees of the field shall clap their hands. Instead of the thorn shall come up the fir tree, and instead of the brier shall come up the myrtle tree," ensuring that the Lord's name will be honored through the fulfilling of His promises and "for an everlasting sign that [Israel] shall not be cut off."

● **Isaiah 56:1–8 Both Israelites and Gentiles will be gathered as the Lord's people and receive exaltation.** Those who watch for the coming of the Lord are assured that "my salvation is near to come, and my righteousness [will] be revealed" (v. 1). In preparation for that great day, "Thus saith the Lord, Keep ye judgment, and do justice. ... Blessed is the man that doeth this, and the son of man that layeth hold on it;

Word will go to all nations

that keepeth the sabbath from polluting it, and keepeth his hand from doing any evil" (vv. 1–2).

This applies not only to the Israelites but also to Gentiles who convert and gather with the Lord's people. "Neither let the son of the stranger, that hath joined himself to the Lord, speak, saying, The Lord hath utterly separated me from his people: neither let the eunuch say, Behold, I am a dry tree. For thus saith the Lord unto the eunuchs that keep my sabbaths, and choose the things that please me, and take hold of my covenant; Even unto them will I give in mine house and within my walls a place and a name better than of sons and of daughters: I will give them an everlasting name, that shall not be cut off. Also the sons of the stranger, that join themselves to the Lord, to serve him, and to love the name of the Lord, to be his servants, every one that keepeth the sabbath from polluting it, and taketh hold of my covenant" (vv. 3–6).

Converts who do this "will I bring to my holy mountain [the temple], and make them joyful in my house of prayer" (v. 7). Jesus said, "My house is the house of prayer" in referring to the temple in Jerusalem (Luke 19:46). "Their burnt offerings and their sacrifices shall be accepted upon mine altar; for mine house shall be called an house of prayer for all people" (v. 7). Thus, Isaiah observes, "The Lord God which gathereth the outcasts of Israel saith, Yet will [He] gather others to him, beside those [of Israel] that are gathered unto him" (v. 8).

Israel's Apostasy and Evil Practices

● **Isaiah 56:9–12 Religious leaders are condemned for their selfishness.** While "beasts … devour," watchmen over the flock are "blind" and "ignorant" [without understanding] (vv. 9–10). Like "dumb dogs, they cannot bark; sleeping, lying down, loving to slumber" (v. 10). "Yea, they are greedy dogs which can never have enough, and they are shepherds that cannot understand" (v. 11).

These figures of speech may refer to the Gentiles who reject the gospel, but they may also refer to those who are charged with watching over a flock but do so with greed and without understanding. "They all look to their own way, every one for his gain, from his quarter" (v. 11). "Come ye, say they, I will fetch wine, and we will fill ourselves with strong drink; and to morrow shall be as this day, and much more abundant" (v. 12).

"Kimchi observes, 'The flock is entrusted to the care of these watchmen. The wild beasts come; these dogs bark not; and the wild beasts devour the flock. Thus they do not profit the flock. Yea, they injure it; for the owner trusts in them, that they will watch and be faithful; but they are not. These are the false teachers and careless shepherds.'"[5] This is an accurate description of the Christian world of our day, as prophesied by Nephi (see 2 Ne. 28:3–9) and Moroni (see Morm. 8:31–33, 37–39).

● **Isaiah 57:1–2, 13–21 "There is no peace, saith my God, to the wicked."** A promise of peace is given to the righteous, but evil will come upon the wicked. The wicked will hardly notice or care when righteous people perish, not thinking that they are being taken away "from the evil to come" (v. 1). These righteous souls will "enter into peace: they shall rest in their beds, each one walking in his uprightness" (v. 2).

The wicked in Israel will be overcome and carried away as if by wind, but "he that putteth his trust in me shall possess the land, and shall inherit my holy mountain" (v. 13). The Lord, "the high and lofty One that inhabiteth eternity, whose name is Holy," declares that He will "dwell in the high and holy place, with him also that is of a contrite and humble spirit" (v. 15). Though He was once angry with Israel, the Lord says, "I will not contend for ever, neither will I be always wroth" (v. 16). He was angry because of Israel's wicked and covetous behavior, but in the latter days He will heal and lead Israel once again "and restore comforts unto him and to his mourners" (v. 18).

Among the righteous, the Lord will cry, "Peace, peace to him that is far off, and to him that is near" (v. 19). But "the wicked are like the troubled sea, when it cannot rest, whose waters cast up mire and dirt" (v. 20). "There is no peace, saith my God, to the wicked" (v. 21).

- **Isaiah 57:3–13 A rebuke of the abominations of the wicked.** Those who desire the Lord's favor must avoid idolatry and other sins for which ancient Israel was cut off. Those sins include sorcery and adultery (v. 3), sporting themselves with falsehood (v. 4), "enflaming [them]selves with idols under every green tree" [worshiping in the groves], and "slaying the children in the valleys under the clifts of the rocks" [human sacrifice of children to the god Molech] (v. 5). "Upon a lofty and high mountain hast thou set thy bed: even thither wentest thou up to offer sacrifice" [a reference to sexual intercourse as a form of worship in the groves] (v. 7).

Also, "behind the doors also and the posts hast thou set up thy remembrance" [placed idols in their homes], and then made covenants with those idols by going up into the groves and making their beds there (v. 8). They made offerings to their kings and to foreign kings and "didst debase thyself even unto hell" (v. 9) . The greatness of their sins did not bother them (v. 10), and they were unafraid of consequences because "thou hast lied, and hast not remembered me, nor laid it to thy heart" (v. 11). But "thy works … shall not profit thee" (v. 12); they will be carried into captivity as if by the wind (v. 13).

Proper Fasting

- **Isaiah 58:1–5, 9 Examples of improper fasting.** The Lord instructed Isaiah to "lift up thy voice like a trumpet, and shew my people their transgression" (v. 1). They continued to perform ordinances, taking delight in their national customs (v. 2), but they did so without full understanding. "Wherefore have we fasted," they said unto the Lord, "and thou seest not? wherefore have we afflicted our soul, and thou takest no knowledge?" (v. 3). The Lord answered, "Behold, in the day of your fast [the Sabbath day] ye find pleasure, and exact all your labours" (v. 3). And while fasting they engaged in "strife and debate, and ... [smote] with the fist of wickedness" (v. 4). They could not do these things and expect "[their] voice[s] to be heard on high" (v. 4).

The Lord asked, "Is [this] a fast that I have chosen?" (v. 5). To fast with a complaining attitude (v. 3); to fast while breaking the commandments and oppressing others (v. 4); expecting our prayers to be heard despite our wickedness (v. 4); to fast with a great show of pretended humility so that others will notice (v. 5); or to fast with vanity and while engaged in the criticism of others (v. 9)—none of these things are acceptable to the Lord.

● **Isaiah 58:6–7, 10, 13 Elements of proper fasting.** According to Isaiah, the type of fasting expected by the Lord includes the following.

— Loosening the bands of wickedness [repentance] (v. 6).

— Undoing the heavy burdens of others (v. 6).

— Providing food, clothing, and shelter to those who are without these things (v. 7).

— "Hid[ing] not thyself from thine own flesh" [spending time with family] (v. 7).

— Feeding the hungry and comforting the afflicted (v. 10).

— Keeping the Sabbath day holy (v. 13).

President Spencer W. Kimball said one element of a true fast is giving generous fast offerings: "I think

S. L. BOIZOT, 1785

Proper fasting includes charity

that when we are affluent, as many of us are, that we ought to be very, very generous … [and] give, instead of the amount we saved by our two meals of fasting, perhaps much, much more—ten times more where we are in a position to do it."[6]

● **Isaiah 58:8–14 Promises for those who fast properly.** In his beautiful poetic language, Isaiah listed all the benefits of proper fasting.

— Enlightened minds (v. 8).

— Good health (v. 8).

— Righteousness and companionship of the Lord (v. 8).

— Answered prayers (v. 9).

— Continual guidance from the Lord (v. 11).

— Happiness "like a spring of water, whose waters fail not" (v. 11).

— Becoming part of the Kingdom of God and of His people (v. 12).

— Receiving the blessings of Jacob [temple blessings] (v. 14).

President Joseph Fielding Smith wrote:

> Fasting we may well assume is a religious custom that has come down from the beginning of time, and always associated with prayer. There are numerous customs and practices that were given anciently about which the knowledge became so common that their origin has been lost in antiquity; therefore we cannot give time or place where the first commandment on fasting was given. It was common in the most ancient times, and there are numerous incidents recorded in the Old Testament indicating that it was well established not only among the true worshipers of Deity but also among the heathen nations. All of this indicates the antiquity of fasting, which we may presume was revealed to Adam.
>
> We may obtain the understanding from the writings of Isaiah that fasting and prayer were commanded by the Lord. For their perversion of this doctrine, Isaiah rebukes Israel and endeavors to bring them back to the path of faithful obedience. …

Isaiah points out clearly the intent of the fast. It was observed with a contrite spirit, a humbled heart, before the Lord. Evil was to be forsaken, prayer and supplication offered with a covenant to feed the hungry, clothe the naked, and let the oppressed go free. If they would do this, then, said the Lord, "shall thy light break forth as the morning, and thine health shall spring forth speedily: and thy righteousness shall go before thee; the glory of the Lord shall be thy reward." Israel, however, had perverted the fast and thus merited Isaiah's and the Lord's rebuke.[7]

Proper Observance of the Sabbath

Isaiah turns next to a discussion of the Sabbath day. He does so in the form of "if … then" statements—"if you do this, then God will do this."

● **Isaiah 58:13–14 The law of the Sabbath.** First, Isaiah lists man's part of the law of the Sabbath—the things to avoid and to do on the Sabbath day.

— "Turn away thy foot from the sabbath" [cease from daily tasks].

— "Turn away … from doing thy pleasure on my holy day" [cease from recreation].

— "Call the sabbath a delight, the holy of the Lord, honourable" [a good attitude about it].

— "Honour him, not doing thine own ways, nor finding thine own pleasure, nor speaking thine own words" [worship God and do nothing else].

Isaiah then lists the promised blessings from God if we keep the Sabbath day holy.

— Delight himself in the Lord	Increased self-confidence (D&C 121:45)
— High places of the earth	Communion with God
— The heritage of Jacob	Eternal life and exaltation (D&C 132:37)

- **D&C 59:9–16 A modern-day restatement of this law.** Proper observance of the Sabbath day helps us to "more fully keep thyself unspotted from the world" (v. 9). We will be less worldly and less prone to sin if we remember the Lord's day properly.

— Go to "the house of prayer" [to Church] (v. 9).

— "Offer up thy sacraments" [participate in the sacramental ordinance] (v. 9).

— "Rest from your labors" (v. 10).

— "Pay thy devotions unto the Most High" [worship the Lord] (v. 10).

— "Offer thine oblations" [serve and sacrifice, make offerings] (v. 12).

— "Confess ... thy sins unto thy brethren, and before the Lord" (v. 12).

— Prepare food "with singleness of heart" [in the spirit of the day] (v. 13).

By doing these things, our fasting will be "perfect" and our joy full, and we will be engaged in true "rejoicing and prayer" (vv. 13–14).

It is true that we are not just a Sunday Church. We are to keep our covenants ("vows") "in righteousness on all days and at all times" (v. 11). We are expected to pray and to read our scriptures and to attend to all Church and family duties on *every* day. "But remember that on this, the Lord's day, ... thou shalt do none other thing" (vv. 12–13). In other words, we are expected to live sanctified lives every day while engaged in our daily work. But on the Sabbath day, the Lord's day, we do *no other thing* except worship Him in the ways that Isaiah and this modern revelation suggest.

If we "do these things with thanksgiving, with cheerful hearts and countenances, not with much laughter, for this is sin, but with a glad heart and a cheerful countenance—... the fulness of the earth is yours, the beasts of the field and the fowls of the air, and that which climbeth upon the trees and walketh upon the earth" (vv. 15–16).

The Results of Disobedience

● **Isaiah 59:1–8 Iniquity separates us from the Lord.** Isaiah reminded the Israelites who were complaining that the Lord was not responding to their prayers: "The Lord's hand is not shortened, that it cannot save; neither his ear heavy, that it cannot hear: But your iniquities have separated between you and your God, and your sins have hid his face from you, that he will not hear" (vv. 1–2). "For your hands are defiled with blood, and your fingers with iniquity; your lips have spoken lies, your tongue hath muttered perverseness. None calleth for justice, nor any pleadeth for truth: they trust in vanity, and speak lies; they conceive mischief, and bring forth iniquity" (vv. 3–4).

They seek for ways to harm others, which Isaiah poetically describes as hatching snake eggs and weaving webs (vv. 5–6). But their works of iniquity will lead to death, and will not "cover" them in the coming days of trouble (vv. 5–6). "Their works are works of iniquity, and the act of violence is in their hands. Their feet run to evil, and they make haste to shed innocent blood: their thoughts are thoughts of iniquity; wasting and destruction are in their paths. The way of peace they know not; and there is no judgment in their goings: they have made them crooked paths: whosoever goeth therein shall not know peace" (vv. 6–8).

● **Isaiah 59:9–15 The results of disobedience.** People who live such lives of vanity and wickedness cannot expect the Lord to help them in their times of trouble. Yet, it is often true that when the wicked face death or destruction they suddenly become religious and plead with God to deliver them. But He will not. The consequences must come.

— They "wait for light" but none comes (v. 9).

— They "walk in darkness" & "grope for the wall like the blind" (vv. 9–10).

— They "mourn sore like doves" for salvation "but there is none" (v. 11).

— Transgression increases (v. 12).

— Their sins (which they know) testify against them (vv. 12–13).

— Their judgment [righteousness] disappears (v. 14).

— Equity [mercy] cannot save them (v. 14).

— They become a "prey" to their destruction (v. 15).

THEBIBLEREVIEW.COM, #12

- **Isaiah 63:7–14 A rehearsal of the Lord's goodness to Israel.** For hundreds of years, ever since Moses brought them out of captivity (vv. 11–14), the Lord had shown to Israel "lovingkindness ... , great goodness ... , [and] mercies" (v. 7). "Surely," the Lord said, "they are my people, children that will not lie: so he was their Savior. In all their affliction he was afflicted, and the angel of his presence saved them: in his love and in his pity he redeemed them; and he bare them, and carried them all the days of old" (vv. 8–9). Even after Moses was taken from them (see D&C 84:25), the Lord continued to lead them "to make [Himself] a glorious name" (v. 14).

- **Isaiah 63:10, 15–19 "O Lord, why hast thou suffered us to err?"** Nevertheless, Israel "rebelled, and vexed his holy Spirit: therefore he was turned to be their enemy, and he fought against them" (v. 10). They begged the Lord to "look down from heaven, and behold from the habitation of thy holiness and of thy glory" and renew "thy zeal and thy strength, ... and ... thy mercies toward [us]" (v. 15). They could not understand why the Lord's mercy was now "restrained" (v. 15). "Doubtless thou art our father, ... our redeemer; [and] thy name is from everlasting"

(v. 16). So now, "why hast thou made us to err from thy ways, and hardened our heart from thy fear?" (v. 17).

This "blame the Lord" mentality of the translators is corrected in JST Isaiah 63:17, which reads: "O Lord, why hast thou suffered us to err from thy ways, and to harden our heart … ?" God does *not* compel any man to sin or to harden his heart. The Israelites had chosen this for themselves. Now, under threat of destruction and captivity, the Israelites prayed, "Return for thy servants' sake, the tribes of thine inheritance. The people of thy holiness have possessed [the land] but a little while: our adversaries have trodden down thy sanctuary. We are thine [and our enemies are not]: thou never barest rule over them; they were not called by thy name" (vv. 17–19).

- **Isaiah 64:4–5 The unspeakable rewards that await the righteous.** Isaiah declares, "Since the beginning of the world men have not heard, nor perceived by the ear, neither hath the eye seen, O God, beside thee, what he hath prepared for him that waiteth for him" (v. 4). Other prophets who have had glimpses of God's heavenly abode have quoted this scripture in describing their experience: Paul (see 1 Cor. 2:9) and Joseph Smith and Sidney Rigdon (see D&C 76:10), for example. There, in that celestial world, the Lord "meetest him that rejoiceth and worketh righteousness, those that remember thee in thy ways" (v. 5). And there they will dwell with Him forever.

- **Isaiah 64:5–11 Israel's former righteousness has become like "filthy rags."** "Behold, thou art wroth; for we have sinned" (v. 5). "We are all as an unclean thing, and all our righteousnesses are as filthy rags; and we all do fade as a leaf; and our iniquities, like the wind, have taken us away" (v. 6). Keil and Delitzsch translated this passage: "All our virtues [are] like a garment soiled with blood."[8] God does not despise virtue nor view it as filthiness.

Because "there is none that calleth upon thy name, that stirreth up himself to take hold of thee," the Lord had now "hid [His] face from us, and hast consumed us, because of our iniquities" (v. 7). And now, the chastened and captive children of Israel were left to plead, "O Lord, thou art our father; we are the clay, and thou our potter; and we all are the work of thy hand. Be not wroth very sore, O Lord, neither remember iniquity for ever: behold, see, we beseech thee, we are all thy people. Thy holy cities are a wilderness, Zion is a wilderness, Jerusalem a desolation. Our holy and our beautiful house, where our fathers praised thee, is burned up with fire: and all our pleasant things are laid waste" (vv. 8–11).

ZION IN THE LATTER DAYS

Christil Will Come to Zion

● **Isaiah 59:16–17 Christ is our intercessor with the Father.** He was sent to earth because "there was no man" else who could save us. "Therefore his arm brought salvation ... and his righteousness ... sustained him" (v. 16). "For he put on righteousness as a breastplate, and an helmet of salvation upon his head; and he put on the garments of vengeance for clothing, and was clad with zeal as a cloke" (v. 17).

● **Isaiah 59:18–20 Christ's latter-day coming.** When the Savior comes the second time, He will repay, according to their deeds, "fury to his adversaries, recompence to his enemies; [and] to the islands [the farthest parts of the earth] he will repay recompence" (v. 18). He will "come to Zion"—those that "fear the ... Lord [in] the west"—and will place His Spirit upon them (vv. 19–20).

Elder Orson Pratt said: "Certainly Jesus, when He came eighteen centuries ago, did not turn away ungodliness from Jacob, for they then were filling up their cup with iniquity. They have remained in unbelief from that day to this; hence, there did not come a Deliverer out of Zion eighteen centuries ago. But the Zion of the last days, that Zion that is so frequently and so fully spoken of by the ancient prophets, especially by Isaiah, is the Church and kingdom of God; and out of that Church or kingdom or Zion is to come a Deliverer, who will turn away ungodliness from Jacob after the times of the Gentiles are fulfilled."[9]

Conditions in Zion in the Latter Days

● **Isaiah 60:1–2 The Glory of the Savior will rise upon Zion.** Isaiah said to the latter-day people of Zion, "Arise, shine; for thy light is come, and the glory of the Lord is risen upon thee" (v. 1). While the earth languishes in apostasy, "the Lord shall arise upon thee, and his glory shall be seen upon thee" (v. 2).

"Arise, shine, thy light has come!"

Elder Orson Pratt said: "The Zion that is here spoken of is called upon to 'arise and shine, for the glory of the Lord is risen upon thee.' There is no one thing more fully revealed in the scriptures of eternal truth, than the rise of the Zion of our God in the latter days, clothed upon with the glory of God from the heavens—a Zion that will attract the attention of all the nations and kindreds of the whole earth. It will not be something that takes place in a corner on some distant island of the sea, or away among some obscure people; but it will be something that will call forth the attention of all people and nations upon the face of the whole earth."[10]

● **Isaiah 60:2 Spiritual darkness will cover the earth "and gross darkness the people."** Thus, a Zion people will arise amidst a world of gross wickedness. Such had been the case with Enoch, who built the city of Zion in a day of great wickedness (see Moses 7). And Melchizedek also preached to a wicked generation that eventually joined the city of Enoch (see JST Genesis 14).

— **D&C 45:66–71** The Saints of this dispensation will build the holy city of New Jerusalem in a day of great wickedness. "And it shall be called the New Jerusalem, a land of peace, a city of refuge, a place of safety for the saints of the Most High God; And the glory of the Lord shall be there, and the terror of the Lord also shall be there, in-

Spiritual darkness covered Earth

somuch that the wicked will not come unto it, and it shall be called Zion. And it shall come to pass among the wicked, that every man that will not take his sword against his neighbor must needs flee unto Zion for safety. And there shall be gathered unto it out of every nation under heaven; and it shall be the only people that shall not be at war one with another. And it shall be said among the wicked: Let us not go up to battle against Zion, for the inhabitants of Zion are terrible; wherefore we cannot stand. And it shall come to pass that the righteous shall be gathered out from among all nations, and shall come to Zion, singing with songs of everlasting joy."

President Ezra Taft Benson said: "I am sure you [religious educators] appreciate the fact that you have been given custody of some of the choicest spirits of all time. I emphasize that. These are not just ordinary spirits, but among them are some of the choicest spirits that have come from heaven. These are they who were reserved to come forth in this time to bear off the kingdom triumphant."[11]

● **Isaiah 60:3–7 People will flock to Zion.** "Lift up thine eyes round about, and see," Isaiah says to latter-day Zion, "all they gather themselves together, they come to thee: thy sons shall come from far, and thy daughters shall be nursed at thy side" (v. 4). Then he lists the various groups that will be involved in this gathering.

— Gentiles and kings (v. 3).

— Zion's "sons shall come from far" (v. 4).

— Zion's children will be "nursed at thy side" (v. 4).

— "The forces of the Gentiles" will do the same (v. 5).

— Gold, silver, camels, and dromedaries [symbols of earthly wealth] will be brought to "glorify the house of [God's] glory" as in Solomon's day (v. 7).

Isaiah 60:8 Missionaries will fly to their destinations. "Who are these that fly as a cloud, and as the doves to their windows?" Isaiah marvels as he sees the Lord's emissaries flying toward their destinations. We can only imagine the wonder he must have felt, since air travel was completely unknown in his day.

Flying as doves to windows

Elder LeGrand Richards remarked that the development of the airplane has helped fulfill this prophecy: "Clearly, Isaiah was referring to individuals and not to birds. Surely there has never been a time in the history of this world when men flew 'as a cloud' or 'as the doves to their windows,' until our present time since the advent of the airplane."[12]

Isaiah 60:9–10 Missionaries will cover the earth. The "isles" [farthest points of the earth] will "wait for me" [the gospel], and ships will "bring thy sons from far, their silver and their gold with them, unto the name of the Lord thy God, and to the Holy One of Israel, because he hath glorfied thee" (v. 9). And "the sons of strangers" (Gentiles) will help to build the city of Zion (v. 10).

Isaiah 60:11–18 Zion will be safe from all her enemies Isaiah promises, "Thy gates shall be open

continually; they shall not be shut day nor night" (v. 11). This is an indication of the complete safety in which Zion will dwell. And through those open gates, they will receive "the forces of the Gentiles, and … their kings" (v. 11). "For the nation and kingdom that will not serve thee shall perish; yea, those nations shall be utterly wasted" (v. 12).

"The glory of Lebanon [all needful resources and treasures] shall come unto thee, the fir tree, the pine tree, and the box together, to beautify the place of my sanctuary; and I will make the place of my feet glorious" (v. 13). "The sons also of them that afflicted thee shall come bending unto thee; and all they that despised thee shall bow themselves down at the soles of thy feet; and they shall call thee, The city of the Lord, The Zion of the Holy One of Israel" (v. 14).

Elder Orson Pratt said: "What! no people or nation left that will not serve Zion? Not one. What will become of this great republic [the United States] … which is spreading forth continually? If they will comply with the ordinances of Zion, repent of their sins and be prepared for this great and glorious day, God will save them; but if they will not they will be utterly wasted away. Thus have the prophets declared."[13]

This gathered people, once "forsaken and hated, so that no man went through thee" will then become "an eternal excellency, a joy of many generations" (v. 15) that will "know that I the Lord am thy Saviour and thy Redeemer, the mighty One of Jacob" (v. 16). They will "suck the milk of the Gentiles, and … the breast of kings" (v.16), which means that they will be nurtured and protected by the Gentiles.

Elder LeGrand Richards believes countries like Great Britain have fulfilled this prophecy: "The part that Great Britain played in the liberation of Palestine from Turkish rule is a matter of history which occurred during World War I, in a remarkable manner. The issuance of the Balfour Declaration on November 2, 1917 had great significance. The text reads: 'His Majesty's

Government view with favor the establishment in Palestine of a National Home for the Jewish people, and will use their best endeavors to facilitate the achievement of this object, it being clearly understood that nothing shall be done which may prejudice the civil and religious rights of the existing non-Jewish communities in Palestine or the rights and political status enjoyed by Jews in any other country.'"[14]

Zion will also prosper, with gold instead of brass, silver instead of iron, brass instead of wood, and iron instead of stones (v. 17). Peace and righteousness will reign (v. 17), and "violence shall no more be heard in thy land, wasting nor destruction within thy borders; but thou shalt call thy walls Salvation, and thy gates Praise" (v. 18).

● **Isaiah 60:19–20 The presence of the Savior will light up Zion.** The glory of His presence will cause the sun to be "no more thy light by day; neither for brightness shall the moon give light unto thee: but the Lord shall be unto thee an everlasting light, and thy God [will be] thy glory" (vv. 19–20).

Elder Orson Pratt said:

Zion will not need the sun when the Lord is there, and all the city is lighted up by the glory of His presence. When the whole heavens above are illuminated by the presence of His glory we shall not need those bright luminaries of heaven to give light, so far as the city of Zion is concerned. ...

People round about, dwelling in other cities ... will still have need of the light of the sun and the moon; but the great capital city where the Lord will establish one of His thrones ... will not need this light. ... They will be clothed upon with the glory of their God.

When the people meet together in assemblies like this, in their Tabernacles, the Lord will meet with them, His glory will be upon them; a cloud will overshadow them by day and if they happen to have an evening meeting they will not need … lights of an artificial nature, for the Lord will be there and His glory will be upon all their assemblies. So says Isaiah the prophet, and I believe it. Amen.[15]

● **Isaiah 60:20–22 There will be no death or disease in Zion.** The days of Israel's mourning will be ended (v. 20). "Thy people also shall be all righteous: they shall inherit the land for ever, the branch of my planting, the work of my hands, that I may be glorified" (v. 21). There will be no death and disease, so that "a little one shall become a thousand, and a small one a strong nation" (v. 22).

THE SECOND COMING AND MILLENNIUM

Christ's Mission

● **Isaiah 61:1–3 "The Lord hath anointed me to … " This is a Messianic prophecy concerning the mission of the Messiah.** Part of this was fulfilled in His first coming and Atonement, and Christ announced His ministry by quoting this scripture at Nazareth. The other part remains to be fulfilled when He comes again.

GUSTAVE DORÉ 1896

— His mission during His first coming (v. 1):

* Preach good tidings unto the meek.

* Bind up the brokenhearted.

* Proclaim liberty to the captives [spirit world].

* Open the prison to them that are bound.

— His mission when He comes again (vv. 2–3):

  * Proclaim the … year of the Lord [the day of His Second Coming].

  * Proclaim a day of vengeance upon the wicked.

  * Comfort all that mourn by giving them:

    – Beauty for ashes.

    – Joy for mourning.

    – Praise for the spirit of heaviness.

  * Make all those that are with Him "trees of righteousness."

  * Do all these things so that He (God) might be glorified.

— <u>Dualism:</u> This scripture has been used in a variety of ways:

  * **Luke 4:16–21**   Jesus used it to announce His ministry in Nazareth.

  * **Matthew 11:2–5**   Jesus also used it as evidence of His divinity.

  * **Isaiah 61:3–9**   But it also clearly applies to Zion in the latter days.

  * **1 Peter 3:18–19**   And it also applies to the spirits in prison.

● **Isaiah 61:4–9 The physical restoration of Zion and the priesthood.** The people of Zion "shall build the old wastes, they shall raise up the former desolations, and they shall repair the waste cities, the desolations of many generations" (v. 4). Gentiles will "stand and feed your flocks, and … be your plowmen and your vinedressers" (v. 5). They will be ordained "Priests of the Lord" and "men shall call you the Ministers of our God" (v. 6). They will "eat the riches of the Gentiles," and will be glorified by them (v. 6). They will receive a double reward for all their former shame and confusion, and "in their land they shall possess the double: everlasting joy shall be unto them" (v. 7).

The Lord will "direct their work in truth, and … make an everlasting covenant with them" (v. 8). "And their seed shall be known among the Gentiles, and their offspring among the people: all that see them shall acknowledge them, that they are the seed which the Lord hath blessed" (v. 9).

Another Marriage Metaphor

Isaiah 61:10 Christ as the Bridegroom. Speaking of Zion like a bride about to be married to the Lord, Isaiah declares, "I will greatly rejoice in the Lord, my soul shall be joyful in my God; for he hath clothed me with the garments of salvation, he hath covered me with the robe of righteousness." Dressed "as a bridegroom decketh

The bride of Christ is the Church

himself with ornaments, and as a bride adorneth herself with her jewels," Zion will await the coming of her "husband," Jesus Christ.

> — **Revelation 19:7–8** Describes "the marriage of the Lamb." "Let us be glad and rejoice, and give honour to him: for the marriage of the Lamb is come, and his wife hath made herself ready. And to her was granted that she should be arrayed in fine linen, clean and white: for the fine linen is the righteousness of saints."

Isaiah 61:11 Righteousness will spring forth from the earth. Just as "the earth bringeth forth her bud, and as the garden causeth the things that are sown in it to spring forth; so the Lord God will cause righteousness and praise to spring forth before all the nations." The Book of Mormon literally sprang forth from the earth. And the kingdom of God [the Church] sprang forth like a newly budded seed in front of all the nations.

Isaiah 62:1–2, 6–7 Zion will possess "righteousness" and offer salvation to the world (v. 1). The Gentiles will "see thy righteousness," and kings will see "thy glory" (v. 2). Zion's "watchmen upon thy walls … shall never hold their peace day nor night" (v. 6). Isaiah says to them, "Ye that make mention of the Lord, keep not silence, And give him no rest, till he establish, and till he make Jerusalem a praise in the earth" (vv. 6–7).

● **Isaiah 62:2–5 The marriage metaphor continues.** As the Lord's bride, Zion will be called by a "new name" (v. 2). Like a "crown of glory in the hand of the Lord, and a royal diadem in the hand of thy God" (v. 3), Zion will "no more be termed Forsaken; neither shall thy land any more be termed Desolate: but thou shalt be called *Hephzi-bah* ['delightful' or 'my desire is for her'], and thy land *Beulah* ['union' or 'married wife']: for the Lord delighteth in thee, and thy land shall be married [unified]" (v. 4; emphasis added).

Just like "a young man marrieth a virgin, so shall thy sons marry thee: and as the bridegroom rejoiceth over the bride, so shall thy God rejoice over thee" (v. 5). The phrase "so shall thy sons marry thee" is changed in the Joseph Smith Translation to "so shall thy God marry thee." Thus, Zion will once again be married to the Lord, and "as the bridegroom rejoiceth over the bride, so shall [our] God rejoice over [Jerusalem's restoration]" (v. 6).

Christ's Second Coming

● **Isaiah 34:1–10 The great destruction of the enemies of Jerusalem.** Isaiah invites all the nations of the world to "come near [and] hearken" to his warning concerning the fate of the wicked nations that will attack Jerusalem at the Second Coming.

— It will be "the day of the Lord's vengeance, and the year of recompences" for sin (v. 8).

— The indignation of the Lord will be upon all nations (v. 2).

— His fury will be upon all their armies, which He will utterly destroy (v. 2).

— Their dead bodies will be "cast out, and their stink shall come up out of their carcases, and the mountains shall be melted with their blood" (v. 3).

— "And all the host of heaven [the sun, moon, and stars] shall be dissolved" (v. 4).

— "The heavens shall be rolled together as a scroll" (v. 4).

— The "host [stars] shall fall down [upon the earth] as a falling fig from the fig tree" (v. 4).

— The Lord's sword, "bathed in heaven," will "come down upon Idumea [the world]" (v. 5).

— The earth will be filled with the blood of dead animals (sacrifices) (vv. 6–7).

— Streams will be "turned into pitch [tar]" (v. 9).

— The dust will become "brimstone [sulfurous burning]" (v. 1).

— The land will become like "burning pitch" (v. 9).

— "It shall not be quenched night nor day; the smoke thereof shall go up for ever" (v. 10).

— Their land will "lie [in] waste," and "none shall pass through it for ever and ever" (v. 10).

● **Isaiah 63:1–6 Christ's robe will be red** with the blood of the unrighteous whom He will destroy at the Second Coming. Though He will be "glorious in his apparel, travelling in the greatness of his strength … [and] mighty to save" (v. 1), yet His robe will be red "like him that treadeth" red grapes into wine (v. 2). And He will declare at His coming:

√ "I have trodden the winepress alone; and of the people there was none with me: for I will tread them in mine anger, and trample them in my fury; and their blood shall be sprinkled upon my garments, and I will stain all my raiment. For the day of vengeance is in mine heart, and the year of my redeemed is come" (vv. 3–4).

√ "Treading the winepress" is symbolic of our Lord's Atonement, with which "there was none to help … [and] none to uphold" (v. 5). He had to bring salvation to humankind alone by paying personally [with "mine own arm"] for their sins (v. 5). For those whom He will destroy at the Second Coming, His Atonement will have been wasted. Therefore, He will "tread down the people in mine anger, and make them drunk in my fury, and I will bring down their strength to the earth" (v. 6).

— **D&C 133:46–48** This latter-day revelation also makes mention of the Savior's red robes. "And it shall be said: Who is this that cometh down from God in heaven with dyed garments; yea, from the regions which are not known, clothed in his glorious apparel, traveling in the greatness of his strength? And he shall say: I am he who spake in righteousness, mighty to save. And the Lord shall be red in his apparel, and his garments like him that treadeth in the wine–vat."

Elder Joseph Fielding Smith said: "Isaiah has pictured this great day when the Lord shall come with His garments, or apparel, red and glorious, to take vengeance on the ungodly. ... This will be a day of mourning to the wicked, but a day of gladness to all who have kept His commandments. Do not let any one think that this is merely figurative language, it is literal, and as surely as we live that day of wrath will come when the cup of iniquity is full. We have received a great many warnings. The great day of the Millennium will come in; the wicked will be consumed and peace and righteousness will dwell upon all the face of the earth for one thousand years."[16]

● **Isaiah 63:7–9 The Lord's lovingkindness to the righteous.** In the midst of this recitation of destruction for the wicked, Isaiah pauses to "mention the lovingkindnesses of the Lord, and the praises of the Lord, according to all that the Lord hath bestowed on us, and the great goodness toward the house of Israel, which he hath bestowed on them according to his mercies, and according to the multitude of his lovingkindnesses" (v. 7). These also "in his love and in his pity he redeemed them; and he bare them, and carried them" (v. 9). These are His people, "children that will not lie," and He will be "their Saviour" (v. 8). Thus, the very same day that will bring sorrow and great suffering to the wicked will be a day of rejoicing and peace to the righteous.

Elder John Taylor said: "When He comes again He comes to take vengeance on the ungodly and to bring deliverance unto His Saints [Isaiah 63:4]. It behooves us to be made well aware which class we belong to, that if we are not already among the redeemed we may immediately join that society, that when the

Son of God shall come the second time with all the holy angels with Him, arrayed in power and great glory to take vengeance on them that know not God and obey not the gospel, or when He shall come in flaming fire, we shall be among that number who shall be ready to meet Him with gladness in our hearts and hail Him as our great deliverer and friend."[17]

● **Isaiah 64:1–3 Great physical changes to the earth at His coming.** Isaiah longs for the day of the Lord's coming in glory: "Oh that thou wouldest rend the heavens, that thou wouldest come down, that the mountains might flow down at thy presence, As when the melting fire burneth, the fire causeth the waters to boil, to make thy name known to thine adversaries, that the nations may tremble at thy presence!" (vv. 1–2). It will be a day when the Lord will do "terrible things" that are unexpected as the "mountains flow … down at [His] presence" (v. 3).

— **D&C 133:37–45** Gospel messengers will offer their last warnings before thee great day of the Lord's coming (vv. 37–39). The destructions that will accompany His appearance will include a "melting fire that burneth, and … which causeth the waters to boil" (v. 41) and the mountains to "flow down" (v. 44). And in the midst of these destructions, all the wicked will "tremble at [His] presence" (v. 42).

— **D&C 88:87–91** "The earth shall tremble and reel to and fro as a drunken man; and the sun shall hide his face, and shall refuse to give light; and the moon shall be bathed in blood; and the stars shall become exceedingly angry, and shall cast themselves down as a fig that falleth from off a fig-tree. … Earthquakes … shall cause groanings in the midst of [the earth], and men shall fall upon the ground and shall not be able to stand … , [and] the voice of thunderings, and the voice of lightnings, and the voice of tempests, and the voice of the waves of the sea heaving themselves beyond their bounds. And all things shall be in commotion; and surely, men's hearts shall fail them; for fear shall come upon all people."

— **D&C 49:23** The heavens will "be shaken, and the earth [will] tremble and … reel to and fro as a drunken man, ... valleys [shall] be exalted," mountains will be "made low," and "rough places [will] become smooth—and all this when the angel shall sound his trumpet."

— **D&C 133:22** God's voice "shall break down the mountains," so that "the valleys shall not be found."

Elder Charles W. Penrose declared:

> He comes! The earth shakes, and the tall mountains tremble; the mighty deep rolls back to the north as in fear, and the rent skies glow like molten brass.
>
> He comes! The dead Saints burst forth from their tombs, and "those who are alive and remain" are "caught up" with them to meet Him [see 1 Thes. 4:17]. The ungodly rush to hide themselves from His presence, and call upon the quivering rocks to cover them.
>
> He comes! with all the hosts of the righteous glorified. The breath of His lips strikes death to the wicked. His glory is a consuming fire. The proud and rebellious are as stubble; they are burned and "left neither root nor branch" [see Mal. 4:1]. He sweeps the earth "as with the besom [broom] of destruction" [see Isa. 14:23]. He deluges the earth with the fiery floods of His wrath, and the filthiness and abominations of the world are consumed. Satan and his dark hosts are taken and bound—the prince of the power of the air has lost his dominion, for He whose right it is to reign has come, and "the kingdoms of this world have become the kingdoms of our Lord and of his Christ [see Rev. 11:15]."[18]

The Millennium

The Millennium will last a thousand years, which is what "millennium" means. It will be an incredibly beautiful time, living alongside our resurrected family and friends in a society of absolute peace and righteousness. Isaiah describes many of the blessings of that day.

● **Isaiah 65:17–19 A new heaven and a new earth.** The Lord declares, "For, behold, I create new heavens and a new earth: and the former shall not be remembered, nor come into mind" (v. 17). But rather than fear this, we should "be ... glad and rejoice for ever in that which I create: for, behold, I create Jerusalem a rejoicing, and her people a joy. And I will rejoice in Jerusalem, and joy in my people" (vv. 18–19).

Elder Joseph Fielding Smith said:

The earth as it is now, this mundane earth covered all over its face with wickedness will not be remembered when this change comes. We will be glad to get rid of this condition, and we will not bring it up to mind. Remember, in speaking of the heavens he is not referring to the sidereal heavens. He is speaking of that which pertains to our own earth, the heavens in which the birds fly. ...

You can see that [Isaiah 65:17–20] does not have any reference at all to the earth when it is celestialized. The new heaven and earth have nothing to do at all with this earth as it will be after it dies and is raised in the resurrection to be a celestial body because then there will not be any death at all. It is going to be restored as nearly as possible to what it was in the beginning. This is coming to pass when Christ comes, and that's part of this restoration.[19]

● **Isaiah 65:19–23 Sorrow and death will cease.** "The voice of weeping shall be no more heard in her, nor the voice of crying. There shall be no more thence an infant of days, nor an old man that hath not filled his days: for the child shall die an hundred years old [in the twinkling of an eye]" (vv. 19–20). Because of this, "they shall build houses, and inhabit them; and they shall plant vineyards, and eat the fruit of them. They shall not build, and another inhabit; they shall not plant, and another eat: for as the days of a tree are the days of my people, and mine elect shall long enjoy the work of their hands. They shall not labour in vain, ... for they are the seed of the blessed of the Lord, and their offspring with them" (vv. 21–23).

- **Isaiah 65:24 The Lord will dwell among us.** He promises that "it shall come to pass, that before they call, I will answer; and while they are yet speaking, I will hear" (v. 24). This is because He will be right there with us, able to respond to our needs face to face and immediately.

- **Isaiah 65:25 There will be absolute peace.** "The wolf and the lamb shall feed together, and the lion shall eat straw like the bullock: and dust shall be the serpent's meat. They shall not hurt nor destroy in all my holy mountain, saith the Lord."

THEBIBLEREVIVAL.COM. #12

Elder Joseph Fielding Smith said: "When the Lord comes to rule on the earth in His own right, and all kingdoms become subject unto Him, and the earth is renewed and again receives its paradisiacal glory, death shall be removed as far as it possibly can be removed before the resurrection, and while mortality remains. During the Millennium the earth will be transformed into a 'new earth' with a new heaven, as Isaiah has declared. It will no longer be a telestial earth, but will become a terrestrial earth. Infants will not die until they become old and then death shall be the transition to the immortal from the mortal state in the twinkling of an eye. This day is near at hand, 'speaking after the manner of the Lord,' and then shall come the time of the entire separation of the wicked from the righteous."[20]

Elder Smith also said: "This new heaven and new earth are our own earth and its heavens renewed to the primitive beauty and condition. This is not the great last change which shall come at the end of the earth, but the change to take place at the coming of Jesus Christ. Moreover, when this change comes all things will be set in order. Enmity between man and man and beast and beast will cease."[21]

There are many other scriptures with regard to the Millennium—too numerous to list and consider here. But some of the most interesting include these:

— **1 Thes. 3:13**   Christ will bring His Saints with Him.

— **A of F 1:10**   Christ will reign personally and the earth will be renewed.

— **D&C 101:23–31**   All flesh will see His coming simultaneously.

In summary, from all the above scriptures, and from others, we know that:

— Every corruptible thing will be consumed

— Everything will be new

— All enmity will cease

— Every desire will be granted

— Satan will have no power to tempt us

— There will be no sorrow

— There will be no death; every child will live a long life

— "Death" will be an instantaneous change to immortality

— All things will be revealed

— The righteous will be taught and prepared for exaltation

— Righteous members of the Church from the days of Adam to the present will associate with one another and with Christ.

Elder Bruce R. McConkie wrote: "Great and marvelous though the changes will be incident to life during the millennial era, yet mortality as such will continue. Children will be born, grow up, marry, advance to old age, and pass through the equivalent of death. Crops will be planted, harvested, and eaten; industries will be expanded, cities built, and education fostered; men will continue to care for their own needs, handle their own affairs, and enjoy the full endowment of free agency. Speaking a pure language (Zeph. 3:9), dwelling in peace, living without disease, and progressing as the Holy Spirit will guide, the advancement and perfection of society during the Millennium will exceed anything men have supposed or expected."[22]

The Prophet Joseph Smith said: "While in conversation at Judge Adams' during the evening, I said, Christ and the resurrected Saints will reign over the earth during the thousand years. They will not probably dwell upon the earth, but will visit it when they please, or when it is necessary to govern it. There will be wicked men on the earth during the thousand years. The heathen nations who will not come up to worship will be visited with the judgments of God, and must eventually be destroyed from the earth."[23]

● **Isaiah 66:5–14 Israel will be redeemed and the wicked destroyed at the Second Coming.** Speaking to Israel, Isaiah prophesies that the Lord will "appear to your joy, and [the wicked] shall be ashamed" (v. 5) as He "rendereth recompence to his enemies" (v. 6).

Like a woman ready to give birth, the earth will be "delivered of a man child" (v. 7). This metaphor was used by the Apostle John on the Isle of Patmos:

— **Revelation 12:1–7** A woman is depicted as struggling in travail to give birth and brings forth "a man child." This child is identified by the Joseph Smith Translation as the millennial kingdom of God (JST Revelation 12:7).

"Who hath heard such a thing? who hath seen such things? Shall the earth be made to bring forth [the millennial kingdom] in one day? or shall a nation be born at once? for as soon as Zion travailed, she brought forth her children" (v. 8). Yes, the Lord will cause it to happen and we will all "rejoice ... with Jerusalem, and be glad with her, all ye that love her: rejoice for joy with her, all ye that mourn for her" (vv. 9–10).

The people of the latter-day Zion will "be delighted with the abundance of her glory" (v. 11). The Lord will "extend peace to her like a river, and the glory of the Gentiles like a flowing stream" (v. 12). Like a suckling child being borne upon his mother's side and "dandled upon her knees," the Lord will comfort His people (vv. 12–13). "And when ye see this, your heart shall rejoice, and your bones shall flourish like an herb: and the hand of the Lord shall be known toward his servants, and his indignation toward his enemies" (v. 14).

Elder Charles W. Penrose said:

> His next appearance will be among the distressed and nearly vanquished sons of Judah. At the crisis of their fate, when the hostile troops of several nations are ravaging the city and all the horrors of war are overwhelming the people of Jerusalem, He will set His feet upon the Mount of Olives, which will cleave and part asunder at His touch.

> Attended by a host from heaven, He will overthrow and destroy the combined armies of the Gentiles, and appear to the worshiping Jews as the mighty Deliverer and Conqueror so long expected by their race; and while love, gratitude, awe, and admiration swell their bosoms, the Deliverer will show them the tokens of His crucifixion and disclose Himself as Jesus of Nazareth, whom they had reviled and whom their fathers put to death. Then will unbelief depart from their souls, and "the blindness in part which has happened unto Israel" [see Rom. 11:25] be removed. "A fountain for sin and uncleanness shall be opened to the house of David and the inhabitants of Jerusalem" [see Zech. 13:1], and "a nation will be born" unto God "in a day" [see Isa. 66:8]. They will be baptized for the remission of their sins, and will receive the gift of the Holy Ghost, and the government of God as established in Zion will be set up among them, no more to be thrown down for ever.[24]

● **Isaiah 66:15–17, 24 The final scenes at Jerusalem.** Jerusalem will be in the midst of a horrible attack from her enemies, who will be in a position to destroy her with all her people. But then, "the Lord will come with fire, and with his chariots like a whirlwind, to render his anger with fury, and his rebuke with flames of fire. For by fire and by his sword will the Lord plead with all flesh: and the slain of the Lord shall be many" (vv. 15–16). The wicked (those that "sanctify themselves, and purify themselves" while engaging in impure practices) "shall be consumed together" (v. 17).

GUSTAVE DORÉ, 1865

The people of God will marvel at what God has done to the wicked. "They shall go forth, and look upon the carcases of the men that have transgressed against me," and "their worm shall not die, neither shall their fire be quenched" [they will not be able to get it out of their mind] because the sight of it will be utterly abhorrent to them (v. 24).

Just as with the Millennium, the scriptures abound with prophesies concerning the final battle at Jerusalem. There is not time or space to summarize them all here, but some of the most interesting ones include the following:

— **Jer. 25:31–33**   Earth will be swept clean of the wicked

— **Ezekiel 38:17–23**   Destruction of the armies of Gog

— **Ezekiel 39:1–16**   Destruction of the armies of Magog

— **Joel 3:1–2;11–14**   The battle of Armageddon

● **Isaiah 66:18–23 The righteous will be gathered from all nations.** The Lord will "gather all nations and tongues; and they shall come, and see my glory" (v. 18). From among this people, the Lord will send missionaries "unto the nations … that have not heard my fame, neither have seen my glory; and they shall declare my glory among the Gentiles" (v. 19).

These converts will be brought "for an offering unto the Lord out of all nations … to my holy mountain Jerusalem," and "as the children of Israel [they will] bring an offering in a clean vessel into the house of the Lord" (v. 20). They will be made "priests and … Levites," and will remain faithful there (vv.

21–22). "And it shall come to pass, that from one new moon to another, and from one sabbath to another, shall all flesh come to worship before me, saith the Lord" (v. 23).

— **Zechariah 14:16–21** Zechariah also prophesied that the heathen nations who survive will eventually turn to Jehovah, and great holiness will prevail in Jerusalem among God's people. Evidently many will then join the Church, for the Lord said He will take of the Gentiles "for priests and for Levites" (Isa. 66:21); in other words, they shall receive the priesthood.

Notes:

1. In *Journal of Discourses*, 19:359.

2. In Conference Report, Apr. 1943, 14.

3. In Conference Report, Oct. 1949, 39, 43–44.

4. In *Journal of Discourses*, 1:368.

5. Adam Clarke, *The Holy Bible ... with a Commentary and Critical Notes*, 6 vols. [1973], 4:212.

6. In Conference Report, Apr. 1974, 184.

7. *Answers to Gospel Questions*, comp. Joseph Fielding Smith Jr., 5 vols. [1957–66], 1:88–90.

8. *Commentary on the Old Testament*, 10 vols. [1996], 7:2:470.

9. In *Journal of Discourses*, 14:64.

10. In *Journal of Discourses*, 16:78.

11. "The Gospel Teacher and His Message," address to religious educators, 17 Sept. 1976, in *Charge to Religious Educators*, 3rd ed. [1994], 11.

12. *Israel! Do You Know?* [1954], 101.

13. In *Journal of Discourses*, 14:355.

14. *Trial and Error: The Autobiography of Chaim Weizmann* [1949], 208, in *Israel! Do You Know?*, 206.

15. In *Journal of Discourses*, 14:355–56.

16. *Church History and Modern Revelation*, 4 vols. [1946–49], 1:175.

17. In *Journal of Discourses*, 10:116.

18. "The Second Advent," *Millennial Star*, 10 Sept. 1859, 583.

19. *The Signs of the Times* [1952], 36–37.

20. *Church History and Modern Revelation*, 2:6.

21. *The Restoration of All Things* [1945], 23.

22. *Mormon Doctrine*, 2nd ed. [1966], 496–97.

23. *History of the* Church, 5:212.

24. "The Second Advent," *Millennial Star*, 10 Sept. 1859, 583.

About the Author

Randal S. Chase spent his childhood years in Nephi, Utah, where his father was a dry land wheat farmer and a businessman. In 1959 their family moved to Salt Lake City and settled in the Holladay area. He served a full-time mission in the Central British (England Central) Mission, 1968–1970. He returned home and married Deborah Johnsen in 1971. They are the parents of six children— two daughters and four sons—and an ever-expanding number of grandchildren.

He was called to serve as a bishop at the age of 27 in the Sandy Crescent South Stake area of the Salt Lake Valley. He served six years in that capacity, and has since served as a high councilor, a stake executive secretary and clerk, and in many other stake and ward callings. Regardless of whatever other callings he has received over the years, one was nearly constant: He has taught Gospel Doctrine classes in every ward he has ever lived in as an adult—a total of 35 years.

Dr. Chase was a well-known media personality on Salt Lake City radio stations in the 1970s. He left on-air broadcasting in 1978 to develop and market a computer-based management, sales, and music programming system to radio and television stations in the United States, Canada, South America, and Australia. After the business was sold in 1984, he supported his family as a media and business consultant in the Salt Lake City area.

Having a great desire to teach young people of college age, he determined in the late 1980s to pursue his doctorate, and received his Ph.D. in Communication from the University of Utah in 1997. He has taught communication courses at that institution as well as at Salt Lake Community College and Dixie State University for 21 years. He is currently a tenured full-time faculty member at Dixie State University in St. George, Utah.

Concurrently with his academic career, brother Chase has served as a volunteer LDS Institute and Adult Education instructor in the CES system since 1994, both in Salt Lake City and St. George, where he currently teaches a weekly Adult Education class for three stakes in the Washington area. He has also conducted multiple Church History tours and seminars. During these years of gospel teaching, he has developed an extensive library of lesson plans and handouts which are the predecessors to these study guides.

Dr. Chase has published three-volume study guides on each of the standard works, all titled *Making Precious Things Plain*. They are designed to assist teachers and students of Gospel Doctrine classes, as well as those who simply want to study on their own, our wonderful scriptural legacy of faith and revelation during every dispensation of the earth.